sexual
hegemony

STATECRAFT, SODOMY, AND CAPITAL IN THE RISE OF THE WORLD SYSTEM

edited by Max Fox, and with an introduction by Christopher Nealon

THEORY Q   A series edited by Lauren Berlant and Lee Edelman

sexual hegemony

CHRISTOPHER CHITTY

Duke University Press   *Durham and London*   2020

Designed by Courtney Leigh Richardson
Typeset in Minion Pro by Copperline Book Services

Library of Congress Cataloging-in-Publication Data
Names: Chitty, Christopher, [date], author.
Title: Sexual hegemony : statecraft, sodomy, and capital in the rise of
the world system / Christopher Chitty.
Other titles: Theory Q.
Description: Durham : Duke University Press, 2020. | Series: Theory
Q | Includes an index.
Identifiers: LCCN 2019054735 (print)
LCCN 2019054736 (ebook)
ISBN 9781478008675 (hardcover)
ISBN 9781478009580 (paperback)
ISBN 9781478012238 (ebook)
Subjects: LCSH: Queer theory. | Homosexuality—Political aspects. |
Capitalism—Social aspects. | Philosophy, Marxist. | Marxian
economics. | Socialist feminism.
Classification: LCC HX550. H65 C45 2020 (print)
LCC HX550. H65 (ebook)
DDC 306.76/609—dc23
LC record available at https://lccn.loc.gov/2019054735
LC ebook record available at https://lccn.loc.gov/2019054736

COVER ART: Jesse Mockrin, *Some Unknown Power* (2018). Image
courtesy of the artist and Night Gallery. Photo by Marten Elder.

contents

foreword

MAX FOX /

The following text represents both a precious record and a bitter loss. Though a thrilling and innovative piece of scholarship, it is incomplete and full of the impossible promises of further writing. Compiled and edited from drafts retrieved after their author's early death, the text attempts to present the theoretical innovations that Christopher Chitty had been laboring with over the course of his academic career, in the hope that his insights might be shared and spur others to take up the fruits of his discoveries.

After he died in the spring of 2015, I was granted access to what his family and friends were able to gather from his digital files: early drafts of chapters, essays submitted as coursework, notes for further refinement or research, research he had conducted but not incorporated into a text—that sort of thing. I asked friends and comrades if they had any copies of papers I didn't know about, and I transcribed MP3s of conference presentations that, mercifully, archivists had secured online. Painfully, I mined my own inbox for the drafts of essays on which we had attempted to collaborate but that had gone nowhere (one, I am now astounded to recall, was a review of a recently published book by Foucault titled *Speech Begins after Death*), hoping not to have to look too long at the last email I sent him, an invitation to a friend's film screening, which is where I was when I got the news.

Christopher Chitty was a brilliant young scholar and activist, endowed with a rare eye and mind and deeply beloved by a genuinely wide community. He was nearing completion on his PhD in the History of Consciousness program at University of California, Santa Cruz, when he killed himself. His dissertation, posthumously recognized under the title "Sexual Hegemony, Early Modern Republics, and the Culture of Sodomy," was a far-ranging attempt to think through the failure of sexual liberation by "returning the history of sexuality to a history of property," as he put it, splicing world-systems theory's account of the transition to capitalism from feudalism with advances in the study of sexuality made since the heyday of Foucault.

Chitty was convinced that the historical emergence of cultures of male same-sex eroticism as a problem within bourgeois polities belied a key aspect of such formations' new form of rule: sexual hegemony. Sexual hegemony, in his words, "exists wherever sexual norms benefiting a dominant social group shape the sexual conduct and self-understandings of other groups, whether or not they also stand to benefit from such norms and whether or not they can achieve them." These groups were not communities defined by sexual identity, a category whose history he endeavored to illuminate, but classes. While he deployed this concept to analyze a number of premodern social forms, most crucially, the concept of sexual hegemony allowed him to historicize sexuality as such. For him, "sexuality could only become a problem for societies in which communities of producers have been separated from their means of production" because such a separation "decouples biological reproduction from the reproduction of ownership" of such means.

Broadly following Giovanni Arrighi's schematic in *The Long Twentieth Century*, Chitty looked for evidence of the link between sexual hegemony and social form in crackdowns on public cultures of male sodomy in Arrighi's four hegemonic centers: Florence, Amsterdam, London, and New York, adding Paris for its role in the development of the bourgeois state. He found that periods of financialization (which in Arrighi's understanding signal the decline of one hegemonic center and the rise of the next) tracked with periods of increased policing of homosexuality. This allowed him to argue that homophobia is not a timeless or religious prejudice that stands by waiting for any arbitrary moment in which to flare up; instead, the problem of male homosexuality represents the form taken by a particular political contradiction or antinomy in bourgeois society, one which economic crises can inflame but not defuse without contingent political antagonism. His stance can be summed up in the following passage:

In short, human sexuality is not only malleable and historical; indeed, at certain points in history, such transformations of human nature were central to the forces of production and certain objectives of statecraft. The problem of sexual hegemony is both a question of establishing whether same-sex attraction, solidarity, and erotic attachments, as such, presented an antagonism to particular relations of force that required neutralization and a question of what relations of force in a particular conjuncture enabled its repression or allowed it to exist unperturbed. These considerations have less to do with a "phobia" or "panic," without regard to political and institutional context, than with an uneven process of development in which dominant groups, who viewed sexual regulation and repression as in their interests, intervened in these relations of force to effect such transformations.

This was the insight with which he wrestled over the course of his writing. It is clear, however, that at the time of his death Chitty was still ambivalent about the form his argument should ultimately take. He drafted and redrafted the chapter on northern Italy, sometimes centering his theoretical apparatus, sometimes staging scenes that performed more of the argumentative work, sometimes pausing to conduct an analysis of a Florentine painting or novel. The later chapters, too, expanded and contracted in scope over various revisions, sometimes dilating on the immediate antecedents of postwar gay identity in the period of American hegemony—the coordinates of which described the limits of the gay liberation movement that occupied much of his thinking—and sometimes diving into later historiographical debates. I found chapter outlines that posited whole new sections or concerns that were evidently never written or which, perhaps, I simply couldn't dig up. A friend told me recently that the last thing Chris told her about the project was that he'd written a new introduction and was reconceptualizing the whole project as something "sleek," which, god bless them, the manuscripts he left us decidedly were not.

In assembling the following text, however, I did try to condense the exposition of his thought. Given that it was written as his PhD dissertation and not a book for wider publication, there were plenty of passages intended mainly to demonstrate his fluency with the literature. He had it. Attentive to the long tradition of political philosophy from which his innovations emerged, Chitty was an unsurpassed reader of Foucault as a close reader of Marx, the latter of whom he, too, could boast of a rare understanding. In a paper delivered at a conference in 2013, framed by an exploration of Foucault's "sins" vis-à-vis the intellectual formation of queer theory that sprung up after him, Chitty wryly observes the following about his two signal thinkers, which could equally well describe his own approach:

> Foucault read *Capital, Volume I*, and he read it very carefully (definitely a sin). . . . I use the term *sin* here somewhat facetiously, but considering how Foucault was attacked by Sartre for being "the last rampart the bourgeoisie can erect against the revolution," and considering all of the facile leftist critiques of him for lacking any kind of theory of revolutionary praxis or something, it's ironic that Foucault's own conceptualization of history as a process without a subject is derived from none other than Marx himself. I am suggesting it's kind of dangerous, in some circles of Marxism, to read *Capital* too closely.

He goes on to read *Capital* very closely, proposing an equivalence between Marx's account of the real subsumption of labor by capital and Foucault's "biopolitical threshold of modernity," in which sexuality plays a central role. But Foucault's *History of Sexuality* omitted most of what was necessary for modern, bourgeois sexuality to consolidate itself historically, he argues, and much of the text published here represents Chitty's long effort to correct the errors that Foucault had, wittingly or not, allowed to stabilize into something like a dogma, both within the study of sexuality and, negatively, within more Marxian treatments of bourgeois rule that fail to address sexuality as one of its key components. I have tried to combine from his drafts only those passages that most starkly lay out what is compelling about this argument, in a form that respects the architecture he seemed to keep intact over the many revisions.

This has meant excising whole chapters, which it distresses me to imagine no one else will never read. But this isn't simply a collection of papers dedicated to his memory, intended to be of interest only to those who knew him. His intellectual achievement is singular and deserves to be presented as such even if he weren't survived by comrades and interlocutors who love and miss him, and his insight is legible and generative even though its full exposition is now impossible.

While working to piece this text together, I have approached it as would an editor rather than a scholar. This means, in general, that I have privileged the argumentative cohesion, rather than, say, its historical or theoretical soundness, which I have had to leave up to the material he assembled. I tracked down nearly all of his sources and was able to verify their accuracy (or fix his citations), but between him and me and each of our limitations, there are bound to be errors for which we share responsibility. Where he deviated from what I could find in the record or formulated something in a way I found suspicious, I, as a rule, reworded as minimally as possible to add the most clarity while leaving its initial sense in place. Still, it is impossible to characterize this work as exactly what he would have written or ended up with himself. I was keenly aware that, every time I intervened on the page, there was no one from whom I could seek validation for my editorial choices, and so in a sense that I can't fully shake, this is also my own, very partial reading of his unfinished work and a record of where my own investments lie.

But it was also Chris who taught me how to read these kinds of texts in the first place. I met him when I was a barely formed undergraduate, seeking to reconcile a desire to treat my sexuality as both an important and unremarkable center of my identity with a desire to join the tradition of doing intellectual combat with capital, which, whatever its intentions, clearly treated homosexuality as outside the arena. Chris was an electrifying, shining example of how to do the two at once. He embodied for me the cutting knowledge of the genius fag in its most vivid, world-burning force. Early on, he fixed me with wide eyes and recounted the lost universe built by gay liberation, one which held a revolutionary kernel but whose defeat through biopolitical counterinsurgency had left unprocessed trauma among survivors and installed a class of ideologues whose function was to justify their betrayal of this past. I had known about this world but not its promise, and I had sensed the deathly energies of its usurpers without knowing what end they were serving. But Chris had the gift of Benjamin's historian for "fanning the spark of hope in the past," and he convinced me that even the dead were not yet safe.

Nor, ultimately, was he. In grasping at him and his project, trying to save it at least from disappearing irretrievably, I know I risk siding with the world that hurt him so much. When I tell people what I've been working on, I have to steel myself against the optimistic but stomach-rending response that this project is generous or selfless. My fear, in fact, is that publishing his unfinished work selfishly exposes him to criticism and judgment he can't answer on the basis of a project he remained unsatisfied with. But I couldn't let go of him; I needed his intellect to exist beyond my private experience of it, and I know I'm not alone in feeling this way. And when I was submerged in his efforts, trying to impose some order on the undated drafts, I couldn't keep from marveling at what he had already achieved.

Unavoidably, the following text is limited to a reconstruction of what this work could have been. Had Chitty lived to finish it, the project might have taken an entirely different form. His argument presumes the existence of equally rich veins of history corresponding to other moments in the succession of sexual hegemonies, many of the source documents and narratives of which are already in circulation but that he had not run through his analytic. There remain omissions he seemed to be hoping to fill in after having set up this theoretical architecture—most notably, in my view, what to do with the assumption that the equally historically contingent and co-implicated concepts of race and gender will function stably precisely in these moments when they, like sexuality, are crossing the "biopolitical threshold of modernity" and assuming their familiar form. But his central insight—the nature of the link between sexual hegemony and the social form of bourgeois rule—remained durable enough across the various iterations of this text that I feel confident in uniting what I have into an introduction to his intellectual project, so that the work he started might continue.

introduction

CHRISTOPHER NEALON /

Christopher Chitty's *Sexual Hegemony* gives us a new way to think about the history of sexuality. It is primarily a book about male homosexuality, though it has implications for understanding forms of sexual life far beyond that particular form. It is also a book about the role of the policing of homosexual activity in the era of the rise of capitalism—or, to be more precise, the role played by the classes that would become the modern bourgeoisie in strategically weaponizing "sodomy" in a struggle against both the aristocracy it hoped to displace and the peasant, proletarian, and lumpen classes whose capacity for labor it needed to manage.

Sexual Hegemony is shaped by a remarkable theoretical and methodological sophistication, and its structure has a complexity born both of its ambition and its incompleteness, but at its root it tells a straightforward story. The book tracks the history of the displacement of young men from Mediterranean peasant lifeways in the transition to capitalism, paying particular attention to how these men were partially and unstably absorbed into a range of new social relations, especially apprenticeships in the cities and maritime labor in the era of its great expansion. Chitty suggests that these forms of absorption were only ever imperfect and involved the constant danger of superfluity and uselessness to the men who had been driven into them. And he argues that these early forms of proletarianization not only shaped what historians of later periods would come to think of as "working-class homosexuality," but also became the focus of ongoing projects of statecraft that continue to influence sexuality down to the present.

In order to make this argument, Chitty drew on a range of theoretical resources that is remarkable for seeming, at first glance, not to address sexuality at all. He also developed a narrative arc that spans distinct—in terms of disciplinary boundaries—historical periods. I'd like to outline the theoretical terrain for a moment, then turn to what is special about Chitty's historical narrative, moving on to some observations about the politics that emerges from the project, and finally providing a brief reflection on the work *Sexual Hegemony* leaves undone and the kind of work I hope it will inspire.

As its title suggests, *Sexual Hegemony* draws on the work of Antonio Gramsci, specifically the writing in *The Prison Notebooks* that concerns the bourgeois project of managing potentially insurrectionary working and lumpen populations. Many readers will have a working understanding of the Gramscian idea of hegemony as a kind of ideological "soft power" that is a necessary supplement to state-sanctioned force in the maintenance of capitalist class relations—and this is indeed the idea Chitty relies on when he suggests that the manipulation of the charge of sodomy in late-medieval Florence, for instance, was a tool in exactly this kind of class agon. But Chitty takes this a bit further, by turning to Gramsci's sense of the importance of historical contradiction for understanding how hegemony works. Gramsci, that is, sees contradiction both as a collision of forces no single class can control, and as material for tactical (if imperfect) manipulation by a ruling class. For Chitty, the archive of Florentine sodomy prosecutions can be seen as the record of an innovative conflict-management system, in which both cross-class and same-class homosexual contact was liable to disrupt the social order: apprentices attempting to seek revenge on abusive masters, or political rivals seeking to discredit each other, could turn to accusations of sodomy to exacerbate conflict or bring it out in the open. Relying on the work of historian Michael Jesse Rocke and others, Chitty notes that Florence's distinction from places like Venice, where sodomy prosecution meant spectacular punishment and execution, was that it deployed a system of fines. As Chitty puts it, "The city monetized sodomy" (38). In doing so, he suggests, the ruling class of Florence not only profited from the ongoing sexual entanglements among the city's men, but also began to develop a form of "hegemony" that linked emergent forms of "homosexuality" to property relations and to manipulate it in strategically contradictory ways: it could be seen as a quiet, open secret from behind the protections of

2   INTRODUCTION

property, even a sign of privilege, just as it could be a scandalizing mark of dispossession—the mark of someone too poorly behaved to participate in the extraction of wealth, in the elite case, or too unruly to deserve work, in the proletarian one.

Already here we are in remarkable new territory: homosexuality being rethought in terms of property relations, and property relations being thought not only in terms of some linear accumulation of wealth or as the static antagonism between two ancient, self-similar classes, but as the contradiction-driven circulation of labor and early forms of capital, to which access is blocked or proffered, in both inter-elite competition and the survival-struggles of the labor market. In his introduction to the book, Chitty suggests that turning to this particularly open-ended version of Gramscian hegemony has implications for how we think about the category of the "queer." Referring to his method as a "queer realism" that is neither utopian n or melancholic, Chitty writes,

> Queer realism takes its cue from the idea of an "open Marxism," one inspired less by restrictive orthodox principles than by the ways in which Antonio Gramsci and others have sought to relate developments in the relations and forces of production to cultural developments and back again. In his *Prison Notebooks*, Gramsci makes the case that Marx's (and Machiavelli's) philosophical significance was to conceive of politics as operating according to principles and rules other than those of religion and morality. Princes make use of pieties when it's favorable to do so and abandon them when it's not. (27)

This practical, tactical deployment of scandal, Chitty suggests, can key us in to a history of homosexuality that assumes a transhistorical "homophobia" repressing a submerged but eventually triumphant gayness. Linking homosexuality to property relations, and seeing property relations as driven by contradiction, he writes,

> The "queer" can then be recast as a narrower descriptive category, signifying the lack of such status property: the way in which norms of gender and sexuality get weakened, damaged, and reasserted under conditions of local and generalized social, political, and economic crisis. The queer would then imply a contradictory process in which such norms are simultaneously denatured and renaturalized. Rather than marking some utopian opening up of these logics for self-transformative play, the queer would describe forms of love and inti-

macy with a precarious social status outside the institutions of family, property, and couple form. (26)

Queerness as outsiderhood will be familiar to readers of the queer theory of the last twenty years; the crucial difference here is Chitty's bidirectional sense of historical movement—he will argue later in the book that norms can get weaker and stronger, by turns, or at once, in different locales—and his sense that this contradictory movement is itself traceable to conditions of "local and generalized social, political, and economic crisis."

This brings us to another of Chitty's theoretical and historical coordinates, which is the body of work known as world-systems theory. Chitty makes particularly innovative use of the scholarship of the economist and historian Giovanni Arrighi, whose 1994 volume *The Long Twentieth Century: Money, Power, and the Origins of Our Times* has proven widely influential in periodizing capitalist crisis. By linking the Gramscian attempt to understand class hegemony to the world-systems theorists' investigation of the dynamics of capitalist crisis, Chitty opens up the possibility of new periodizations in this history of sexuality as well as new political optics for it.

For Arrighi, "hegemony" names the dynamic by which, since the fifteenth century, capital accumulation has been organized by the dominance of single political-economic bodies, which have succeeded each other across a series of "long centuries"—or, as he puts it, "cycles of accumulation." The historical scheme Arrighi lays out for this succession runs chronologically from a "Genoese-Iberian" hegemony (fifteenth through seventeenth centuries) to a Dutch one (late sixteenth to the late eighteenth centuries), then to British (mid-eighteenth to early twentieth centuries) and finally American dominance (late nineteenth century to the recent past).[1] Each cycle is more globally extensive than the last.

The transfer of such power over accumulation from one hegemon to another involves, for Arrighi, a tipping point in which the profitability of material expansion reaches a conjunctural limit: there is only so much more infrastructure to invest in; there is only so much more of key commodities to sell to saturated markets. This tilts the hegemon, and the system organized around it, away from material expansion and into financial expansion, which is to say, into speculation on future material possibilities. Such periods of financialization are politically unstable (as we have seen, since 2008), and for Arrighi they have historically marked the beginning of a transfer of power from one hegemon to the next, usually in the thick of "systemwide chaos" and war.[2]

Chitty's intuitive stroke of genius is to ask: If the history of capitalist production has indeed been structured this way, what does capitalist reproduction look like in such periods? This question structures the unusually ambitious historical arc of *Sexual Hegemony*, which roughly tracks the Arrighian narrative by beginning with a study of the class dynamics of sodomy prosecutions in fifteenth-century Florence, moving to the Dutch cities of the seventeenth century, and then to revolutionary and nineteenth-century Paris, before reflecting on the dominance and limits of late twentieth-century, American-style LGBT identity politics. Because so much scholarship on the history of sexuality has followed a modernity-framework that differs from the history Arrighi outlines, it is all but impossible for Chitty not to turn to the political character of sexuality in revolutionary France—itself the source of many of our historical stories about the birth of modernity. But his focus, even there, is on the question of what pressures might be shaping social reproduction—and through it, sexuality—in periods of political-economic crisis.

It was highly generative for Arrighi to construe "hegemony" in terms of inter-state relations, but *The Long Twentieth Century* is not primarily focused on the closer-to-the-ground, intranational class dynamics of "hegemony" in Gramsci's original sense. Nor is it focused on the peasant lifeways that subtended the transition to capital and that were so dramatically reorganized by it. For help with this, Chitty turns to the historian Fernand Braudel, whose pathbreaking work on the rise of capitalism in the Mediterranean basin is a key source for Arrighi as well. Following Braudel, Chitty isolates a key moment in the transition to capitalism in the Mediterranean world of the twelfth through the fifteenth centuries for its significance to social reproduction (such a long "moment" is typical of the Annales school of civilizational history to which Braudel contributed foundational methods). This period is epochal for Braudel partly because it involves the massive restructuring of peasant and agricultural lifeways, and Braudel tells its story with a layered historiography that superimposes archival discoveries about daily life with long-term civilizational transformation. In yet another remarkable and ambitious intuitive leap, Chitty takes advantage of the possibilities afforded by this layered historiography to pursue its implications for a history of homosexuality left unattended to by Annales-style scholarship. For Chitty, the rise in the extent and complexity of circum-Mediterranean textile manufacture that Braudel and others track is important because it drives a separation from peasant forms of production that is also a separation from their forms of reproduction. As he puts it:

The production of a propertyless condition is the decisive factor in the transition from economic production centered around mastery, reproductive marriage, and agricultural community to one based on impersonal market-mediated relations in towns and cities. The compulsion to produce for an employer or for the market is a form of life that produces surpluses, leading to the further development of the forces of production. It is a form of life that emerged on the periphery of peasant proprietorship, a population superfluous with respect to inheritance and land. (132)

For Chitty, it is this separation from production and reproduction, along with the forms of migration and journeying they generate, that gives us the matrix of modern sexuality:

Alternate or queer sexualities . . . emerged within the interstices of transformed property relations, through population displacements from the countryside and the subsequent concentration of those workers who were superfluous to agrarian production in urban centers, as well as within the institutions that attempted to manage or capture these surplus populations—factories, workhouses, standing armies, policing and punitive apparatuses, naval and merchant fleets, and colonial territories. (129–30)

The shift in this paragraph from an attention to queerness in relation to property, initially, to an emphasis on queerness in relation to institutions and settings that we might think of as catchments for labor—this shift indexes Chitty's other remaining theoretical coordinate: the work of Michel Foucault. Readers of Foucault will no doubt find aspects of the passage above familiar—the references to policing and punishment, say—and Chitty was indeed a deep, attentive reader of Foucault. But the differences are crucial. In *The History of Sexuality, Volume 1*, Foucault argues that sexual identities—including the precursors of those we'd now think of as "alternate," or "queer" —emerge as a result of the rise of sexual science, which itself is a product of the historical bourgeoisie's long attempt to displace older, aristocratic forms of authority and organization. Because Foucault is focused on developing a theory of power that is immanent to social relations, rather than merely elaborating a theory of power as the exertion of force by rulers upon the ruled, it is important that he distinguish this bourgeois project of sexual science from simple repression or domination. Sexual science was part of that class's quest for a firm understanding of itself, the "self-affirmation of one class rather than the enslavement of another."[3]

Foucault specifically counterposes this idea to what he seems to think would be a Marxist understanding of discipline, that is, the bourgeois discipline of workers:

If one writes the history of sexuality in terms of repression, relating this repression to the utilization of labor capacity, one must suppose that sexual controls were the more intense and meticulous as they were directed at the poorer classes; one has to assume that they followed the path of greatest domination and the most systematic exploitation: the young adult man, possessing nothing more than his life force, had to be the primary target of a subjugation destined to shift the energy available for useless pleasure toward compulsory labor. But this does not appear to be the way things actually happened. On the contrary, the most rigorous techniques were formed and, more particularly, applied first, with the greatest intensity, in the economically privileged and politically dominant classes. The direction of consciences, self-examination, the entire long elaboration of the transgressions of the flesh, and the scrupulous detection of concupiscence were all subtle procedures that could only have been accessible to small groups of people.[4]

This is a counterintuitive story, or at least an unexpected one. And it is not necessarily an anti-Marxist one. But it is easy to imagine a Marxist rejection of such a passage: no, this reply would go, the bourgeoisie really did discipline workers' sexuality first. Another Marxist reply to Foucault's counterintuitive idea might be that this story of bourgeois self-experimentation, which later spreads to the working classes, leaves aside something too important to ignore, which is a history of the at least semi-autonomous working-class sexualities that existed on the periphery of the bourgeois world, sometimes in defiance of it. The first reply would be an insistence on the intellectual, historical, and political primacy of exploitation rather than "power"; the second would be an insistence on the importance of recognizing the spaces and practices of freedom developed dialectically out of that exploitation.

Chitty takes neither of these routes (I am tempted to say he doesn't take the bait), because his Marxism is not primarily shaped by a desire to assert the moral primacy of the working classes. He simply notes that because Foucault makes the bourgeoisie his starting point, he misses something about the history of class struggle: "[Foucault's] theory of the emergence of modern sexual categories proceeds by assuming bourgeois sexuality to be hegemonic, rather than rigorously accounting for how it came to be so" (156).

When Foucault describes a gradual transformation from bourgeois indifference about the lives and deaths of the laboring class to a meticulous concern for its health and well-being, he does so using a broadly functionalist language: the bourgeoisie needed healthy populations to operate complex, heavy machinery, for instance.[5] While this functionalist language has the advantage of not allowing moral outrage to cloud an analysis of class conflict, it has the disadvantage of linearizing the history of that conflict. The project of capital accumulation did not just demand the management of workers' health after a long unconcern with it in a simple, unidirectional, or monolithic shift of attention. Capital accumulation has always been in continuous flux, down to this day, pitting workers who labor without managerial care for their health against those whose health is monitored and managed, producing a stratified working class according to the demands, not of machinery, but of the intercapitalist competition that compels the use of machinery in the first place.

What this means is that while Chitty is deeply sympathetic to Foucault's critique of power-as-repression-from-above, he is also committed to holding off on telling the story of the bourgeois management of populations as the story of a single epochal shift driven by new forms of technical knowledge about the self. His dialectical sense of sexual history leads him to argue, instead, that homosexuality in its forms as a recognizable identity are inseparable from processes of proletarianization that redounded even to the styles of homosexuality practiced by elites. This has political consequences. As the last part of *Sexual Hegemony* makes clear, Chitty shares with Foucault a skepticism that modern "gayness" is either innately leftist or liberatory, or even simply "freer" than some earlier, supposedly "closeted" or repressed innate homosexuality. Indeed, he is clear that he owes some of this skepticism to Foucault. But I want to venture that he gives us more to work with than does Foucault when it comes to recognizing that homosexualization, if we want to call it that, is dialectically enmeshed with the reproduction of class struggle, in that it cuts across the divide between styles of gayness that "reek of the commodity," as Michael Warner once put it, and styles of gayness that are rooted in displacement from the reproduction of capital. These working-class gay styles are harder to pin to sexuality exclusively; they are closer to the kind of "trade" that John Rechy describes in *City of Night*, or that Whitman identifies with when he calls himself "one of the roughs" in *Leaves of Grass*. The two styles—the two classed lifeways—are of course enmeshed at every level, including that of erotic fantasy: for every working-class camp subculture that ransacked the opulence of aristocratic style to build its own queerness, there is a patrician gayness that seeks re-lease in contact with rough-hewn laboring masculinity (one literary lineage of this would run from E. M. Forster's *Maurice* to Alan Hollinghurst's *The Swimming-Pool Library*).

Queer theory has tended to read these styles in polar rather than dialecti-cal terms (this is less true of gay historical scholarship, as I will suggest be-low). Mid-2000s queer academic debates about the "anti-social thesis" were a kind of summary and climax of this polarity—the question of the day was: Are LGBT folk innately ill-suited to the norms of social reproduction because their sexuality is unignorably internally riven, and they therefore represent unwelcome evidence that all sexuality, including self-congratulatory het-erosexuality, is riven and unviable too? Or are LGBT people opposed to such norms because their non-self-identicality opened onto the possibility of un-expected forms of social connection, more horizontal, less hierarchical? At its root this was a highly literary debate about the place of psychoanalysis in queer practices of interpretation, pitting Lacan's pathos of self-splitting against Deleuze's more optimistic sense that each "split self" was in fact part of a potentially multisubjective subjectivity. Though the parties involved did not frequently cite it, these debates found their impetus in Michael Warner's 1999 volume *The Trouble with Normal*, which was in part a riposte to jour-nalist and commentator Andrew Sullivan's 1995 *Virtually Normal*, which made a widely read conservative argument in favor of the assimilation of gay men (and to some extent lesbians) into traditional forms of family and citizenship. Though the activist Urvashi Vaid had made decisive histori-cal arguments against Sullivan-style bids for assimilation in her 1996 book *Virtual Equality: The Mainstreaming of Gay and Lesbian Liberation*, it was Warner's popularization of the theoretical term "heteronormativity" that served to orient academic critiques of the assimilationist impulse in the U.S. LGBT movement. Outside literary queer studies, scholars like Lisa Duggan extended this assimilationist-resistant binary by popularizing the term "ho-monormativity," which was meant to designate the politics of well-to-do white gay men who happily accepted racial exclusion, patriarchal privilege, and class power from the state in return for its acceptance of certain expres-sions of homosexuality. In this line of argument, "homonormativity" was opposed to a politically rebellious homosexuality that was antineoliberal, antiracist, and antipatriarchal.

These binaries tended to congeal into polar opposites during the course of academic debate, and they have always had a lightly prescriptive tone and a preoccupation with something like the moral question, Who should "we"

LGBT and queer folk be? Should we be good citizens? Or radical opponents to society as it is? Such binaries are not merely academic: they are often expressions of tactical decisions and concrete struggles in social movements. What makes Chitty's scholarship so interesting in this regard is his willingness, having studied some of the deep history preceding these dilemmas, to let go of the possibility of and the desire for a "we" based in either an identitarian-communitarian "homosexuality" or an abstractly antinormative "queerness." This is because he sees the vicissitudes of capital accumulation as analytically and historically prior to the formation and deformation of classes and views those processes as themselves prior to any identitarian experience of sexuality. It is also because he sees homosexuality's identitarian expressions only barely masking a class conflict with homosexuals on both sides, a conflict that runs deeper than individual identity and that obviates any attempt to make "gay people" or "queer people" an anticapitalist identity category tout court.

So rather than ask what kinds of politics homosexuals should have, Chitty begins with an anticapitalist politics that is committed to abolishing the forces that produced "gay people." He is agnostic about what forms of sexual life would outlive capital: he does not make an abolitionist argument per se, suggesting that "homosexuality" should disappear as an identity category; and he does not make a '70s-style utopian argument that, after some social revolution, "we" would all be bi- or pansexual. Rather than predict a future or prescribe a politics for homosexuality, Chitty closes *Sexual Hegemony* with a set of startling reflections on the recent past, which suggest alternatives to earlier scholarship on the relation between male homosexuality and capitalism. Let me describe briefly what some of that past scholarship has established.

Though Chitty refers to influential arguments made by scholars like George Chauncey, Jonathan Ned Katz, David F. Greenberg, and Jeffrey Weeks about male homosexuality and capitalism, he highlights the work of John D'Emilio as closest to his own. For D'Emilio, the social movement that marks its appearance on the national stage with the Stonewall riots of 1969 has important origins in both the same-sex intimacies enjoyed by soldiers in World War II and in the changes to the urban landscape of places like San Francisco after those soldiers' demobilization. In his landmark 1983 volume *Sexual Politics, Sexual Communities*, D'Emilio suggests that separation from the strictures of the nuclear family afforded young men and women the opportunity to experiment with nonprocreative sexuality as more than a series of isolated experiences. In an essay slightly predating this volume, called "Capitalism and Gay Identity," D'Emilio is clear that capitalist social relations have a contradictory relationship both to the nuclear family and to the homosexual identity that he thinks breaks free from it:

> On the one hand, capitalism continually weakens the material foundation of family life, making it possible for individuals to live outside the family, and for a lesbian and gay male identity to develop. On the other, it needs to push men and women into families, at least long enough to reproduce the next generation of workers. The elevation of the family to ideological preeminence guarantees that capitalist society will reproduce not just children, but heterosexism and homophobia. In the most profound sense, capitalism is the problem.[6]

In the conclusion to his essay, D'Emilio draws on his historical argument to make some political remarks from the perspective of a democratic socialism, remarks that scale down from the contradiction between capitalist accumulation and homosexual identity to another binary, that between homosexuality and family. Because they provide a useful contrast with Chitty's approach, I will quote them in full:

> The instability of families and the sense of impermanence and insecurity that people are now experiencing in their personal relationships are real social problems that need to be addressed. We need political solutions for these difficulties of personal life. These solutions should not come in the form of a radical version of the pro-family position, of some left-wing proposals to strengthen the family. Socialists do not generally respond to the exploitation and economic inequality of industrial capitalism by calling for a return to the family farm and handicraft production. We recognize that the vastly increased productivity that capitalism has made possible by socializing production is one of its progressive features. . . .
>
> We do need, however, structures and programs that will help to dissolve the boundaries that isolate the family, particularly those that privatize child-rearing. We need community- or worker-controlled daycare, housing where privacy and community coexist, neighborhood institutions—from medical clinics to performance centers—that enlarge the social unit where each of us has a secure place. As we create structures beyond the nuclear family that provide a sense of belonging, the family will wane in significance. Less and less will it seem to make or break our emotional security.

In this respect gay men and lesbians are well situated to play a special role. Already excluded from families as most of us are, we have had to create, for our survival, networks of support that do not depend on the bonds of blood or the license of the state, but that are freely chosen and nurtured. The building of an "affectional community" must be as much a part of our political movement as are campaigns for civil rights. In this way we may prefigure the shape of personal relationships in a society grounded in equality and justice rather than exploitation and oppression, a society where autonomy and security do not preclude each other but coexist.[7]

Writing at the dawn of the Reagan era, D'Emilio remains hopeful for a socialist politics that would gently abolish "family" as a stand-alone category by organizing a struggle whose aim is to draw on the productive plenty of which he feels presocialist capitalism has been capable. In one regard, D'Emilio is prescient here—on the other side of the long economic downturn that began in the years before D'Emilio's essay, the end of American hegemony has given U.S.-based democratic socialism its highest profile in a century, and left-democratic proposals for job guarantees and a "Green New Deal" are attracting wide attention. At the same time, however, D'Emilio's soft-abolitionist position regarding the family skips over the ways in which capitalist productivity does terrible harm not just because its products are poorly distributed, but because capitalist accumulation produces and requires labor regimes built on violence, subjugation, and the stratification of the workforce. And when he writes hopefully that "there may very well be more gay men and lesbians in the future," he is imagining a political success in terms that Chitty has abandoned.[8] Instead, Chitty writes drolly, "Gays and lesbians got a shot at dreams of the good life in the period of American hegemony precisely at the moment of its political-economic liquidation" (173). At this late stage of Chitty's argument it is clear that, for him, the global downward mobility of labor will pull not only gays and lesbians but "gay and lesbian" identity into its gravity as well.

As Max Fox notes in his preface to this volume, there is a painful dovetailing at the end of Chitty's manuscript between the historical present into which he's brought us, across so many centuries, and the abrupt end of his own life. Any reader of this book who takes its claims seriously will wonder what a more fully fleshed-out account of the present Chitty might have offered, in the last part of his argument, had he felt able to continue writing. This is true of his account of the past as well: readers will no doubt feel the range of ways in which this dazzling work remains unfinished. In closing, then, let me describe what I take to be the most important underexplored aspect of Chitty's argument and then briefly place him in a promising contemporary tendency.

A pressing question for any student of the history of sexuality who reads *Sexual Hegemony* will surely be its relationship to feminism and to lesbian studies. Chitty's attention to scholarship on these questions is peripheral to the book's focus on male homosexuality, but he is clear that women's labor and women's role in social reproduction are at the center of the historical forces that produce that sexuality. Writing about the beginning of the five-hundred-year period he adopts, Chitty attends to how homosexuality emerged in the interzone between act and lifeway on the margins of a peasant subsistence in which women's reproduction of children is constantly at issue; when he turns his attention toward more recent history, he notes that women's entry into the industrial workforce in the nineteenth century produced reverberations for male sexuality in tandem with transformations in women's. He turns to scholarship by historians like Janet Zollinger Giele and Kathleen Canning to support these observations, and when he brings the book around to the recent past, he turns to the work of scholars like Lillian Faderman, Martha Vicinus, Gayle Rubin, and Sharon Marcus for support in thinking about the political relationship between lesbians and gay men who experience their sexualities as identities. Reflecting on Adrienne Rich's classic 1980 essay "Compulsory Heterosexuality and Lesbian Existence," he touches on the contradictory character of this political alliance, which amalgamates different relations to productive and reproductive labor in a tactical alliance with the state:

Rich confronts us with another paradox of sexual hegemony: the extension, by analogy, of an epistemology of male homosexuality [the equation of "homosexuality" with male gayness] to women-identified women erases their unique political existence and history. Politically, however, this elision has made possible new forms of solidarity between gay men and lesbians for the achievement of formal equality, same-sex marriage, and the radical politicization of AIDS. Political mobilization around AIDS drew upon feminists' crucial experience in making women's health issues visible to medical bureaucracies. Feminist affinity with male homosexuality often involved solidarity with gender-variant types and with oppressed axes of class, racial, and sexual identity from which the mainstream movement for gay rights sought to distance itself. Although the feminist tradition continues to emphasize the vital importance of particularity in understanding experiences and histories of oppression, the price of legal recognition for gays and lesbians as a class involved glossing over such particulars. (146–47)

Nonetheless, it is hard to read *Sexual Hegemony* without a sense of its unfinished exploration of feminist scholarship. This is true in terms of both period-specific and longue durée work. A deeper engagement with work like Marcus's *Between Women: Friendship, Desire, and Marriage in Victorian England,* for instance, would have shed light on the limits of Rich's continuum model of women's relationships: Marcus amply demonstrates that, in the mid-nineteenth century, such relationships demonstrated a range of textures and a variety of roles which would find no place in a continuum model but which, if we were to cross-reference Marcus with Chitty, we would recognize as reproductive in a broader sense, and dialectical. That is, Marcus shows that female friendships could serve as material support for heterosexual marriage, or even as its ideal model, while also bequeathing habits of couplehood and kin-building to future women who would think of themselves, as modern "lesbians," in terms more opposed to nuclear family and marriage. Chitty's work, in turn, allows us to reread *Between Women* with a clearer sense of the class-hegemonic character of the social projects that both shaped women's relationships and afforded them unexpected leeway.

Similarly, it seems undeniable that *Sexual Hegemony* would only have benefited from engagement with feminist work on the longue durée such as Silvia Federici's *Caliban and the Witch: Women, the Body, and Primitive Accumulation* or Maria Mies's *Patriarchy and Accumulation on a World Scale.* To take Federici as an example: like Chitty, she is committed to developing a historical account of sexuality linked to the epochal transformations of European agrarian life that led to the birth of capitalism. And like Chitty, she identifies a flexible capitalist strategy which spans the entire period and which shapes sexuality as necessary. For Federici that strategy is primitive accumulation, rather than statecraft; and it is clear that Chitty's sense of male homosexuality's emergence from the disruption of peasant forms of subsistence and reproduction would only have been deepened by attention to the archive Federici assembles of political struggles over those peasant forms—not least struggles led by women in the name of both actual and possible forms of communalism. Federici's welcome feminist universalism leads her to underplay the history of the development of a heterosexual-homosexual divide, but it affords an emphasis, not only on capitalism, but also on active, conscious struggle against it; Chitty's keen historical awareness of the adaptability of capital, not least in its making and remaking of states as well as identities, leads him to give only passing attention to anticapitalist struggle. The two volumes are very productively read in tandem.

Sexual Hegemony also forms part of a contemporary wave of Marxist scholarship that is providing fresh ways to think about gender, sex, race, and revolutionary practice. Key writing from this moment has been published in the communist journal *Endnotes*, and much (though hardly all) of it emerges from cycles of political struggle in Santa Cruz and the San Francisco Bay Area dating to around 2010. But the new wave of scholarship is wider than the *Endnotes* project and is linked, if sometimes only implicitly, by an attention to what Marx called "The General Law of Capitalist Accumulation."

In chapter 25 of volume 1 of *Capital* (the chapter that goes by the title "The General Law"), Marx develops an argument about how the organic composition of capital—that is, the value ratio between means of production and labor-power—shifts with the tides of intercapitalist competition, always tugged in the direction of more efficient machinery, with the result that the production process comes to involve less exploitable human labor. Because this expulsion of labor-power from the production process is also the expulsion of the source of that process's profitability, capitalists have to maintain profitability in a range of other ways, from finding new markets to pushing wages as low as possible. This is why, in the second half of chapter 25, Marx shifts from a discussion of the pressures on the composition of capital to his famous account of the "reserve army of labor." Here he provides a schematic description of negative relations to the wage—what he calls stagnant, latent, and floating reserves—as well as a brief account of sheer pauperdom. This relative surplus population is the product of a dynamic of exploitation by which capitalists continually try to reduce the number of workers they employ and create, in the process, a population of formerly and intermittently exploitable people.

Marx closes out chapter 25 with brief empirical analyses of gang-labor in English agriculture and of impoverishment in Ireland. But it's not hard to see how we might expand the frame of his analysis to think, for instance, about capitalism's global dynamics, or about the household arrangements that have accompanied the rise of the wage relation. For me, this is where the rubber hits the road today. If the revival of interest in Marx after the 2008 financial crisis first led us to try to understand financialization and the contradictions in the money form, it was very soon accompanied by a revival of interest in aspects of the Marxist tradition that had lain understudied by Marxists for decades, not least the political and intellectual work of Black and anticolonial Marxists, and of Marxist feminists. Returning to this work and bringing it into contact with a range of contemporary Marxist thinkers is providing us an opportunity to develop a stronger, more flexible account of capitalism, one that takes into account the waves of struggle since 2008 from Occupy to Black Lives Matter to #NoDAPL to #MeToo as well as conversations about universal basic income, robotization, and job guarantees. It goes without saying that this more robust Marxism, one that keeps exclusion from the wage in a close relation to the compulsion to work, can also help us think about processes of environmental degradation, since the waste products of capital are the sources of that degradation, just as the populations capital wastes are the objects of its indifference.

Work like this could help us move past old divisions between a Marxism that saw capital through the lens of a narrow version of "class," on the one hand, and a range of social movements, including so-called identity movements, that rightly suspected this Marxism of deprioritizing struggles outside the industrial workplace or, worse, taking the wrong side in struggles to oppose racism, sexism, and colonial subjugation. The rising superfluity of the kinds of labor that built global middle classes is affording an opportunity to see links between different moments in the history of capitalist exploitation: the ejection of wider and wider swaths of the global population from a stable wage could and should make us take notice of the history of the shaping of other unwaged, intermittently waged, and surplus populations long before our time. Chitty's work in *Sexual Hegemony* does just this: one of the most startling effects of reading the book, for me, was the realization that the specific prehistory of male homosexuality that makes the most sense for thinking about its contemporary contradictions is less the modernity-story of the rise of sexual science than the long story of labor-seeking migration that is most visible in the United States today in political struggles over immigration.

This is just to say that, as *Sexual Hegemony* begins its future in print, it has many fellow-travelers. Readers of this volume will benefit from thinking of it alongside work on racial capitalism by Nathan Connolly, Donna Murch, and Nikhil Singh; on the abolition of "race" as one aim of anticapitalist, antiracist struggle, by Chris Chen; on "the logic of gender" and on revolutionary motives by *Endnotes* and by Jasper Bernes; on settler-colonial violence by Iyko Day and Glen Coulthard; on the production of waste frontiers by Jason

Moore; on the accumulation strategies of energy regimes by Andreas Malm; and on the longue-durée rhythms of anticapitalist struggle by Joshua Clover.

I was an outside reader on Chitty's dissertation in the History of Consciousness program at the University of California, Santa Cruz; that work is this book. We only met once, in a café on Shattuck Avenue in Berkeley in 2014; Chitty wanted to outline his work for me to see if I might be interested in serving on his committee. I didn't know what I was in for. My excitement grew as Chitty described the ambit of his thesis; before he was finished, I was already imagining the range of scholars whose work would be altered by such a project. I had no idea that the work would remain unfinished, of course. But my effort here has been to suggest the riches you can find in this work, if you are patient with it. The chapters are of sharply varying lengths; it is clear that the final reflections might have made better sense as part of a sustained introduction; passages notionally focused on one period contain long asides on other periods altogether; and the citational apparatus will never be what it should be or could have been. The text digresses, leaps, and speculates, sometimes on the basis of the archive, sometimes on the basis of intuitions whose sources are invisible. It is not polished. But it is extraordinary, even singular—and my hope is that it will change the way we think about sexuality and anticapitalist struggle alike.

PART I sexual hegemonies of historical capitalism

1

It is categories in the mind and guns in their hands which keep us enslaved.
—LARRY MITCHELL, *The Faggots and Their Friends between Revolutions, 1977*

HOMOSEXUALITY AND CAPITALISM

Since Michel Foucault's critique of the repressive hypothesis, historians have been largely agnostic toward the politics of sexual liberation. A caricature of how that politics understood the dialectic of sexual freedom and constraint is opposed to liberationists' own, perhaps exaggerated, portrait of a sexually repressive society. The resulting history of sexuality proceeds like something of a masked drama, with comedic or tragic significance depending on one's perspective. "Doctors, reformers, Christians, educators," Françoise Barret-Ducrocq writes in *Love in the Time of Victoria*, were drowning in an "insistent discursive tide" ebbing beneath the apparently modest surface of "speech, gesture, and clothing."[1] Theirs was a culture marred by hypocrisy, Jeffrey Weeks writes, where "verbal and visual delicacy marched arm and arm with a flourishing pornography."[2] "Mingling contradictions" appear in some of the first portraits of the Victorian age from this side of the war that brought about its end: "a vision of strange characters," we read in Lytton Strachey's *Eminent Victorians*, "moved by mysterious impulses, interacting in queer complication, and hurrying at last—so it almost seems—like creatures in a puppet show to a predestined catastrophe."[3]

The American century, too, witnessed a striking tableau of "mingling contradictions." Organized political repression of pornography and alternate sexualities peaked during the Great Depression and through the two decades following the Second World War; however, this same period generated the "vanguard" of a particular form of "homosexual freedom," argues Andrew Sullivan in *Virtually Normal*, "despite its tradition of fundamentalist Christianity, despite its capitalist system, despite its allegedly oppressive influence in world culture."[4]

"So it was that our society assembled," writes Foucault in the first volume of *The History of Sexuality*, "a whole machinery for speechifying, analyzing, and investigating."[5] "We, Victorians," or so the familiar story goes.[6] "Speechifying," exactly. Who would dare make such proclamations today? The proximity of the "Victorians" with "our society" was already something of a jest in the mid-1970s. Bourgeois sexual norms—do they exist anymore?

From a sociological perspective, the present is marked by an "end of the European-family marriage boom."[7] With significant national variations, intimate arrangements under late capitalism now display a variegated pattern of precarity: informal coupling, serial marriage, delayed marriage, and single life. Parenting has been delinked from pairing. This pattern, Göran Therborn writes, is "remarkably synchronized across the Western part of the continent, and even across the oceans, including the North American and Pacific New Worlds, and at least parts of Latin America, such as Argentina and Venezuela."[8] In retrospect, nothing appears to have been historically "normal" about middle-class nuclear family norms; these were quite extraordinary.

Outside the privileged classes, capitalism supported these peculiar customs for coupling and raising offspring for a brief period beginning with the sexual chaos initially unleashed by industrialization, reaching its peak in the mid-nineteenth century, and continuing until the social upheavals of the 1960s and collapse of the USSR—little more than a century. And even this short century of middle-class nuclear-family norms was uneven. War and depression eroded this sexual hegemony in the first decades of the twentieth century, raising the specter of freer sexual mores and necessitating state repression to curb unruly working-class sexual cultures. As these wars tended to level social hierarchies, whether through the creative destruction of capital or the mobilization of populations for war, disinhibition and an increasing optionality of sexual norms were the rule, creating sexual cultures more closely resembling those of the present period than some Victorian puppet show of tarts and prudes.

The achievement of gay rights only seems like a dramatic about-face from a perspective that views homophobia as a timeless force of social exclusion. The forms of repression against which the gay and lesbian rights movement struggled were, on the contrary, "of recent origin and of short duration," as historian George Chauncey writes.[9] Homosexual repression, as such, was largely the product of an expanded state bureaucracy, increased police power, and capital's twentieth-century concern for the welfare and health of working populations.[10] The goals of the gay and lesbian rights movement were posed internally to the developmentalist state, which incentivized nuclear family norms to curb various male excesses, forge an immensely more productive labor force, and foster adjustment to new kinds of work around the middle of the twentieth century. A transnational imagined community of queers established itself in response to organized state repression.[11] During the postwar period, gays and lesbians struggled against the censorship of lifestyle magazines, pornography, films, and pulp novels. They forged political alliances with neighborhood businesses and other minority groups to oppose police brutality and raids on bars and other public spaces. State repression galvanized a political consciousness known to no other period in the existence of such institutions.[12]

Since the 1970s, Perry Anderson writes in *The Origins of Postmodernity*, the "democratization of manners and disinhibition of mores advanced together."[13] A vertical dedifferentiation of the social order has unraveled norms of discipline and restraint at every level of society. As developmentalist states encouraged and promoted middle-class nuclear-family norms in order to facilitate working populations' adjustment to more demanding labor processes, it's not so surprising that this hegemony should break apart during a period of flexible employment, declining real wages, debt-fueled consumption, and successive asset bubbles. High-income societies became morally apathetic toward perversions and differences of sexual taste as enduring intimacy and stable families became anomalies in the lives of ever more people. In some places this waning of sexual affect has enabled an extension of marriage and family rights to gays and lesbians. Once excluded as sexual outlaws from the hallowed institutions of family and property, same-sex couples now represent model neoliberal citizens in many high-income countries.

Although the picture is not so consistent, or so rose-tinted, everywhere in the world, increasing sexual options were a global phenomenon in the late twentieth century. Two great fertility declines—the first, accompanying industrialization and the French and American Revolutions, and a second, corresponding to the postwar developmentalist state and anticolonial movements—index the global impact of emancipatory movements in terms of increasing sexual freedom and life options.[14] These epochal transformations, long obscured by the rhetoric of the culture wars, fundamentally altered the terrain of sexual politics. Economic development accounts for a significant part of this story; however, political contingency has also played a crucial role.

A consideration of the politics of homosexuality prior to the rise of middle-class nuclear-family norms requires some alternative to the modernization thesis in which sexual freedom develops alongside commodity production. Urban, interclass cultures of sex and intimacy between men flourished at the historic centers of the early modern capitalist world system: Florence and Venice in the fourteenth century, the United Provinces and London in the seventeenth and eighteenth centuries, and Paris and other great cities in the late eighteenth and early nineteenth centuries. This episodic character, corresponding to what Karl Marx identified as periods of primitive accumulation, suggests a new periodization for the history of sexuality. These periods organize the structure of the chapters that follow. Each chapter considers these episodes from the perspective of their economic and geographic conditions of possibility, how sodomy accusations and regulations figured in republican political experiments, and how the cultural artifacts left behind by these formations reflect a struggle between residual and emergent social forces.

The study attempts to throw light on these earlier moments in which conservative, middle-class sexual norms and categories had not yet achieved dominance in the combined and uneven transition to capitalism. These norms formed part of the field of struggle of national bourgeois formations against elements of the old regime for control over state and civil society. The social visibility of cultures of sodomy made sex between men into an object of scandal and a target for state repression, and such politicizations revealed the same social fault lines that animated the political upheavals of each period. Urban, interclass political alliances sought to reactivate the republican political forms of antiquity, just as urban cross-class cultures of sodomy understood themselves as reactivations of classical forms of love between men.

Aside from a few introductory and concluding thoughts, I have limited myself to these early modern examples in which the tensions between residual and emergent lifeworlds began to crystallize into something like modern sexual categories, norms, and cultures. This "something like modern sexual categories, norms, and cultures" has been a contentious topic in theory and history since the social turn of the 1960s.[15]

The remainder of this introduction attempts to make a path through what has become an overgrown thicket of interpretations by advancing a methodological, aesthetic, and political approach I call "queer realism." By considering cultures of sex between men in light of the temporality of attempts to establish early modern republics—a cycle of revolution, interregnum, and restoration—I foreground the role of contingency in the history of cultures of sodomy. I close with a précis of the account that unfolds over the succeeding chapters.

Queer Realism

A relationship of sexual hegemony exists wherever sexual norms benefiting a dominant social group shape the sexual conduct and self-understandings of other groups, whether or not they also stand to benefit from such norms and whether or not they can achieve them. Sexual norms operate at the level of aspirational fantasy and as a form of social status. Habituation to such norms has sometimes secured wealth and prestige for socially dominant groups and a wider sphere of influence for those in subaltern groups. Deviation from them has, at other times, altered these relations of force very little, and no strong relationship of sexual hegemony can be identified. Groups have achieved sexual hegemony with force and consent, repression and persuasion. At certain crucial points in its history, sexuality has provided a weapon for the strong and the weak in struggles for legitimacy and power.

Normalized sexual arrangements sometimes produced predictable, stable, and productive workforces, ensured national cohesion, and provided a rationale for extending state welfare assistance. Sexual norms also functioned in more oblique ways to impose a moral order upon public spaces and domestic arrangements, setting up sanitary geographies in which some bodies mattered and others didn't. They have, at other times, been neutral with respect to these relations of power and matters of life and death.

The problem of sexual hegemony: whether and how sexuality outside marriage and property relations congealed into opposition, defiance, or open antagonism toward socially dominant groups and their institutions.

Put differently: How has sexual anarchy propped up such dominant groups and institutions by enhancing their prestige? How has marriage functioned to transmit property—and thus, the social dominance of one class over another—from generation to generation? How have the formation and dissolution of sexual hegemonies been politically and economically necessary despite whatever moral hackles they raised?

I call my approach to this very broad problem-field "queer realism" for a number of methodological, aesthetic, and political reasons.[16] Queer realism is not a call for a return to positivism, as the term "realism" has sometimes been used. Methodologically, queer realism is not a theory of how power works to shape sexuality, according to some schema of repression or that which is typically proposed using concepts of "normativity" and "homophobia."

Overt societal repression of sexuality—in terms of the ability to detect, prevent, exclude, punish, and prevent sexual deviance—may be one function of sexual hegemony, but this power has historically accompanied the growth of state bureaucracies. It makes for a poor basis of comparative analysis with the early modern period, for increasing sexual repression only ever indexes the growth and penetration of state apparatuses into the social tissue of everyday life.

The normal will not be understood as "normativity"—some free-floating, regulative idea, perhaps taking shape in particular institutions, according to which human activities are monitored and judged. I will instead conceive of the normal as a status, one which—given certain concrete socioeconomic conditions—accrues material advantages to those who achieve it or happen to be born into it.[17] This understanding restores a sociological significance to the term by reframing whatever cultural competences it marks as extensions of status property. As Pierre Bourdieu writes, "Only those who ought to have it can really acquire it and only those who are authorized to have it feel called upon to acquire it."[18]

The "queer" can then be recast as a narrower descriptive category, signifying the lack of such status property: it captures the way in which norms of gender and sexuality get weakened, damaged, and reasserted under conditions of local and generalized social, political, and economic crisis. The queer would then imply a contradictory process in which such norms are simultaneously denatured and renaturalized. Rather than marking some utopian opening up of these logics for self-transformative play, the queer would describe forms of love and intimacy with a precarious social status outside the institutions of family, property, and couple form. This critical redefinition of the categories of the normal and the queer has political implications for present, ongoing analyses of the intersection of gender, privilege, race, class, and sexuality.[19]

Queer realism takes its cue from the idea of an "open Marxism," one inspired less by restrictive orthodox principles than by the ways in which Antonio Gramsci and others have sought to relate developments in the relations and forces of production to cultural developments and back again.[20] In his *Prison Notebooks,* Gramsci makes the case that Marx's (and Machiavelli's) philosophical significance was to conceive of politics as operating according to principles and rules other than those of religion and morality. Princes make use of pieties when it's favorable to do so and abandon them when it's not. My argument seeks to unsettle a commonplace that creeps into histories and theories of sexuality: that moral or religious ideologies are at the core of sexual intolerance and oppression, which, in the final analysis, boil down to a kind of irrational superstition or phobia awaiting the right conditions to break out. This kind of ideology critique frequently winds up renaturalizing the very cultural phenomena it was meant to explain.

The socialist tradition sought to portray sexual nonconformity as a logical outcome of the ruthless drive of capital toward greater profit, turning a liberal bourgeois atmospherics of scandal and titillation against itself. If property ownership incentivized stable family formations, then the development of capitalism had a tendency to generate a quasi-universal condition of propertylessness in which there was no basis for normal family life. This was especially true for the earliest phase of industrialization, during which Marx and Engels undertook their analyses.

Marx's own term for this propertyless condition—the "proletariat"—drew upon an analogy with the status of the propertyless citizens of ancient Rome. The *proletarii* of the Roman Constitution referred to free men who lacked sufficient property for full enfranchisement in the political community. Merely contributing a supply of human life to the polity (and occasional muscle for the Roman galleys) through their biological reproduction, they sustained the growth and expansion of the Empire.[21] From this choice of words, it's clear that Marx sought to distance himself from the moralism of his day in order to grasp the political significance of the destructive forces unleashed by capitalist development. Despite whatever liberal pieties were pronounced, the liquidation of traditional subsistence economies was a barbarous and ongoing process, providing a constant supply of new laborers to replace those destroyed by perilous working conditions and disease in cities.[22]

During the 1840s and especially following the revolutions of 1848, middle-class reformers fretted over the effects of this propertyless condition as if it were a metaphysical "crisis of the family." In stark contrast to the nostalgia of early bourgeois sociologists such as Frédéric Le Play and Wilhelm Heinrich Riehl, who contrasted the instability of industrial society with the bucolic sexual innocence and patriarchal power of peasant families, Engels's *The Condition of the English Working Class* (1844) and *The Origin of the Family, Private Property, and the State* (1884) and Marx's conscription of reports generated by factory, housing, and children's labor inspectors in *Capital* (1867) sought to aesthetically estrange readers from liberalism's affective tonality for registering sexual and moral differences. To do so they juxtaposed the alarmed reports of bourgeois reformers with a steely prose, assessing the structural causes and abstract, impersonal compulsions driving such apparent moral disorder. Oscar Wilde's withering formulations in *The Soul of Man under Socialism* (1890) and George Orwell's more introspective *Road to Wigan Pier* (1937) provide later, more self-critical examples of the technique. As representational interventions, these texts sought to demonstrate, by way of an estrangement from learned structures of feeling, that moral responses to abjection and poverty were themselves part of the problem.

These old socialist representational strategies may no longer be suited to the present period of moral permissiveness and of widespread cynicism toward traditional ideologies. Queer realism sets for itself the modest task of dedramatizing the kinds of stories we tell about the sexualities of the past. To do so is to short-circuit the connection between individual fantasy and collective identification. As in Bertolt Brecht's dedramatization of epic theater with juxtaposition, anecdote, and cut-up, the desired effect of this aesthetic realism is deflationary.[23] Its purpose is to reopen the place for "big enough history," as James Clifford writes: "Realism works self-consciously with partial histories, alert to their constitutive tensions."[24]

Dedramatization eschews the whiggish and tragic cathexes of history that inhere to liberal and romantic models, respectively. The intellectual formation thrown up by the gay liberation movement has for decades been divided, the efforts of one tendency fixed on the prize (and discontents) of formal equality and those of the other captured by overwhelming losses and defeats. One tendency tells a story that mercilessly paves over such defeats with a yellow brick road of progress. The other speaks of this past in a melancholic trance, weighed down by the immeasurable losses of life that brought an end to the gay counterculture of the 1970s.[25] To unburden sexual history from the imperative that it answer to present sexual identities and cultures is to relieve it from the sense of urgency of an earlier period. Although that sense of urgency was generative, this disburdening seems to be a necessary starting point for experimenting with alternate kinds of historical narrative and collective belonging.

My appeal to realism is thus a performative intervention. "Realness" was initially queer slang for the face one had to wear in the straight world—less deception or disguise than a disengaged persona and form of comportment. According to this slightly cynical understanding, realness has the meaning of subjectivating a sense of what is possible. This kind of realness has historically provided queers with rhetorical strategies for questioning dominant ideologies while nonetheless moving within them. The importance of a disengaged persona deserves a place alongside that often dreamy appeal to some queer utopian imaginary, however politically important and worth defending that may also be.

Contingency and the History of Homosexuality

Names can be tricky, especially where sexual institutions are concerned. Even Aristotle's *Politics*, which takes the union of man and woman as the basis of all forms of society, furnishes no unique name for this institution.[26] Émile Benveniste, who along with fellow structuralists Georges Dumézil and Claude Lévi-Strauss laid the intellectual groundwork for the nominalism of Georges Canguilhem and Michel Foucault, admits in *Le Vocabulaire des institutions indo-européens* that relations of kinship are "lexical anomalies" without ur-sources for their various appellations.[27] If the terminology of so "universal" an institution as exogamous marriage between man and woman discloses so little about a common origin and remains so resistant to etymological analysis, it is reasonable to expect that a nominalist account would fail to account for the origins of marginal sexual institutions.

Nonetheless, historians have attempted to establish a basis for cross-cultural histories of homosexuality with a narrative of the succession of modes of production influenced by classical political economy. Each mode of production has been associated with its own garden varieties of "homosexuality": homosexual shamanism and fraternal bonding amid nearly universal exogamy in hunter-gatherer societies; a general sexual stability with room for eccentricity (bestiality, bastardy, incest, polygamy, polyandry, homosexuality, etc.) within pastoral societies; homosexual warriors and priests alongside various occultations of the family in the first Indo-European agricultural settlements.[28] Same-sex eroticism has been documented in most artisanal classes in which age and status hierarchies subjected male youths to the direct domination of adult men in handicraft production.

In each social form there is evidence of a sacred (or ridiculed) gender-variant type and a profane, non-gender-variant, warrior type of male same-sex behavior, neither of which seems to have upset the order of things in traditional societies. Same-sex eroticism in the context of artisanal production—often called pederasty, after the Greek fashion—centered around youths, who were expected to play the passive-receptive role, and arose with a certain level of economic development and a certain social importance placed upon the division of labor. These institutions and relations, fraught with social power, could be quite troublesome for social hierarchies.[29] Thus, according to a sort of Dumézilian mythopoetics in which the third term turns out to be the dynamic one, the comparative history of social forms has turned up sacral, martial, and economic same-sex eroticism, accounting for each of the tripartite social functions of Indo-European societies.[30]

This world-heritage approach has made for some questionable history. Same-sex attraction and sexual activities are not actually historical according to this paradigm. Specificities get presented as mere curiosities of custom according to a sort of relativism, but the behavior appears universal, more or less common to all social forms, modified here and there by various institutional, cultural, and economic contexts. This historicism can suggestively string together a diverse collection of costumes and set pieces reconstructed from the artifacts deposited by some gradual process of accretion and erosion; however, these layers ultimately appear static and two-dimensional. The perspective can account for neither the social forces giving rise to the colorful procession nor the interest of its audience in the unfolding tableau.

A set of questions goes unanswered. Two central ones are of concern here: Why did sex between men become so problematic within social forms that placed such great importance upon a division of labor? And how did the political and social struggles that characterized such social forms generate and transform cultures of sex between men? Early modern cities are of crucial importance for these questions. The growth of civil institutions of governance, trade in raw materials, the production of finished goods, and large urban populations generated some of the first socially visible cultures of sodomy in early modern cities. The problem of how these cultures became socially visible gets to the nub of the political and social struggles that accompanied urban growth. Thus, an approach able to take into account both the structural conditions of possibility for cultures of sex between men and the contingent effects of political struggles upon such cultures could provide a new basis for comparative history.

Eve Kosofsky Sedgwick, who criticized the unilinear narrative temporality of David Halperin's *One Hundred Years of Homosexuality* and Michel Foucault's *History of Sexuality, Volume 1*, may also be credited with providing a clever, if obvious, psychoanalytic reading of genealogical thinking.[31] Far from being "queer," she writes, genealogy is remarkably "Oedipal":

> The dogged, defensive stiffness of a paranoid temporality, after all, in which yesterday can't be allowed to have differed from today and tomorrow must be even more so, takes its shape from a generational narrative that's characterized by a distinctly Oedipal regularity and repetitiveness: it happened to my father's father, it happened to my father, it is happening to me.

And so on. "But isn't it a feature of queer possibility—only a contingent feature, but a real one, and one that in turn strengthens the force of contingency itself—that our generational relations don't always proceed in this lockstep?"[32] The problem of the plural possessive pronoun in "our generational relations" remains the hinge of ambivalent queer senses of belonging, possibility, and temporality outside "generational narratives" rooted in the family romance. What sort of belonging is this? If not identity with the past, then what?

In his essay "On the Concept of History," Walter Benjamin associated the temporality of narrative succession with social democracy and its limited vision of history as progress. He thought that by registering the past as a "dialectical image," containing a "multiplicity of histories," the concept of history could be liberated "from the schema of progression within an empty and homogeneous time."[33] To do something more than present the past "the way it was," the historical materialist "has to brush history against the grain—even if he needs a barge pole to do it."[34] For Benjamin, as for Sedgwick, Proust's model of epiphanic recollection, in which "mnemonic shocks" produce "a climactic series of joy-inducing truths about the relation of writing to time,"[35] provided an alternative to "historicism's bordello" by relating a "unique experience with the past."[36]

The relation of memory and writing to time, which Benjamin identified with a dialectical conception of history, bears an isomorphic relation to the temporality of emancipatory struggles, which, Benjamin writes, take place under the sign of "enslaved ancestors rather than the ideal of liberated grandchildren."[37] This temporality isn't against a future. Its ecstatic and epiphanic relation to the past remains far more open to possible futures than the ways in which fixations on forward and backward movement, babies and death, tend to limit social imaginaries.

Benjamin's articulation of the relation between political form and temporal models helps explain why contemporary sexual history has tended to favor a progressive, unilinear temporality. As the historian Dagmar Herzog points out, this literature was mostly written during the late twentieth-century ascendance of a "liberalization paradigm," which presumes "the gradual overcoming of obstacles to sexual freedom" but "leaves us with few tools for making sense of moments of renewed sexual conservatism."[38] Compared to the relative sophistication of histories of political forms, Herzog argues, existing theories and models of sexual history have great trouble with periods of restoration and interregnum. Against a model of progressive liberalization and its recoil, analogous to the archaeological model of impassable epistemic breaks, Herzog proposes a *syncopated* quality of sexual developments in Western Europe": rhythmic alternations, starts and stops, periods of calm punctuated by dramatic reversals.[39]

"Syncopated sex"—sure. The metaphor is suggestive. Most readers of sexual history would probably agree with Herzog's judgment that contingency has played a far more important role than is generally allowed in the usual modernization story of cumulative accretion and development. But to what drummer has sexual restoration marched? The question requires more than the identification of periods and patterns of reaction to sexualities falling outside middle-class sexual norms—although this is a necessary starting point. It requires a theoretical framework that can account for how and why public cultures of homosexuality and prostitution were perceived as threatening. Was there an actual basis for such perceptions? How did the regulation of these cultures effectively prop up a formation of sexual hegemony favoring middle-class norms? How was sexuality different before the rise of national bourgeoisies?

The twentieth-century story is illuminating to consider. The theory of moral panics has been adept at describing periods of homophobia and sexual reaction, revealing an episodic structure to such politicizations. Social crises with obscure causes provoke a politics of scapegoating in the public sphere, mobilizing irrational fears and anger into a morally regulative force, elaborating new techniques of discipline and social repression. This or that figure of deviance—or "folk devil"—is imagined to pose a threat to the social order, shoring up the forces of repression.[40]

However illuminating, the theory of moral panics has been unable to account for the *differentia specifica* of homosexuality in this role. The paradigm has tended to assume that antihomosexual sentiment is a sort of timeless ideology given vent by social crisis. Tolerance gets negatively conceived as the absence of homophobia; however, the very publicness of cultures of sodomy suggests that something more than the absence of fear and panic allowed such cultures to flourish, something positive or constitutive, perhaps solidarity with sexual outlaws, or opposition to the dominant culture. Despite the limitations of the moral-panic paradigm, it has laid the groundwork for reintegrating microhistories of periodic sex panics back into a more systematic framework of analysis.

The closet, as late twentieth-century gay activists and intellectuals understood it—a subjective interiority into which homosexuality was forced by epistemological structures prohibiting its public expression—can no longer be understood as some universal social experience of homosexuals. It was the experience of a privileged class of homosexuals who are overrepresented in the literary archive. A highly public culture of same-sex love flourished in working-class, immigrant, and African American enclaves of New York and other cities in the late nineteenth and early twentieth centuries.[41] The relative oblivion into which those cultures and lives have fallen suggests the limitations of historical models emphasizing a progressive story.

The repression of New York's fairy subculture provided an outlet for middle-class male resentment toward wider transformations in the mode of production: work in large corporate firms in which these men were increasingly subject to the management of other men, the employment of female office workers, the precarity of traditional breadwinning identities during a period of depression and war, and threats from organized labor all menaced white middle-class male status property.[42] The same culture of effeminate, working-class fairies that once confirmed the normalcy of middle-class men toward the end of the nineteenth century now reflected back these same men's feminization, embodying a range of threats to middle-class men's status in a vertically differentiated society.[43]

The normalization—that is, extension of the form of status property in sexuality—of working-class families provided a basis for a wider hegemony of middle-class understandings of deviant sexualities. In the early twentieth century, the nuclear family became a powerful regulatory instrument for reproducing a reliable, regimented laboring population. To counteract the high turnover of labor in Ford's factories, the paradigmatic industrial enterprise created a Department of Sociology to investigate its workers' family life and ensure the ethnic immigrants of Detroit had been transformed into proper "Ford men."[44] The discipline in Ford's factories expanded to target areas of housing and family life that had historically been a matter of indifference to the concrete production process.

As the conditions of social and economic crisis were shared by most highly developed countries following the First World War, such a pattern of mid-twentieth-century American repression of working-class sexuality held true in Western Europe, Japan, Russia, and other countries. Socially repressive forces were brought to bear on proletarian cultures of lawlessness; prostitution and homosexuality were increasingly subject to police power and pathologizing discourses. This process led to an extension of bourgeois sexual hegemony over working-class norms and self-understandings.[45]

In the last few decades of the twentieth century, social historians produced a remarkable history of homosexual cultures whose principle of unity and intelligibility across a long span of time was highly socialized and public sexual contact between men from different classes, ethnic groups, and national origins. Whatever continuities can be established between these cultures were less the result of some organic reproduction of memory and tradition from one generation to the next, less the product of some stable consumer identity mediated by markets, technology, or print culture, than the consequence of codes, behaviors, and affects transmitted from body to body within particular institutions, reproducing these social practices and institutions of interclass sexual contact.[46] A shared grammar of sexual possibility and availability produced by practices of cruising public spaces for this contact gave these particular codes whatever continuity or legibility they held across time and place. Homosexuality was thus reconceptualized as an active, counterhegemonic appropriation of urban space generating public cultures of interclass sociality centered around stranger intimacy.[47]

These historians' insights into the structural and contingent features of twentieth-century politicizations of homosexuality provide a model for thinking about the longer history of commercial capitalism and its periods of transition and crisis. The establishment of bourgeois sexual hegemony—which facilitated both middle-class and working-class men's adjustment to developments in modes of production by confining sexuality within private spaces and forms of intimacy revolving around the family—was tantamount to a kind of enclosure, forming one episode in a long history of accumulation by dispossession. Such a reconceptualization of the dialectic of sexual freedom and constraint in terms of primitive accumulation returns the history of sexuality to a history of property, where the connections between sexuality and social form become clearer.

Overview of the Argument

My hypothesis concerning the relation between sexual repression and the origins of capitalism in forms of primitive accumulation stands on two related but distinct suppositions, which form the warp and woof of the historical narrative that follows. First, cultures of sex between men were politicized amid much wider forms of dispossession during periods of geopolitical instability and political-economic transition; they are therefore world-systemic phenomena. Second, such politicizations turned on a passional dialectic, and male homosexuality became a lightning rod for popular anger because it reflected the general form of social power during periods of crisis.

Unraveling the full significance of these two suppositions has required reading social histories of homosexuality in light of political history and world-systems theory's account of the "combined and uneven development" of capitalism.[48] This approach to the longue durée of sexuality, social form, and economic development requires bracketing many of the literary tropes through which we've come to think about the "modernity" of homosexuality.

Historical periods of intensive politicization of homosexuality correspond to what Giovanni Arrighi and others have identified as periods of world-systemic crisis, periods in which a hegemonic power has entered a phase of financialization, deepening internal social divisions and destabilizing the wider geopolitical balance of power, which had been the basis of its cycle of capital accumulation and rise to hegemony. The terminal phases of northern Italian, Dutch, British, and American hegemonies of capitalism were each marked by a heightened sense of moral crisis in which municipal authorities cracked down on the institutions of sexual contact between men at the central nodal points of the world system. These periods of economic and geopolitical destabilization and the subsequent periods of "restoration"—in which a balance of power was reestablished within the system under the hegemony of a single world power—were central to the disruption and establishment of the sexual orders in Western societies. The historical terrain of conjunctures of political and economic crisis is thus a privileged site for examining how sexual categories and behaviors were undone and remade, and for examining which social forces were brought to bear upon this process.

Institutions and cultures of love and sex between men were products of a contradictory field of reality. Residual and emergent lifeworlds vied with one another for dominance over the moral order of cities.[49] This dominance was never total in reach. Older, partially socialized familial relations for the organic reproduction of an agrarian way of life were dissolved, allowing for the expansion of capitalist social relations in which social reproduction was decoupled from the family.[50] Production for the market created wage-dependency for broader swaths of the population, unseating the family as the primary economic unit of self-reproduction and opening up sexual and life options outside its restrictive form.[51] A variety of sexual norms and lifeworlds flourished within the breach between a dissolution of the old regime and an ongoing elaboration of new capitalist social relations.

Cities were sites of contact and conflict between these classes and lifeworlds. They provided a "spatial fix" for capital investment, as David Harvey has argued, creating a dynamic basis for further capital accumulation and geographic expansion of the world system. However, "crises of overaccumulation, technological change, unemployment and de-skilling, immigration and all manner of factional rivalries and divisions both within and between social classes" generated various kinds of "social anarchy" in cities.[52] At times, such volatility produced urban political movements that threatened bourgeois interests. "Political experience," Harvey writes,

> taught the bourgeoisie another lesson that could be used to check the undue radicalism of any urban-based political movement: superior control over space provided a powerful weapon in class struggle . . . increasing ruling-class reliance upon national and, ultimately, international power sources and the gradual reduction of the sphere of relative autonomy of urban-based class alliances.[53]

Cities provided a medium for the existence and flourishing of early cultures of sexual contact between men and a terrain for struggles over the sexual order of public spaces.[54] It is no accident that much of the legal and punitive apparatus constructed to deal with the "social anarchy" of surplus populations—vagrancy laws, forced labor, imprisonment, and impressment—was mobilized to criminalize homosexuality for most of the modern period. Sodomy, as such, was notoriously difficult to prosecute, and some of the earliest laws against sodomy in early modern Europe were associated with vagrancy. Moreover, the criminalization of the poor and working classes in cities provided cannon fodder and cheap labor for the expansion of the world system's catchment area and the geopolitical competition between rival capitalist powers.

Modernity becomes a nonteleological category when used to describe multiple, overlapping lifeworlds, sexual norms, and self-understandings produced by an unevenly developing world system. Those lifeworlds and sexual norms that characterized an increasingly residual world of feudal peasantry, small proprietors, urban artisans, and noble classes combined and came into conflict with the emergent norms and lifeworlds of cities, proletarian populations, and ascendant national bourgeoisies. Thematizing this unevenness and conflict establishes the disjunctive temporality and shifting borders of change without representing the historical process as some unilinear succession or archaeology settled into impassable, sedimented layers.[55]

The concept of sexual hegemony requires conceiving of the moral geography of urban space as divided into blocks of antagonistic conducts, norms, and self-understandings; in bourgeois societies, wherever public culture reflected deep moral divides, the state stepped in to enforce middle-class sexual norms, establishing footholds in zones of proletarian sexual anarchy. Certain levels of economic development expanded the network of these footholds beyond a handful of local informants to include whole segments of the working class making bids for respectability.

During the period of what have been called "bourgeois revolutions,"[56] the political challenges presented by "pederasty," "buggery," or "sodomy" were articulated within the problematic of good government, which drew comparisons between the city-states of antiquity and early modern experiments in republican forms. In their struggles for dominance over the old regime, the revolutionary classes sought models in the mixed constitutions of ancient republics, which combined the rule of the one, the few, and the many. Even prior to the hegemony of bourgeois sexual morals and impersonal capitalist forms of domination, cross-class cultures of sodomy were problematic to such republican experiments because they dramatized the social hierarchy and inequality of their mixed social form.

Early modern republics politicized socially visible cultures of sex between men because the pursuit of sodomy and its occasional spectacles of punishment gave vent to collective structures of feeling, or passions, which responded to various forms of direct domination. The ambivalence of popular sentiment toward such cultures reflected broader social contradictions. Expressions of collective love and hatred, empathy and revulsion, pleasure and anger, articulated very different conceptions of sexual freedom—and together formed a passional dialectic. The liberty of men of property and status came into conflict with popular classes' desire for freedom from domination, producing often unpredictable collective responses to cultures of sodomy wherever they were exposed to public scrutiny. Without any real intent or power to eliminate such cultures entirely, early modern ruling classes pursued and punished such offenses and institutions in order to sway popular sentiment.

The syncopated structure of the history of homosexuality and its relation to political forms is thus more than a convenient analogy for better historiography. The very same class alliances that sought to found early modern republics also generated institutions for cross-class sexual contact between men. The fortunes of both were bound up in political battles over the moral order of cities. These social struggles and sexual publics were ultimately transformed over the course of the nineteenth century, as middle classes tightened their control over urban space and as economic development gave bourgeois sexual norms greater traction in the working class.

Early modern regulations of sodomy reflected anxieties about the popular forces that the bourgeoisie had mobilized in its struggle with the old regime. In these "unnatural" sexual behaviors, they apprehended the essence of their own destructive powers in an inverted, alienated form. Whereas early modern cultures of sodomy dramatized forms of social hierarchy and direct domination, modern cultures of homosexuality tended to reflect the diffuse, impersonal power of bourgeois societies and the increasing feminization of the labor process. From a passional dialectic (reflecting a sexual culture that was an organic outgrowth of various forms of male sociality and friendship) to a dialectic of enclosure (reflecting a growing alienation and separation of private acts from public spaces), the politicization of cultures of sex between men struck at the core of problems of government (and reflected how such problems were changed by the political dominance of middle classes).

The chapters that follow proceed in roughly chronological order, tracking politicizations of sex between men at the central nodal points of the world system. Each chapter in turn analyzes the socioeconomic preconditions for a particular culture of sodomy, the politics of sodomy accusations and regulations within interclass political alliances, and the cultural artifacts of these formations.

Part I, "Sexual Hegemonies of Historical Capitalism," consists of this introductory chapter followed by three chapters centered on case studies. The first case study, "Sodomy and the Government of Cities," presents an analysis of why cultures of sodomy were able to flourish in the early modern Mediterranean world, and of why they became such a political problem in Florence, requiring a secular regulatory office to hear accusations against citizens. Florence's guilds prefigured (but radically differed from) later bourgeois sexual politics in their choice to regulate sodomy with a special office and a progressive sliding scale of fines. Over its seventy-year history, this office sought to absorb amorous disputes into the state edifice, buffering against the formation of political factions opposed to the Medici regime. Machiavelli's thoughts about such institutions, factions, and conflicts opens up a discussion of the continuities and discontinuities between his own period of republican experimentation and the world of antiquity.

Chapter 3, "Sexual Hegemony and the Capitalist World System," centers around the social and political conditions of possibility for institutions of sex between men during the seventeenth and eighteenth centuries in the Atlantic basin. During the autumn of the Dutch Republic's commercial hegemony and the Restoration following the English Civil War, both polities cracked down on institutions of cross-class sexual contact between men in ways that indicate conflicting notions of sexual freedom and further transformations of the dialectic of passions. Records of these crackdowns indicate the first inklings of bourgeois senses of interiority and demonstrate how these were elaborated in a moral politics concerning the proper use of public space and the appearance of moderation in appetite. This politics came into conflict with the sexualities and self-understandings of noble and popular classes. Each text points beyond its particular national formation, indicating on the one hand a transnational imagined community in which religious persecution and homophobia were understood as forms of dispossession, and on the other hand the beginnings of an equally transnational bourgeois sexuality rooted in property relations and senses of interiority.

The case studies conclude with chapter 4, "Homosexuality and Bourgeois Hegemony," a consideration of the plebeian public sphere of prostitution and sex between men that flourished during the French Revolution. During its rise to power, the bourgeoisie openly declared war on the sexual libertinism of the aristocracy, reflecting a pattern seen in the previous case studies in which scandals of appetite index a wider failure of government. However, the general unruliness of popular classes over the nineteenth century sustained a surprising variety of sexual norms in the capital that resist any progressive modernization story. Forensic medical epistemologies of pederasts followed closely on the heels of cycles of revolution and restoration, furnishing a racial theory of degeneration and same-sex proclivities, lending scientific pretense to the French bourgeoisie's appetite for stories of the underworld. During cycles of restoration, the imperative to turn the revolutionary city into a space of consumption and real estate speculation required a repression of the highly public sexualities of the old regime—turning a discourse about the monstrous sexuality of the noble classes against the artisans and proletarians who formed the shock troops of the revolutionary activity in the streets.

The chapter pauses on a cultural history of public urinals. Public urinals were a restoration architecture, reflecting the enclosure of homosexual activity in urban space. The first models were constructed in Paris during the July Monarchy. Later designs were adopted as part of Hausmann's transformations of Paris. The English sanitary engineer George Jennings's patented urinal was unveiled at the Crystal Palace in 1851, standardizing urinal design for the first time. Thus, the evolution of urinal design and construction in the nineteenth century allows for consideration of how the mass production and wide distribution of a particular architectural form in European cities began structuring forms of sexual contact between men, articulating the anxieties of bourgeois society and reflecting the new freedoms and constraints generated by a dialectics of enclosure.

Part II, "Homosexuality and the Desire for History," enacts a displacement of the object of analysis and historical inquiry, from the problem of a homosexual identity and subculture to a problem of the relation of sexual subjectivity to successive conjunctural crises of hegemony in the capitalist world system, offering a new paradigm for thinking the history of ways in which homosexuality has been politicized, from Renaissance Florence to current breakthroughs in gay rights. These chapters attempt to develop an analysis of the present conjuncture and an analysis of why historical knowledge has mattered to struggles over homosexual representation and bids for respectability.

Chapter 5, "Historicizing the History of Sexuality," asks what was politically at stake in constructivist theoretical and historical accounts of homosexuality's "modernity." What does it matter whether or not homosexuality has a history? And why did a particular conjuncture wind up producing a completely unprecedented historical knowledge of the same-sex practices and identifications of the past? I ask how gay history achieved such an importance to intellectual and political formations and explore how it lent legitimacy to the struggle for gay rights. Such an expanded historical consciousness of homosexuality is considered alongside that of previous intellectual and political formations, and I argue that it became possible due to a declining bourgeois dominant that permitted an understanding of sexual mores as socially constructed, just as previous formations were produced by the rise of a bourgeois dominant following the revolutions of 1848 in Western Europe. After historicizing the intellectual formation, I perform an immanent critique of Foucault's *History of Sexuality, Volume 1*, arguing that his critique of the "repressive hypothesis," however generative it has been, contains a certain number of unresolved philosophical and historical contradictions, leading much of the sexuality studies formation down the path toward a metanarrative emphasizing epistemology over political struggle and bourgeois categories over class analysis. I conclude by assessing the inquiries of social constructivist historians into how capitalism enabled both the repression of homosexuality and its politicization. These accounts successfully established the historicity of "homophobia" as a product of the mobilization for the Second World War but tended to project this vision of homosexuality as a persecuted minority back onto periods of time and into classes in which a bourgeois understanding was not yet hegemonic.

Based on these historical insights, the sixth chapter, "Homosexuality as a Category of Bourgeois Society," reconstructs the conflictual relation of homosexuality to a historically bourgeois public sphere, demonstrating how the shift toward a postmodern cultural dominant greatly diminished the social antagonism once posed by homosexuality. By way of an immanent critique of Michael Warner's theorization of "queer counterpublics" as a counterhegemonic language group, I propose a model for conceptualizing homosexuality as an "imagined community" according to principles not limited to a psychological identity, a sense of interiority, or some synthetic sociological category such as deviancy. This critical analysis allows for a consideration of the plebeian public sphere in which cultures of same-sex sexuality circulated, establishing the crucial importance of class analysis to the history of sexuality. In both cases, the historical imposition of a bourgeois sexual order—and its withering away in contemporary societies—are intelligible to thought only when the social categories and standpoint of critique are themselves subjected to historical analysis.

2

SODOMY AND THE GOVERNMENT OF CITIES

Lorenzo de' Medici, or the Piazzas of Florence

In 1472, the *Ufficiali di notte* of Florence found Pacchierotto, a poor shoe-
maker, guilty of sodomy, issuing threats that the boy would be "led through
the city and through its public places" while wearing a miter on his head
and flogged by the minister of justice. "It happened that he was arrested
as a sodomite," recounts Florentine chronicler Simone Filipepi, "and under
torture he confessed unheard of and extraordinary filth, and also a few petty
robberies." He was whipped and paraded around Piazza della Signoria, the
historic and political center of Florentine life, receiving twelve lashes under
the marble gaze of a Medici lion.

"Then he was led into the very center of the New Market, and here he
was given twelve more. From here he was conducted to the street of the

furriers where he had been caught several times at such ribaldry, and here he got another twelve lashes." Crowds likely greeted Pacchierotto with the same hubbub of hoots, whistles, hollers, and angry storms of vegetables as assailed a man and his boy who were paraded around the very same square in 1503, under Savonarola's regime, with placards indicating their crime—*sodomia*. Pacchierotto was subsequently led to the Stinche where he was "put in the prison of the sodomites, the thieves, and the blasphemers, who were all waiting gaily for him. When he arrived they made him their new captain, merrily singing together for a little fun. As he was so well looked upon by the group, they sat him at the head of the table with another miter, bigger than before."

"Poor Pacchierotto was weeping," Filipepi concludes his account, "because of his shame and because of the pain of the flogging, but seeing among those ribalds some who had their foreheads branded, some without noses or ears, some with only one arm, and others who were worse off than he was, he was somewhat consoled. And thus he remained very honorably in that place for several years."[1]

Pacchierotto—who later associated with the notorious Compagnacci, the "Rude," "Rowdy," or "Ugly Companions," a political faction of young freedom fighters who in 1498 plotted to assassinate the good friar Savonarola in the city's cathedral of Santa Maria del Fiore by setting off explosives during mass but backpedaled after discovering that some of their friends and relatives might be at the service[2]—likely suffered such public humiliations for failing to pay a fine of ten florins.[3] Thus, Lorenzo de' Medici's regime piously performed expiations for the sins of Sodom by publicly humiliating the poor; the Florentine policing of sodomy made enemies of the state and brought an incredible amount of public attention to the vice.

Spectacles of humiliation were not without their political limits, as the sympathy of Pacchierotto's prison admirers and his later involvement in the Compagnacci might indicate. In fact, public punishments for sodomy were exceptionally rare in Florence and occurred only during the most tumultuous political period of transition and political reaction. Were these spectacles symptoms of the end of a declining hegemony of northern Italian cities? Perhaps. Florence mostly pardoned sodomites who turned themselves in and punished those convicted with fines. Florentine magistrates preferred profit to public humiliation.

Florence's municipal records indicate that, during the short period between 1478 and the abolition of the Ufficiali di notte or "Officers of the Night" in 1502, a period of great political tumult—the death of Lorenzo de'

Medici, the invasion of Florence by Charles VIII of France, the sacking of Lorenzo's son Piero, and the rise of a new republic established under the influence of Savonarola, whose moral reforms included harsher sentencing for sodomy convictions—only twenty-three sodomites were pilloried, seven were mitered and whipped through the streets, two flogged, three mitered and branded, and one pilloried and branded. Nine were imprisoned, with most serving a sentence of six weeks to six months. Six were exiled, and three were killed. A total of 553 sodomites were fined, with most paying fines of either ten florins or fifty.[4] Demonstrating the severity of the spiraling currency inflation of the preceding historical period of economic decline, the city collected at most total revenues of 15,780 florins, or approximately 1 percent of Edward III's massive 1339 loan default, which had triggered the "great crash" of the 1340s.[5]

The Officers of the Night frequently pardoned boys and men who confessed to sodomy, citing their inability to pay such fines. As the office would discover over the course of its seventy-year tenure, less severe punishments and sliding scales for penalties tended to drum up higher numbers of confessions and accusations from Florentines. Savonarola's regime, by contrast, presided over a crackdown on the city's taverns, baths, and brothels. The state ordered innkeepers to keep tighter surveillance over their charges and to bar male youths past certain hours of the night. Sentencing for convictions was harsh, requiring public humiliations, time in stockades, or spectacular death for repeat offenders. Under Savonarola, progressive fines were eliminated. Accusations dried up. Boxes for anonymous accusations installed by the Officers of the Night throughout the city fell into disuse relative to the period of lenient punishments under the Medici. In short, citizens refused to accuse their neighbors or to themselves confess as penalties increased. Where legal action failed, Savonarola pursued de facto enforcement of his calls for a purge of Florence's vice. He trained youth gangs and encouraged them to publicly harass and humiliate those frequenting offensive *casini*, taverns, brothels, and known sodomite haunts.

The population of Florence had forced the state to adopt what seems like a surprisingly modern rationality: the city monetized sodomy. Considering the magnitude of such revenues, Florentine merchants' previous persecution of sodomy represented more of a tax or rent collected from its population than a rabid moral campaign of repression and punishment, as was now advocated from the pulpit. Epitomizing that infamous Florentine irony, the tax on sodomites went to provide for the upkeep of a large convent of reformed prostitutes.

CHAPTER TWO

The Commune of Florence had established the Officers of the Night in April 1432, for the express purpose of prosecuting male homosexual acts in the city. Many northern Italian city-states established municipal offices for the policing of public morals in the fifteenth and sixteenth centuries, and these offices inevitably wound up policing homosexual activity in addition to prostitution, gambling, and other "moral offenses." Florence, however, was exceptional in its lenient convictions and punishments. The records generated by the Officers of the Night provide an incomparable window into the socially visible practice of male homosexuality across all classes in Renaissance Florence and demonstrate how intricately these sexual relations were woven into the fabric of everyday life in the wider Mediterranean world. Historian Michael Jesse Rocke, who uncovered this rich archive, writes that

> for seventy years, from the magistracy's founding in 1432 to its suppres-
> sion in 1502, the Officers of the Night provided the Florentine regime
> with a remarkably productive and potent instrument to police homo-
> sexuality. Indeed, judging by the dimensions of the sodomitic activity
> they brought to light, their success—at least in numerical terms—was
> little short of astonishing. Despite lacunae in their records, it can be
> estimated that between 1432 and 1502, nearly twelve thousand different
> men and boys alleged to have engaged in homosexual relations came
> to the attention of the Officers of the Night. Of these the magistrates
> convicted well over two thousand. Probably no other city in late me-
> dieval Italy, if indeed in early modern Europe, matched this record.[6]

The records of the Officers of the Night reveal that sex between men functioned, among elites, as a way to curry political and personal favors and to
secure business deals and patronage. Among the city's young, poor, informal
laborers and among the workmen of the city's lower textile guilds, sex with
other neighborhood boys and men functioned as a way to form friendships
and political affinity groups, as male youths were otherwise denied any form
of representation or participation in the state.

Relations between elite men and lower-class boys were more socially
troublesome and could magnify uneven relations of power. In such cases
sex was exchanged for favors or fine clothes and shoes; such power was easily abused, and the offended boy could cause trouble for the man of status.
In the cities of the Mediterranean basin at this time, these sexual relations
across age and status lines were a normal feature of male sociability and
economic survival; the apprentice system kept youth and boys dependent,
usually into their thirties, in the workshops and houses of masters.

FIGURE 2.1. Albrecht Dürer, *Lot Fleeing with His Daughters from Sodom*, c. 1498, oil and tempera on panel. National Gallery of Art, Washington.

In the rest of Europe during this period, homosexuality was never pursued by church or state on any scale comparable to that of Florence. The counterexample of Venice is illuminating: unlike Florence, whose fortunes fell following the outsourcing of cheaper cloth production to France and England, Venice had effected a smoother transition to finance capitalism, converting its middling classes into rentiers whose ruthless execution of sodomites also had the effect of making its citizens less likely to report the offense.

In 1418, the ruling oligarchs of Venice, the Council of Ten, established a standing subcommittee called the *Collegium sodomitarum* to investigate sodomy in the city. From 1426 to 1500, 411 individuals came to the attention of the Ten for sodomy.[7] As in Rome, Milan, Bologna, Ferrara, and Trieste, the punishment for sodomy in Venice was burning at the stake. Those who confessed to the sin (often under torture) were publicly executed between the two columns of the Lion of Venice and St. Theodore in Piazzetta San Marco where the land meets the water.[8] Sodomites were burned alive in the Piazzetta until 1445, at which time the Council of Ten decided to lessen the barbarity of the punishment in view of the fact that "all the other Christians who deliver justice by fire proceed otherwise," whereupon Venice adopted the gentler way of Christian Europe, decapitating the accused before consigning head and body to the flames. The severity of the punishments for sodomy generated very few convictions; one historian found only 268 convictions, including those who refused to confess and were therefore sentenced to imprisonment, pillory, or banishment.

The Spanish Inquisition is not comparable to the municipal pursuit of sodomy in Venice or Florence in either intensity or scale, as the activities of its offices spanned more than three centuries. Nevertheless, the Spanish Inquisition conformed more to the pattern of Venice than to that of Florence: harsh punishments drummed up fewer accusations and lower rates of conviction for those accused. Records indicate that sodomy across hierarchies of age and status was an inevitability in societies whose economies were structured by relations of dependence and servitude. Sodomy accounted for a small but significant portion of the persecutions of the Holy Office. According to Henry Kamen's influential revisionist account of the Spanish Inquisition, punishments were spectacular but restricted death by burning at the stake to those over twenty-five years old. Minors were typically punished with flogging and or by being sent to the galleys; the sentences for clergy were mild; men of status were given favorable treatment.[9]

Whereas Aragon pursued sodomites with particular zeal, trying nearly six hundred individuals for sodomy, Barcelona and Valencia prosecuted and punished sodomy less avidly. Records from Aragon's Inquisition reveal a pederastic pattern in conformity with the wider Mediterranean world. The historian Cristian Berco writes that

> the three main aspects that determined sexual encounters between men and adolescents in the trials were socio-economic relations of dependence, informal prostitution, and sexual violence. In these three

cases, the confluence of normal social conventions and the private rules of sexual masculinity yields a variety of results. While adults often utilized their social status to coerce adolescents into sexual activity, thus reinforcing public hierarchies . . . the social and economic status of the adult active partner coupled with early modern labour structures that saw young teenagers normally working in relations of dependence often facilitated the use of coercion in sexual activity. Adolescents in the Crown of Aragon and throughout Europe at the time commonly left the parental household at puberty to work as apprentices in various trades. They lived in their master's household while apprenticing and thus were immersed in a labour structure that signaled their dependence to their employer. Never immune to the pressures exerted by their masters, these young men could find themselves the object of sexual advances.[10]

To what purposes were the extensive and completely unparalleled police apparatus of the Officers of the Night mobilized in Florence? Behind this question are several related ones that take us to the heart of the political matter. Why did male homosexuality require regulation at all if it was so familiar and widespread? If unregulated sodomy presented some kind of threat to the political regime, how did early modern Italian city-states perceive this threat? Perhaps the regulation of sodomy in Florence was *politically productive* in addition to being a neutralization or repression of vice. Consideration of the attempt to found a republic in Florence would be crucial to understanding the political logic of the city's attempt to regulate sodomy, opening up a comparative perspective on the politics of sex in other republican polities such as France and the United States.

Another way of posing this question is to ask whether these regulations were established to protect the civic life of Florence against effeminate mores, or *effeminato,* in order to bolster those famously masculine virtues. On the other hand, might this institution have functioned in some other way to govern the humors and passions of the men of Florence? Perhaps the "officers of the sodomites" drew these often violent passions and humors out of men's breasts and into speech and writing, circulating the power to accuse, humiliate, and punish in a sphere of public discourse, which in turn could be manipulated by the regime to direct the flow of this sort of speech in particular directions and to produce certain effects at the level of city governance? Lastly, is there some political paradigm internal to the period itself which would not require us to make recourse to our own explanations by way of some theory of deviancy, social phobia, normativity, or whatever else? As the normalcy of homosexuality in the Mediterranean world is foreign to our understandings of what it means to be "gay" in our own time, so it would be reasonable to expect current explanations for its repression to have little traction.

In fact, the regulation of sodomy in this particular time and place served many purposes, and a consideration of the role played by the Officers of the Night in the tumultuous political history of fifteenth-century Florence will bring us closer to answering some of the above questions. The objective of this regulation could not have been a purely repressive, morally prohibitive, and ultimately negative power over homosexual practices, as the leniency of punishment in Florence for the greater part of the fifteenth century, with only the occasional harshness of public humiliation and exile, never succeeded in a prohibition of any significant scale. In fact, the regulation had the opposite effect: it allowed the conduct to continue in the city unabated and lent it greater social visibility. The governmental paradigm could not have been merely a policing of the norms of acceptable masculine behavior, or *virtù*, through the repression of effeminacy, for homosexual behavior was widespread in Florence—and not exclusively associated with the vanity, luxury, and effeminacy of its ruling classes—and the office was most extensively mobilized against the city's poor and working-class men.

Sodomites were extensively criminalized in Florence after the defeat of the working-class struggles of the fourteenth century, as political power was consolidated in the hands of a single family and financial speculation created the conditions for a building boom in the city. Although members of the nobility and the wealthy elite were convicted of sodomy, many escaped punishment by calling in political favors. From a peak population of about 95,000 people around 1300, the population of Florence slumped to around 30,000 following the Black Death and the economic downturn of the 1340s, stabilizing at around 40,000 to 55,000 until the later fifteenth century. The political and demographic instability of Florence gave rise to a polarized social world in which a very small coterie of merchant elites and upper guildsmen, often quite senior in age, exercised control over the city's political offices.

These elite elder statesmen governed a mostly younger population with no legal standing.[11] In the language of contracts in which this population was named, they were movable assets, *locati*, placed in marriage or nunneries or serving as domestics in the case of most Florentine women, or rented out for hire and labor as apprentices in the case of most young Florentine men. Young males, according to one contemporary moral treatise, "because of their youth no less than because of their nude knowledge [are] equal to the vile females."[12] Reflecting this queer socio-sexual calculus, the Officers of the Night overwhelmingly tended to convict young men from the ages of eighteen to thirty. Sexual roles of activity and passivity were also structured by age and status hierarchies, conforming to a more or less pederastic pattern that has been noted throughout the Mediterranean world.

Boys under the age of twenty, of all classes, worked in all sectors of the economy and constituted a substantial portion Florence's labor force. In the fifteenth century, approximately 40 percent of Florence's total population was under the age of fourteen; boys between the ages of fourteen and nineteen made up 10 percent of the total population. The market had transformed apprenticeship into little more than waged child labor, and a weak corporate structure of guilds in Florence meant that this transitional stage of dependency "introduced the boy much more abruptly to the realities of a labor market dominated by the cash nexus."[13] Masters rarely assumed full responsibility for the boys in their workshops. It is the boy's position at the center of this "cash nexus" that made his eroticization socially problematic in Florence.

Markets, ruling-class family processions, punishments, state ceremonies, patrician horse races, and bullbaiting all ritualized the maleness of public space in northern Italian cities.[14] Fynes Moryson, a seventeenth-century Scottish traveler, remarked that the women of Italy

> know not the price of any thing, or ever goe to Markets (scarce are allowed to go to Church) neither do they trust their servants to make their market, but the richest of all Italy, and most noble (especially in Venice) daily buy their owne victuals and other necessaries. And in all Market-places stand little boyes with baskets, to carry any thing that is bought to their houses, which they easily find, knowing all streetes and allyes, and never faile to perform this honestly, though the buyer leave them, and (according to their custome) goe about his other affaires; for if they should fayle, they cannot escape punishment, being easily found in the Markets where they use daily to stand, and well knowne by face and name.[15]

The streets and markets of the early modern Mediterranean world were predominantly male spaces in which boys filled many of the socioeconomic roles played elsewhere by women. Sexual encounters between men and boys reflected this peculiar sexual geography and primarily took place within networks of acquaintances and familiars of varying degrees of intimacy.[16]

In northern Italian cities, a constant threat of violence directed against women and boys reinforced hierarchies of age, sex, and status in streets, workshops, markets, and all other public and semipublic spaces. Poor and working-class youths exposed themselves in streets, used profanity, and committed indecent acts, in the words of one contemporary, "bringing scandal to women [who] pass on the streets nearby them."[17] In Florence, gangs of youths from all classes, especially the sons of patrician families, sexually assaulted women and boys on the streets.[18] Women's access to legal courts decreased in the oligarchic culture of fifteenth-century Florence; magistracies "simply ceased to bother with many normal, run-of-the-mill assault and battery cases involving women from artisan and laboring families."[19] Gang assaults on boys were "part of a broader context in which the sexual 'possession' of boys by groups of men, whether by force or not, was common and deeply implicated in the fashioning of manly and social identities."[20]

Rivalries between leading families and between rival interest groups in Florence precipitated a political crisis in the 1420s and 1430s that would bring the Medici to power. The *popolo* were at the center of a "triangular struggle," John Najemy writes: on the one side an elite whose arrogance and power it sought to curtail and on the other an array of artisans and workers it was determined to keep at bay. Only in the aftermath of 1378, when the most radical of the popular governments created three new guilds of textile workers and artisans, did the frightened non-elite major guildsmen abandon any further attempts to create popular governments in alliance with the minor guildsmen.[21]

The origins of antisodomy jurisprudence in Florence reflect anxieties surrounding the crisis of feudal property relations prior to the economic downturn of the 1340s and the Black Death. In fact, much of Europe's earliest laws against vagrancy originated during this period. In England, the first laws were enacted after the Black Death in 1348 and 1349; as labor was in short supply and wages increased, vagrancy acts attempted to prevent men from wandering the countryside to find higher wages. In 1349, the Ordinance of Labourers prohibited private individuals from giving relief to able-bodied beggars; in 1388 the Statute of Cambridge restricted movement of all laborers and beggars. Workers required a letter from a local justice of the peace before departing from the "hundred, rape, wapentake, city or borough" where they lived or risked being put in stocks.[22]

The first laws against sodomy in Florence appeared in statutes regulating vagrancy. According to Rocke, "wayfarers or brigands called in Italian *trapassi* or *malandrini*" were the archetypal figures of sodomy:

"Infected with the contagion" of sodomy, according to the arresting imaginary of the 1325 statute, these outsiders came "to the borders of the city of Florence" to "sow their wicked and abominable crimes in the good and decent seedbed" of the Arno city. If residents saw such marginals seizing, striking, threatening or in any way molesting Florentine boys in order to sodomize them, they could capture and beat the foreigners without penalty. Moreover, the statute reserved the punishment of death only for these strangers, while residents of Florence caught in the act of sodomy were to be castrated. This early emphasis on non-Florentines gradually faded, however. In the sodomy law of 1365 the penal distinction between residents and others disappeared. *Trapassi* and *malandrini* are still mentioned in the 1415 statute, but this seems merely conventional, a repetition of past injunctions now emptied of their original meaning.[23]

As in Roman law, where the *exceptio* articulates two juridical demands of the *ius civile* and the *ius honorarium*, so Florence suspended civil law for vagabonds carrying the contagion of sodomy. The exception enshrined in the original 1325 statute concerning sodomy in the city exposed trapassi and malandrini to danger by placing them in a relation of ban. The vagabond sodomite's behavior would be corrected *propter utilitatem publicam*, by customary reprisals rather than by the laws of the city.[24] The punishment reserved for residents, castration, may indicate some fear of overpopulation or some more spiritual concern to force the sodomite into conformity with norms prevailing in the South and East concerning the castration of eunuchs. In any case, exclusion from the reproductive community enabled inclusion in the civic body. Thus the legal exclusion of sodomites, as *homines sacri*, was doubled in turn, capturing even Florentines within a juridical exception.

The vagrancy statutes of this earlier period doubtless reflected anxieties about the strain of human populations on the scant resources of the region. As Wally Seccombe indicates in *A Millennium of Family Change*, human reproduction was limited by feudal property relations. Population increases implied a subdivision of landholdings below subsistence level. The system worked so long as death due to war and disease counteracted human reproduction. There are signs of a population strain upon the land right before the Black Death.[25] In the original statute against the "contagion" of sodomite vagabonds in Florence, the law links two anxieties: the spread of dissolute sexual morals like a contagion and a population in excess of resource capacity, outside of the normal function of the family unit to reproduce feudal property relations. The infectious contagions of excess population and sexual excess were to be arrested at the borders of the city through a suspension of the normal rule of law.

The invocation of the older statute in the law providing for the establishment of the Officers of the Night lent the more liberal statute of 1415 a fearsome precedent. Even the more tolerant establishment of an office for the regulation and taxation of sodomy contains the seed of this originary relation of ban: although the local sodomite was spared the punishment of castration demanded by this earlier law, his ambiguous legal status was much closer to that of the trapassi and malandrini. His offense was frequently subject to the extrajuridical reprisals of the community; by soliciting accusations from citizens, the new magistracy maintained a blurred distinction between ius civile and ius honorarium. Savonarola's regime pushed this exceptional legal status for sodomites to its extremes.

Harsher sentencing laws for sodomy were earlier adopted in 1364 during the Florentine Republic's tumultuous period of labor unrest. Plague, economic downturn, and the outsourcing of cheaper cloth production to northern Europe in the middle of the fourteenth century contributed to the political ferment of the 1378 revolt of the Ciompi. Impoverished clothworkers seized state power and installed a wool comber, Michele di Lando, at its head. As an employer lockout of the rebellious workers attempted to starve them out, they rioted, marching threateningly to the Signoria, where di Lando (himself now aligned with the factional interests of upper-guild workers) turned on them and dealt them a crushing defeat.[26]

At the time, a full third of the Florentine population lived off wages paid by cloth manufacturing. Giovanni Arrighi writes that the lowest strata of the workforce were, over the course of the century that followed, "stripped of all protection and rights of independent organization and thereby turned into a floating mass of surplus labor forced by indigence to seek their daily bread in the building boom of the Renaissance."[27] This surplus population of young, underemployed, and unemployed men was a human by-product of declining investment in the manufacture of coarse wool cloth and more profitable investment in higher-quality lines of production. Most men in Florence married late, if at all. Such economic and demographic pressures contributed as much to the city's incidence of sodomy and casual male prostitution as to its political turmoil.

At its inception in 1432, the Officers of the Night was a formidable political weapon wielded by the Medici in their quest to consolidate power over economic and political rivals in the early 1430s. In fact, having been founded two years before the Medici rise to power, the office made its first accusations against the existing regime. Five of the six officers were selected from among the upper-guild workers, with one member from the lower guilds. Accusations during the period from 1478 to 1502, the period for which there are the most detailed records of men and boy's occupations, reveal that although homosexual relations occurred across lines of trade and generational divides, and among ruling-class families, workers, and the poor, the majority of men and boys convicted were Florence's young *mechanici e poveri*, the tradesmen and the city's poor.[28] These men, who were excluded from the political community and barred from the guilds, shouldered the greater share of the financial burden and humiliation from sodomy convictions.[29] As Rocke notes,

> The workers who proportionally were most likely to be convicted were weavers, dyers, tailors, and wool-washers—men denied full guild rights and in the lower-middle to lower social strata—and butchers. Comparison of the different occupational categories reveals similar inequality. Again the officials were more inclined to punish men who labored in the textile industries, mainly poor wage-earning dependents, or *sottoposti*, of the major guilds, and men who worked in various alimentary trades, both among the poorest sectors of the Florentine population. These two areas alone provided fully 37.9 percent of convicted sodomites, but only 20.8 percent of the men who were absolved.[30]

To some contemporaries, the activities of the Officers of the Night seemed like a campaign of repression against the lower classes of the city, and Rocke observes that complaints about leniency toward the rich frequently appear in the accusals deposited in boxes throughout the city. Citing a particular remark as exemplary of the popular sentiment, Rocke relates one man's accusation of a patrician in 1473 who wrote to the Officers, "You won't make a meal of this one, yet if he were some poor fellow you'd drink his blood."[31]

Pacchierotto, captain of the sodomites, thieves, and blasphemers, was one among nearly a thousand men—mostly young, informal workers and wage-dependent artisans—convicted for sodomy by the Officers of the Night under Lorenzo de' Medici's rule from 1469 to 1499. This campaign against the vice reached its zenith in the first years of Lorenzo's reign, when Florence experienced "the most extensive repression of sodomy in Florentine history."[32] The first five years of his rule account for a remarkable 535 convictions of men for sodomy. This was a period of great tumult, as the Medici's assets dwindled and those exiled in the 1466 conspiracy continued to threaten the regime from abroad; Prato and Volterra revolted in 1470 and 1472. Florence passed measures to limit private and public festivities in the city, curbing Carnival celebrations to quell ribaldry and lawlessness.[33]

Niccolò Machiavelli discusses the episode at length in his *Florentine Histories*. After the insurrection at Prato,

> the citizens of Florence returned once again to their former manner of life; the government was established upon a stable foundation—all suspicion was quieted, and they abandoned themselves to the luxuries of life. All those evils now sprang up in the city which are usually generated by the indolence of peace. The young men were less occupied, and became more dissolute than ever, and wasted their time and fortune in dress, in banquets, in gaming, and in the indulgence of sensual love. . . . These customs were carried to greater excess by the courtiers of the Duke of Milan, who had come to Florence (in fulfillment of a vow it was said) with the Duchess and all the Ducal Court. . . . The duke found the city filled with courtesans, dissoluteness, all manner of corruption; but he left it so much worse at his departure, that the better portion of the citizens esteemed it necessary to regulate the excesses of dress, banquets and ceremonies, by new statutes.[34]

If such are the reasons for Lorenzo de' Medici's campaign against sodomy in the city, according to Machiavelli, it is likely that the campaign was directed toward a neutralization of the basis of insurrectionary activity. The sexual networks that accusations tended to short-circuit were often rooted in neighborhoods, religious associations, clubs, and confraternities between friends and familiars. These were the very same kinds of associations in which youths expressed and gave vent to their discontent.

The crackdown on these networks of homosexual relations risked blowback from a multitude whose consent and fear was essential to the regime's political power, and indeed campaigns against homosexuality turned elements of the population against Lorenzo de' Medici. In April 1478, Lorenzo and his brother Giuliano de' Medici were assaulted by Bernardo Bandi and Francesco de' Pazzi in front of thousands during Easter High Mass at the Duomo. Giuliano bled to death on the cathedral floor, but Lorenzo survived with serious stab wounds and fled the city. The following decade was marked by a return of Carnival festivities and a consolidation of Medici control over the regime as the family's powers were centralized and the old Republic's councils were replaced by loyalists in the Council of Seventy.

FIGURE 2.2. Girolamo Macchietti, *Baths at Pozzuoli*, c. 1570, oil on canvas. Palazzo Vecchio, Florence.

Sodomy convictions during the last decade of Lorenzo de' Medici's reign declined to the lowest rates of any period during the establishment of the Offices of the Night.[35]

What role did same-sex attachments play in such intrigues? Machiavelli had such issues at the forefront of his mind in his discussion of conspiracies against princes. In *Discourses on Livy*, he reasons that to kill one's enemy is better than to threaten him with death, for

> property and honor are the two things that offend men more than any other offense, from which the prince should guard himself. For he can

CHAPTER TWO

never despoil one individual so much that a knife to avenge himself does not remain for him, and he can never dishonor one individual so much that a spirit obstinate for vengeance is not left to him. Of honors taken away from men, that concerning women is most important; after this, *contempt of one's person*. This armed Pausanias against Philip of Macedon; this has armed many others against many other princes.[36]

Although there is no explicit reference above to Lorenzo de' Medici's campaign against sodomy, throughout Machiavelli's discussion of conspiracies in *Discourses on Livy*, he returns to examples from antiquity to explicitly connect the sources of conspiracy against princes with political instabilities generated by the play of same-sex desire across hierarchies of age and status.

In fact, Machiavelli's only explicit reference to Aristotle in *Discourses on Livy* concerns the way in which sexual jealousies and quarrels (over male and female love objects) among men of the ruling class led to the formation of political factions and power struggles.[37] Another passage to which Machiavelli alludes concerns the necessity of tyrants to avoid sexually assaulting (ὑβρίζοντα) youths of either sex and avoid publicizing their bodily enjoyments (ἀπολαύσεις τὰς σωματικάς) in publicly visible orgies and feasts to avoid turning the citizenry against him.[38]

"I say thus that absolute princes and governors of republics," Machiavelli writes, "are not to take little account of this part, but they should consider the disorders that can arise from such an accident and remedy them in time so that the remedy is not with harm and reproach for their state or for their republic, as happened to the Ardeans. For having allowed that rivalry [between nobles and plebs] to grow among their citizens, they were led to divide among themselves; and when they wished to reunite, they had to send for external help, which is the beginning of a nearby servitude."[39]

Thus, Machiavelli writes elsewhere in the *Discourses on Livy* that "there is no example more beautiful or more true" than that of Pausanias's assassination of Philip of Macedon, father of Alexander the Great:

[Philip] had in his court Pausanias, a beautiful and noble youth, with whom Attalus, one of the first men near Philip, was in love. Having often sought to get him to consent to him, and finding him averse to such things, he decided to have by deception and by force that which he saw he could not have by any other direction. Having made a festive banquet to which came Pausanias and many other noble barons, after everyone was full of food and wine, he had Pausanias taken and brought bound, and not only vented his own lust by force, but also for greater ignominy had him reproached in a similar mode by many of the others. Pausanias complained of this injury often to Philip, who, after holding him for a time in hope that he would be avenged, not only did not avenge him but elevated Attalus to the government of a province of Greece. Whereupon Pausanias, seeing his enemy honored and not punished, turned all his indignation not against the one who had done him the injury but against Philip, who had not avenged him.[40]

Machiavelli offers a historically new thought about cultures of male violence and sodomy in the time-honored guise of commentary on antiquity, singling out this passion as threatening to the foundations of modern political power, as intimately bound up with the hatred of tyrants and love of freedom. He offers a key to deciphering what was historically new about Florence's attempt to regulate sodomy.

There can be little doubt that the cultural rediscovery and veneration of antiquity in Renaissance Italy played no small role in aesthetically authorizing the practice of love for boys and male youths. In fact, a growing body of literature, considering a much wider variety of sources from ancient Greek city-states than were available to Renaissance scholars, has revealed much variety in practices of boy-and-man-loving—*paidophilein*, *philetairos*, and *hetairos*, to name only a few.[41] A broad scholarly consensus no longer considers the open practice of same-sex love and its related institutions—formal education, a democratic army, nude exercises, homoerotic art and literature, baths, intense male friendships and bonding—to be some timeless social feature or truth of "the ancient Greeks." In fact, all available evidence indicates that the practice took off only in the seventh and sixth centuries, during the period of Athens's rise to military and commercial hegemony.[42] Against the findings of some initial studies that followed some of Kenneth Dover's assumptions about the institutions of pederasty, more recent scholars have now established that a major transformation took place within Greek society, sometime around 650 BCE, in which pederasty was institutionalized in armies and athletics, symposia and gymnasia, alongside the institution of norms of late marriage for most men and seclusion for women.[43]

Three decisive historical events are responsible for this explosion of same-sex eroticism. The Dorian invasions of the seventh and early sixth centuries led to impoverishment and agrarian subsistence crises.[44] The technological adoption of iron democratized war, as the chariots and spears of Homeric epic gave way to semipopular infantries. Iron also provided incentives for the development of greater craft production, the expansion of trade networks, and the establishment of Greek colonies overseas.[45] All of these contributed to a class struggle in seventh- and sixth-century Athens between rich and poor; the armed strength of the hoplites, so necessary for the defeat of the Dorian armies, also made possible the eviction of aristocrats and the cancellation of debts.[46] Investment in craft production in fifth-century Athens and sixth-century Corinth began to break with the residual mode of agrarian production, one based on slavery and debt, by encouraging a system of capital investment in craft production and trade.[47]

Thus, the "homosexualities" of "ancient Greece" must themselves be considered the contingent outcome of a history of class struggle, war, and the first democratic and republican polities. The ancient association of same-sex eroticism with the hatred of tyranny, which had become a commonplace by the time of Aristotle, here finds its originary meaning: it was only after the overthrow of tyrants in the Greek city-states, after the fall of despotism, that open cultures of same-sex eroticism could flourish. Pederasty was subsequently institutionalized in the political-economic form of handicraft production, which prolonged young males' social dependency long into adulthood.

Many of these historically specific preconditions for "ancient Greek homosexualities" were reproduced in northern Italian cities at the height of their hegemony. Machiavelli would have considered the idea that Florentine pederasts were aesthetic copies or imitations of the pederasty of antiquity—that of the court of Philip of Macedon or the exemplary Athenian tyrant-slayers Aristogeiton and Harmodius[48]—to be akin to the superficial antiquarianism of his Florentine contemporaries who collected ruins of statues in their homes. Nonetheless, he thought that the historicity of human life and customs could only emerge through juxtapositions of old and new, by comparing the *deeds* of ancients and moderns. This juxtaposition of deeds and passions occurs throughout the passages on conspiracies against princes, where the Pazzi conspiracy against Lorenzo de' Medici is named as the opposite number of a homoerotic example from antiquity.

I have cited these examples and quoted them at length to show that Machiavelli's freedom to discourse upon the erotic intrigues of the ancients is matched only by his relative silence upon these same issues in his own time. There is a sly irony to his disparagement of contemporaries for not attaining to the virtuous masculinity of antiquity; Machiavelli's own historical discourse permits a discussion of present controversies—but only in a register that would not offend.[49] Modern truths were best appreciated from a distance, concealed beneath the patina of ancient wisdom. Machiavelli's silence on the sodomitical intrigues of his own time indicates how danger-ous they may have been to discourse upon. "Persecution," as Leo Strauss reminds us with Machiavelli in mind, "gives rise to a peculiar technique of writing, and therewith to a peculiar type of literature, in which the truth about all crucial things is presented exclusively between the lines. That lit-erature is addressed, not to all readers, but to trustworthy and intelligent readers only."[50]

The above discussion of Machiavelli's commentary on the political in-trigues of his own day from the distant perspective of antiquity brings us closer to the political rationality behind Florence's regulation of sodomy. Although same-sex eroticism rarely figures in commentaries on Machia-velli or on the political scene of Renaissance Florence, the centrality of this sexual culture to the civic life of Florence suggests that any such commen-tary failing to incorporate same-sex eroticism is fundamentally limited in its approach. In fact, the public regulation of sodomy in Renaissance Florence through the establishment of a special office for sodomy accusations offered Machiavelli a window into a deeper set of questions concerning the politics of men's passions. One needn't read too far between the lines to discover that the Officers of the Night loomed large in Machiavelli's thought by the time of his composition of the *Discourses on Livy*.

To threaten the city's sodomites with death, as was customary throughout the rest of Europe during this period, would surely have backfired in Flor-ence. Popular sentiment was essential to the Medicis' influence over other ruling elites, and sodomy was a normal feature of civic life. This explains why campaigns against sodomy in other cities of the Mediterranean world failed to accomplish their repressive ends. Too many convictions, seem-ingly disproportionate convictions of poor rather than rich men, and pun-ishments that might be perceived as excessive threatened to turn the lower strata of the city against the regime. Sodomy confessions provided occasions for the regime to pardon its poorer citizens of apparently serious crimes and disgrace its economic and political rivals to appease the poor.

Instead of adopting policies that Machiavelli calls *liberalità*, Florence adopted a radically new approach to sodomy, turning guildsmen, workers, and nobles against one another in order to arbitrate petty amorous disputes through the establishment of a special office, absorbing these feuds and fac-tions into the state edifice and protecting informants by shielding their identi-ties and giving them legal immunity.[51] Neither lenient nor ruthless in extract-ing its tax from sodomites, the Medicis perfected a mean, manipulative touch, soliciting sexual discourse and recriminations from Florentine men.

The nub of the political problem of regulating sex between men in Florence turned upon the *omore*, or humors, at the root of both pederastic sexual relations and republican government more generally. If pederastic sex across hierarchies of class and age created opportunities for the abuse of power, privilege, and status, then the Florentine state provided an outlet for venting these frustrations by punishing the rich. If the powerful felt slighted by pretty young things, they could turn them in to the Officers of the Night rather than seeking satisfaction through other means. Sodomy accusations against the nobility and convictions of Florence's elite formed a small but significant portion of the Officers' activities. The accusation and conviction of the powerful provided an outlet for popular anger in much the same way that, according to Machiavelli, the disunity of the Plebs and the Senate in the Roman Republic secured freedom and imperial power for the city.

Dissenting from the commentaries of Cicero and others who viewed this disunity as bad for the stability of a free polity, Machiavelli understood the phenomenon as an index of a republic's political strength, for like some hydraulic pressure–regulating system, a public forum for grievances balanced the humors and desires of the nobility against those of the people and prevented either force from threatening the continuity of political power. He writes, "If one considers the end of the nobles and of the ignobles, one will see great *desire to dominate* in the former, and in the latter only *desire not to be dominated*; and, in consequence, a greater will to live free, being less able to hope to usurp it than are the great."[52] Although either desire could be identified as the source of political upheaval—and Machiavelli isolates a complex dialectic between the two—the noble humor, the "desire to dominate," is far more threatening as "[the nobility's] incorrect and ambitious behavior inflames in the breasts of whoever does not possess the wish to possess so as to avenge themselves against them."[53] This blueprint of republican political power, at odds with ancient commentary, provides a political anatomy of the function of sodomy accusations in Florence.

Sex between men across hierarchies of age, status, and power materialized the "desire to dominate" and "desire not to be dominated" by providing occasions for these appetites to meet and play out across an economy of pleasure and pain, profit and punishment, power and humiliation, transgression and shame. Sodomy inscribed these political humors and their ambiguous hydraulic movements upon and within the bodies of those engaged in its pursuit. Through a reciprocal movement, the establishment of a special office for accusations against sodomites inscribed the play of these forces, this economy of flesh, back into the edifice of state power. The desire to dominate and the desire not to be dominated played out over the course of a life's trajectory, offering the possibility of further transgressions: from the pleasure of assuming a sexually passive role while still young and while such pleasure was still socially acceptable to the pleasure of assuming the sexually active role in one's manhood, the partners in these exchanges traded power and status for pleasure. Sodomy thus reflected, in the most immediate and embodied form of submission to penetration, the very structure of political-economic power itself.

Before proceeding any further with this line of inquiry, it is important to recall from the above discussion that Machiavelli's only explicit reference to Aristotle concerned cases of sexual abuse. Such an explicit reference indicates that he felt compelled to cite an authority on the matter—and thus, perhaps an anxiety concerning his own authority—where on all other matters pertaining to Aristotle's teaching he chose to remain silent on his source. His commentary on the Pausanias incident indicates how, among men who consider themselves free, anger at the sexual abuse of someone connected to the regime is easily transferred into a hatred of the regime itself for not avenging the offense. Just so, the Officers of the Night were suppressed in 1503, after the execution of Savonarola and the ascent of Piero Soderini to *gonfaloniere* of the Florentine Republic. The office was abolished for many reasons, some of which will be discussed further below, but given the Medici family's long history of mobilizing the office toward political ends, it is likely that it was abolished at least in part in the new spirit of republicanism. As second chancellor of the Republic, Machiavelli would have been very close to such deliberations but likely felt constrained in speaking of them directly; both *The Prince* and the *Discourses on Livy* were published after the sacking of the Florentine Republic by Spanish troops and the restoration of the Medici. As is well known, the texts were written following Machiavelli's imprisonment and torture for conspiracy; we might expect his language to be heavily veiled when addressing himself to such issues as the fall of the Florentine Republic, so as to give little ammunition to his enemies.

Machiavelli's correspondence with his close friend Francesco Vettori, which comprises some of the most widely read letters in the Italian language, give a crucial indication of Machiavelli's own political and intellectual development following the fall of the Republic and shed light on the widely remarked differences between *The Prince* and the *Discourses on Livy*. As John Najemy has demonstrated in his remarkable exegesis, *Between Friends*, of the whole correspondence with Vettori, Machiavelli's writings on the humorous foibles of love came to leaven his relationship to political language, leading to the adoption of a more poetic way of writing about politics that can be registered, for the first time, in the *Discourses*.[54] In a letter to Vettori, who was then in Rome, dated February 25, 1513, Machiavelli relates "a ridiculous metamorphosis," but, fearing that someone might "feel hurt," he tells the story "hidden under allegories." The letter must have been written from the prison cell of his torturers, or else immediately upon his release.

In the letter, Machiavelli draws an elaborate allegory between a bird hunt and one Giuliano Brancaccio's cruising of Florence for chance sexual encounters with beautiful male youths:

> He crossed the Bridge alla Carraia, and by way of the Canto de' Mozzi came to Santa Trinita, and having entered Borgo Santo Apostolo, went twisting around a bit in those alleys that surround it; not finding birds that waited for him, he turned toward your goldbeater, and near the Parte Guelfa crossed the Mercato and through the Calimala Francesca came under the Tetto de' Pisani, where looking carefully at all those hiding places, he found a little thrush, which with the bird-swatter and the light and the bell he stopped and cleverly brought it into the depth of the thicket near the cave where Panzano was living. Detaining his bird there, and finding its disposition generous, and kissing it many times, he straightened two feathers of its tail and at last, as many say, put it in the bird-basket hanging behind him.[55]

Abandoning the metaphor beyond this chase, Machiavelli relates to Vettori that the hunted boy was the son of a man of standing, and that the hunter Giuliano played a trick on the boy by giving the name and address of some shopkeeper as his own, requesting that the boy come by the shop for his payment on the following day. The boy sends a friend whom the shopkeeper turns away, denying any connection with the boy. When the boy himself boldly returns the following day, demanding payment and threatening to speak ill of the shopkeeper about town, the man is forced into a dilemma whose internal dialogue, as recounted by Machiavelli, reveals a sensitive appreciation of the political and ethical dilemma of this form of sexual deception:

> Because he said: "If I keep still and satisfy Michele with a florin, I become his vineyard, make myself his debtor, confess the sin, and instead of innocent become guilty; if I deny it without finding out the truth of the thing, I have to stand in comparison with a boy; I have to justify myself to him; I have to justify myself to the others; all the

harm will be mine. If I try to find the truth, I must blame somebody for it; I may guess wrong; I shall bring on hostility over it, and with it all I shall not be justified."[56]

Correctly guessing the man who played the trick on him to be Giuliano, the shopkeeper arranged for the boy to be led into a square to identify him by the sound of his voice:

> Coming up from behind, having seen Brancaccio, who was sitting in the middle of a big crowd telling stories, he managed that the boy got so close to him that he heard him speak; and on turning around and seeing him, Brancaccio, all confused, made off. So to everybody the affair seemed plain, in such a way that Filippo is now cleared and Brancaccio spoken ill of. . . . To your letter I have nothing to reply except that you should continue your love with loose reins, and the pleasure you take today you will not have to take tomorrow; and if the thing stands as you have written to me, I envy you more than I do the King of England. I beg you to follow your star, and not to let an iota go for the things of the world. . . . It is better to act and repent than not to act and repent.[57]

As to what real events prompted Machiavelli's veiled allegorical telling, we will probably never know, and to my knowledge, no commentators have yet ventured a guess as to the identities of those in question. In the reading that follows, I propose that we adopt Machiavelli's interpretative stance, and see its staging of the political drama of sodomy accusations as an allegory of the fall of the Republic.

In the *Discourses on Livy* Machiavelli argues for the necessity of an official institution for making accusations in a republic so that "those alternating humors that agitate it can be vented in a way ordered by the laws."[58] In support of this conclusion, in addition to Titus Livy's example of the ancient Sparta of Coriolanus, in which military culture institutionalized pederasty and erased outward signs of difference in status, and the example of contemporary Venice that had effected a smoother transition to finance capitalism, he writes,

> One could also cite in support of the conclusion written above the incident that also occurred in Florence regarding Piero Soderini, which occurred entirely because in that republic there was no mode of accusation against the ambition of powerful citizens. For to accuse one powerful individual before eight judges in a republic is not enough;

the judges need to be very many because the few always behave in the mode of the few. So if such modes had been there, either the citizens would have accused him, if he were living badly, and by such means they would have vented their animus without having the Spanish army come; or, if he were not living badly, they would not have dared to work against him for fear of being accused themselves. And so from each side the appetite that was the cause of the scandal would have ceased.[59]

In other words, Machiavelli suggests that the fall of his own patron, Piero Soderini, and the ensuing political crisis was triggered by the absence of official institutions through which citizens could have accused him for "living badly."

Although these allusions are heavily veiled, we would expect nothing less concerning accusations against Machiavelli's patron. He refuses to confirm or deny whatever the charges were against Soderini, but the tone of the discussion and Machiavelli's close association of homosexual offenses with conspiracies against princes elsewhere suggests that the text refers to the Officers of the Night, which had been suppressed in 1502. A decade of petty amorous slights and injustices would have accumulated without any pressure valve for their release. By declaring that the "eight judges," or *Otto di guardia*, whose authority over general criminal concerns continued well into the seventeenth century, were "not enough" of a vent for the animus against Soderini, and arguing that "the judges need to be very many because the few always behave in the mode of the few," Machiavelli signals that the elimination of certain municipal offices contributed to the downfall of Soderini. Following the suppression of the Officers of the Night, the "eight judges" were indeed the only authority to which Florentines could appeal for justice concerning sodomy.

Florentine chronicler Filipepi recounts a group of defamatory denunciations for sodomy in 1496, following the war with France, in which Piero Soderini was named and denounced for the practice.[60] The harsher penalties meted out by the Otto di guardia under the new republic were of central concern to the pro-Medicean youths who overthrew Piero Soderini's regime and invited Spanish soldiers to occupy the city.

On August 31, [1512,] with Spanish and Medicean troops at the city gates, some thirty young partisans of the Medici led by twenty-three-year-old Anton Francesco degli Albizzi invaded the government palace and forced the gonfaloniere Piero Soderini to resign. According to

Cambi, the youths then stormed into the chambers of the bewildered priors—who were "like a fly without a head," as he put it—and demanded that they revoke the sentences of those who had been exiled or deprived of office for sodomy.[61]

Under Giuliano de' Medici those exiled or barred from office were reinstated. The episode demonstrates the double danger of how sodomy accusations functioned politically, as calumny, and how punishments for sodomy could inflame men's passions against a political regime. Far from some "marginal" or "closeted" phenomenon, sodomy formed a crucial hinge of political power in Florence. Same-sex desire was so central to the fate of the Republic that Machiavelli's veiled commentary on its fall is completely incomprehensible without an understanding of the history of attempts to regulate the practice.

RECORDS INDICATE THAT BETWEEN 2,500 and 3,000 men and boys—for the most part poor servants, unskilled workers, and increasingly superfluous artisans from minor Florentine guilds—were convicted in a city where the population, after successive plague epidemics, never recovered above 50,000. The political power to make the city's homosexuality visible was the result of a governmental organ that absorbed petty (and also very grave) slights and power struggles into the state edifice. By making sentences lower and providing men with a way out—confession granted an individual immunity from accusations—the Officers of the Night ensured a constant flow of accusations, greater social control over homosexuality, and better knowledge of its locations, persons, and practices. In addition to its primary function of policing the poor and the workers, its regulation provided a pressure valve for outrage at abuses of power that included, among other things, the sexual abuse and humiliation of boys and young men by nobles. Following the suppression of the "Officers of Sodomites" the regime unraveled, as such tensions between "nobles and ignobles" found no other vent than the calumnies pronounced in piazzas and loggias. By providing an outlet for putting sodomy into discourse and by multiplying this discourse throughout the population, the Florentine state extended power over the sexuality of its male population. It was able to regulate pederasty without repressing it, to neutralize the threat generated by volatile sexual encounters between men of different strata, to break apart the solidarities that formed among men who had sex with men—turning friend against friend, lover against lover—

and, most crucially, to provide incentives for the betrayal of one's self to the state.

Discourse about sex between men was, in other words, an absolutely essential instrument for extending the political hegemony of the ruling classes over the poor and working classes in Florence. By abolishing this special office, one associated with the tyrannies of the Medici family and Savonarola alike, the Republic lost a central tool for governing men's passions. In the absence of this organ, accusations against its leader found no outlet and fomented into open rebellion. Within the ebb and flow of these discourses and recriminations, sodomy was a weapon that changed hands in a "war of position" that quietly raged in fifteenth-century Florence, following closely on the heels of the "war of maneuver" of the fourteenth.[62]

The edifice of our received historical narrative that associates "homosexuality" with a singular modernity—owing much to the nominalist historiographic leanings and epistemological assumptions of Michel Foucault, Paul Veyne, and their intellectual mentor George Canguilhem—threatens to collapse beneath the accumulated weight of the above examples and analysis. For a long time, the medieval sodomite was thought to be the product of another order of words and things; the modern figure, it is said, was determined by scientific schemas dividing the normal from the pathological. The body of the accused and confessed sodomite sometimes committed to the fire in early modern cities was, according to this view, only a grotesque figure pronounced by a unitary discourse revolving around belief in God; he was perhaps an occasional casualty of the moral theology of flesh and concupiscence, but more frequently manifested a behavior that was revealed and atoned for from behind the grill of confession. An impassable historical and epistemological break is supposed to have separated the nineteenth-century homosexual from these sodomites of the past. The medieval mind is supposed to have considered sodomy a *sin* of the sensuous East, perhaps even a luxurious excess of the mythopoetic "cities of the plain" whose name he bears. Sodomy was supposed to have been "a type of forbidden act, whose author was merely a juridical subject," habitual sodomites merely recidivists or relapses; the modern homosexual, by contrast, was "a personality: a past, a history and a childhood, a character, a form of life."[63]

In fourteenth- and fifteenth-century Florence, however, sodomy was far from a confused legal category. Juridically speaking, it included only men who had sexual relations with other men. The population of Florence knew very well how to identify men who were having sex with other men; the sheer number of accusations demonstrates that the category was not the purview of an eccentric pseudoscience, as it may have been for the nineteenth-century homosexual and his "possibly mysterious physiology"; in fact, sodomites were readily identifiable among all classes of Florence. They were identifiable not only for their stereotypical outward appearance, in some cases mixing elements of the masculine and feminine—long hair, fine clothes, jewelry. This type coexisted alongside less gender-ambiguous ones. Their sexual escapades were often stumbled upon by neighbors, as sodomites conducted their affairs in the shops, squares, baths, taverns, inns, bars, and other public and semipublic spaces of urban life. Sodomites in Florence were infamous personalities, immortalized in satire and poetry by men of letters.[64]

Habitual homosexual behavior was, in its actual practice and in the way in which it was conceived, *a form of life*. It had a childhood, conforming to certain expected patterns of sexual passivity or receptive roles, and an adulthood conforming to certain expectations of sexual activity or insertive roles, all according to Florentine customs of acceptable masculine behavior. Like all social rules and expectations, these customs were made to be broken. Moreover, knowledge of the flourishing northern Italian culture of same-sex eroticism was not limited to southern climes. At the time that the Medici closed their last bank in Bruges, the city of Florence typified the vice: it was common in fifteenth-century German to equate the vice with Florence and its coin—to sodomize was *florenzen*, the sodomite a *Florenzer*.[65] As with the association of the practice with the cities of Sodom and Gomorrah, its association with Florence after its spectacular economic decline around the turn of the sixteenth century reflects a political-moral equation of excess and riches with injustice. This moral-political equation at the end of northern Italy's hegemony in the world economic system should give us pause, as the script of this morality play—and its scapegoating of financiers, Jews, and homosexuals—would remain unchanged throughout each instance of the decline of a world hegemonic power, from Italy to the United Provinces to London to the United States.

In the iconography of Sodom and Gomorrah, as represented in Italian and Flemish genre paintings of the period, it is hard not to see, in the distance, beyond the ugly scene of the drunken, besotted patriarch Lot and his incestuous daughters all dressed up in the trappings of the merchant class, the object upon which the gaze of the pillar of salt, the dead mother, is fixed for all eternity (see figures 2.1, 2.2, and 3.2). The line of sight along which the composition of the familiar landscape pulls even a casual observer is toward the brilliant sight of cities in a littoral, burning like beacons signaling the excesses and ultimate demise of the Mediterranean world.

Girolamo Macchietti's *Baths at Pozzuoli* (1570; figure 2.2), in which the foreground has been populated with male bathers and bath attendants, gives the viewer a local perspective on those infamous vices, perhaps even a cynical or satirical moral portrait. Lot's wife has been replaced by a central statuary figure of a bearded man, arrayed in the fashion of imperial Rome, frozen and fixed in the gaze of a serpent wrapped around his extended hand. The perspective remains but the moral lessons become more ambiguous as the fire and brimstone is reduced to a volcanic eruption, just barely visible beyond the baths. These paintings are modern in the perspective into which the viewer is drawn, the perspective of the historical witness. The standpoint is that of the retrospective glance where "lo, the smoke of the country went up as the smoke of a furnace";[66] we share the perspective of the pillar of salt that was once Lot's wife, a backward glance that refuses to heed God's command to "escape for thy life; look not behind thee, neither stay thou in all the plain; escape to the mountain, lest thou be consumed."[67] Such a perspective, one of historical retrospection, is that of a transgression; its danger is that of being consumed or frozen into place by that which it beholds.

Perhaps we too are frozen by this horrified sympathy or, alternately, by an aversion to the cities' going up in smoke, to the oblivion of things. Whatever its dangers, it remains the standpoint of lost innocence and illusions, the starting point of a secular historical consciousness. But there is within this perspective perhaps another standpoint, perhaps a dialectic between this disabused standpoint and some other one. The other perspective is that of the historical materialist, who maintains an eye for the "zero hour," or *Still-stellung*, a universal history in which "thinking suddenly halts in a constellation overflowing with tensions, [and] there it yields a shock to the same, through which it crystallizes as a monad." The perspective of the *Stillstellung* recognizes the sign of a "revolutionary chance in the struggle for the suppressed past. [The historical materialist] perceives it in order to explode a specific epoch out of the homogenous course of history; thus exploding a specific life out of the epoch, or a specific work out of the life-work."[68]

Perhaps this other perspective sees in the image of destruction and the overthrow of cities the possibility of precisely this revolutionary éclat or perhaps its defeat. The abuses of power, the hubris of empire, the social visibility of gross inequality, and the lack of kindness toward strangers are all articulated in the Old Testament mythopoetics of sodomy and conspicuous wealth in the cities of the plain. These injustices must have burned with clarity to contemporaries of the Renaissance, as they do to us in this familiar image.

Whether beautifully painted by masters for rich patrons or described in broad strokes from the pulpits of Bernardino de Siena, Girolamo Savonarola, Martin Luther, or John Calvin, these smoldering cities, sunken ships, and bursts of fire from heaven provide an ambivalent moral-political fable: even the passages in Genesis and the accompanying traditions of rabbinical commentary contain great ambiguity as to the real sins of Sodom. Wealth, inhospitality, social injustice, and sexual violence have all been proposed in various allegorical interpretations. To the poor, the riches of the war-mongering cities of the plain must have appeared strikingly similar to the class divide apparent in their own social world. The mythopoetic disaster must have confirmed that the path of excess and injustice leads to ruin. The iconography probably resonated very differently with the merchant elite of northern Europe: the decline of Italian cities probably confirmed their own senses of entitlement and divine election, the justice of their newfound fortunes. In conjoining conspicuous riches, abuse of power, and the pederasty of the Mediterranean world with divine moral justice, the image likely resonated on another level among those classes prey to priest, noble, and burgher alike.

This image was popular in paintings and sermons because it resonated as an allegory of the rise and fall of civilizations; it resonated with very different intensities and meanings for the ruling classes and for the oppressed who received its message. For the Abrahamic traditions of faith, Sodom figures as the arche-mythology of civilization, economic surplus, corruption, decadence, and pride. Despite this polysemy, the image resonates as the first critical stance on economic development, one that was immediately recognizable to all who heard its story told. Its wide currency throughout Europe at the end of the Italian city-states' hegemony reflects a new historical consciousness of the oblivion of markets and civilizations. And unlike with the fall of Rome, there were no invading barbarians to blame.

IT IS VERY LIKELY that the Ufficiali di notte were dissolved in 1502 for the ironic reason that the magistracy itself, far more than the city's actual practice of sodomy, had come to be seen as an embarrassment for having made such a public spectacle of the vice. In 1497, at the height of the Piagnone spiritual awakening—bonfires of vanities, religious revivals, processions, and Carnival spectacles—the silk merchant Domenico Cecchi proposed a platform of reforms that included ridding the city of the sodomy officers. He wrote, "Before all else, for the honor of the city, abolish the Officers of the Night so that it cannot be said, 'Florence has a magistracy over sodomites,' for those who hate the city believe that here we do nothing else, and it gives us a bad reputation."[69] Even friar Savonarola avoided mentioning the office by name in his appeals for "justice" for sodomy, naming only the Otto di guardia. Perhaps Machiavelli was merely following the customary conventions of politesse in avoiding mention of the Ufficiali di notte out of shame for the infamy that Florence had acquired throughout Europe, as this magistracy aired the city's dirty laundry so publicly. One can only imagine the hilarious puns on Soderini's name that accompanied the slanderous discourse against him in the taverns and piazzas of Florence. If sodomy remained the butt of jokes in the squares of Florence and at the banks of Bruges and Antwerp, it was the office—far more than the sin—that dared not speak its name.

The nominalists and others might counter that despite such facts and observations, these remain only anecdotes, and Florentine sodomites were not coequals in their relations with one another. They might push these examples further back along the sociohistorical timeline toward the pederasty of ancient civilizations in the Mediterranean world, further away from a "modern" homosexual. These seemingly innocent temporal maneuvers, shuffling events along the continuum of empty homogeneous time, might be excusable if they weren't symptomatic of serious political disavowals.

It is true of course that these fifteenth-century Florentine sexual relations were shot through with relations of power structured by hierarchies of age, class, and status, and that they only occasionally took place between men of the same age and status, or, at least, only occasionally came to the attention of authorities for doing so. Perhaps it was precisely the interclass relations that were politically and morally troublesome in the first place. There are many indications that sexual relations between men of equal status were less socially troublesome and therefore came to the attention of authorities far less frequently.

The argument for nudging these practices further down the continuum of empty homogeneous time toward antiquity indulges a little too much in the trope of Sodom, engages a little too much in a childish and speculative historicism of antiquity, what Benjamin called "the whore called 'Once upon a time' in historicism's bordello."[70] It belies false assumptions about the nearer past, as if sexual relations between men and boys in nineteenth-century Europe were somehow free of power, free of class, status, and age hierarchies. These assumptions are politically blind to all forms of homosexual behavior in the contemporary world that do not conform to the progressive liberal ideal of relations between coequals—to master-slave or daddy-boy scenes, to sex among prisoners, nonconsensual sex, prostitution, sex between individuals with healthcare and those without healthcare, to interracial sex, not to mention the complex relations of dependency and mastery internal to the couple form itself. This moral and political assumption of liberalism is not only patently false, it has inscribed into our discourses on the historicity of sex a sad caricature of social thought and criticism, a disempowering conception of human freedom, implying that self-reflection and subjectivity, sexual or otherwise, could only begin when the psychiatrist or some other pseudoscientist pronounced it to be so. How free is this apparently critical perspective on the values of enlightened scientific knowledge from the belief of the prior episteme, centered around a belief in God, in which the world existed because some entity "said let there be" x, y, or z, "and it was so"?

If not scientific rationality, what then accounts for this early entry of sexuality into the discourse on princes and good government? If the above historical sketch has brought to light some of the contingent political motivations for the establishment of a special office for sodomy accusations in fifteenth-century Florence and exposed a perhaps wider Mediterranean set of geopolitical preconditions for ubiquitous male homosexual behaviors and identifications, it has only begun to indicate the weakness of our existing models for historicizing this world and has, so far, refrained from offering an alternate hypothesis.

The evidence presented so far, however suggestive, is probably not yet enough to quiet some of the objections that could be made from either the nominalist historical perspective or its liberal political counterpart. After all, northern Italian cities were the exception to rather than the rule of European societies during this period. To dispense with these objections once and for all would require a careful reconstruction of the conditions of possibility for the apparently ubiquitous homosexuality of the centers of handicraft production and trade in the Mediterranean world and an analysis of how these conditions of possibility were at variance with the wider pattern of feudalism throughout continental Europe. Until now, my exploration of the political rationale for the regulation of homosexuality has only begged this larger question: What accounts for the apparently ubiquitous homosexuality of the Mediterranean world?

3

SEXUAL HEGEMONY AND THE CAPITALIST WORLD SYSTEM

Richard Burton, or Port Cities

The geophysical position of northern Italian cities—along maritime trade routes between the Levant and the ports of northern Europe—and these cities' early naval prowess made them hegemonic centers of an emerging world system of cities, war and merchant capitalism.[1] Florentine-finished wool was exchanged for spices, dyes, and other Asian products from the east, while Florentine ships carried cloth and debt obligations to distant ports of call in the west and north, clothing the elite in finery and financing their battles for territorial sovereignty. The ubiquitous cultures of sodomy known to many Mediterranean societies resulted from their demographic peculiarities, extreme class polarization, and such an early circulation of men and goods from distant lands.

A consideration of the Mediterranean—as defined by its geographic, climatological, and cultural boundaries—and the Mediterranean social world opens up a perspective on how the production of a particular kind of world-space, favoring port towns along coastal trade routes, created one of the necessary preconditions for a homosexual lifeworld. In the Mediterranean, the climate is consistent across the region, favoring the same crops and establishing the same rhythms of life: a winter season with rain and winds, when shipping mostly came to a halt, rendering its maritime labor temporarily superfluous, and a summer season in which heat and traffic brought discomfort and disease.[2] This perspective permits a backward glance into the immediate past, the surrounding world of agrarian life under feudalism, and the more distant past of the ancient world. It opens up a unique perspective on the sexuality of the transition to capitalism, the continuities and discontinuities with the sexuality of the ancient world.

It is illuminating to consider this geography in light of Richard Burton's controversial idea of a "Sotadic Zone," first raised in the terminal essay to his translation of *Thousand and One Nights*.[3] Inspired by having the occasion to "make enquiries and to report upon" brothels of boys and eunuchs in Karachi, and following later "enquiries in many and distant countries," Burton concludes that the geographic space of the Mediterranean basin, its complex cultural interactions over trade routes with the civilizations to the east and their traffic with Spice Islands, created a nearly universal practice, which he terms "Pederasty," at variance with the sexualities of northern Europe and sub-Saharan Africa.

Although he has been criticized by some scholars for having a "racial" understanding of homosexuality, such a criticism does not hold up under further investigation. This charge loses sight of the insight and world-historical sweep of Burton's essay and of the materials it furnishes to anyone looking for a geographic argument that would unsettle cultural and political distinctions between Eastern *ars erotica* and Western *scientia sexualis*—at least one of the purposes of Edward Said's *Orientalism*.[4] Burton's essay argues that homosexual practices among warrior classes and third-gender types—often associated with priestly or shamanic ritual—existed as features of all civilizations, suggesting a universal basis for the practice and a universal perspective from which to question both northern European and sub-Saharan African sexual mores and gender binaries as exceptions rather than historical rules. Recent historical research has comported with many of Burton's central hypotheses concerning the Mediterranean world, the Japanese shogunate, and many cultures of North, Central, and South America.

In Richard Trexler's history of the concept and political function of the *ber-dache*, he demonstrates the social and symbolic significance of this type in the discovery of the New World. The intellectual history of the berdache concept reveals that a spatial epistemology of homosexuality in terms of a third-gender person, mixing elements of the feminine with the masculine, circulated from at least the tenth century to as late as the sixteenth century in the Mediterranean world.[5]

This geographic perspective on the cultural distribution of same-sex sexuality is indebted to an imperial view of the world-space; it is an epistemology possible at the close of the nineteenth century only due to the bloody conquests and subjugations of colonial subalterns under the British hegemony of capitalism.[6] It is also true that Burton relied on ethnographic reports containing no small amount of essentialism; he argues, however, against the grain of these texts, that race cannot be understood as a determining factor in the formation of the Sotadic Zone. He rejects all the popular scientific theories of the nineteenth century concerning the biological or physiological basis of sexuality as the bunk pseudosciences that they were, according them little significance, explanatory or otherwise, and he instead favors social and geographic explanations for cultures of pederasty. Burton holds that the geographic particularity of the greater world of and just beyond the Mediterranean is the cause of its peculiar sexuality and sexual consciousness. Although he provides brief summaries of the sexuality of indigenous civilizations of North and South America and offers brisk encounters with India, China, and Japan, the Mediterranean world constitutes the bulk of his evidence and argument for a geographic determination of pederasty.

What is it about the geography of the Mediterranean world and the world to which it was connected by trade routes that favored pederasty? An answer to this question would begin to unravel the longue durée of early commerce, naval warfare, and political-economic institutions such as craft production and markets. The geography of the Mediterranean favored a very early development of port cities. The scant natural resources of both mountain and ocean environments in the region required constant interaction between mountains and sea in the littoral. A concentration of class power and massive outlays of capital investment in transforming the land was necessary to clear out the malarial swamps and establish habitable cities by the sea. Great earthen works of ditches, canals, trenches, and pumps—although never as advanced as those of the Dutch engineers of the seventeenth century—remained constant indexes of human effort, and provided some way of draining swamps and guarding against floods and disease. Earthworks of this scale required large amounts of capital and could only be funded with the profits of trade or the spoils of war; accordingly, the tracts of reclaimed land in the plains became the property of wealthy patricians and became habitable only with great civilizational effort.[7]

In his seminal essay on the subject, Karl Polanyi wrote that ports of trade developed into one of the most enduring and global economic institutions. The institution developed as "a universal institution of overseas trade preceding the establishment of international markets."[8] Archaeological excavations, Polanyi continues, have revealed that

> ports of trade were in evidence on the north Syrian coast ever since the second millennium B.C., in some Greek city-states of Asia Minor and the Black Sea in the first millennium; in the Negro kingdoms of Whydah and—later—Dahomey on the Upper Guinea coast and of Angola on the Lower Guinea coast; in the Aztec-Maya region of the Gulf of Mexico; in the Indian Ocean and on the Malabar Coast, in Madras, Calcutta, Rangoon, Burma, Colombo, Batavia as well as in China.[9]

Geographically speaking, port cities are border phenomena, emerging along the edge of ecosystems but not limited to sites where land meets water—coasts of oceans and seas, rivers and lagoons—for even sites bordering the desert, "that *alter ego* of the sea," might qualify according to Polanyi's ideal-typical criteria as ports of trade. "The caravan cities of Palmyra and Petra, Karakorum, Ispahan and Kandahar may be said to have fallen into the category of *quasi* ports of trade."[10]

The Mediterranean, in other words, realized a very early concentration of capital employed in the transformation of arable land, urban development, and state- and war-making apparatuses. Its dense trade network and concentration of wealth formed a geographic sink for the products of industry, raw materials, and resources of the hinterlands immediately to the north, south, and east.[11]

Commerce and communication between coastal cities united the Mediterranean in a vast network of roads and urban centers, connecting imperial lines of force with strategic nodal points for commerce and military offensives. The rapid geographic spread of the Black Death by infected crews from the Italian merchants' last trading station in the Crimea to the ports of Europe in October 1347, its transit across or around the Alps, striking Paris within six months and southwest England by June, reflects the vast interconnected web of humanity. These networks formed a cohesive "human unit," according to Braudel:

> In the sixteenth century no other region in the world had such a developed urban network. Paris and London were just on the threshold of their modern careers. The towns of the Low Countries and southern Germany (the latter bathing in the reflected glory of the Mediterranean, the former stimulated economically by merchants and sailors from the South), further north the industrious but small towns of the Hanseatic League, all these towns, thriving and beautiful though they might be, did not make up a network as closely knit and complex as that of the Mediterranean, where town followed town in endless strings, punctuated by great cities: Venice, Genoa, Florence, Milan, Barcelona, Seville, Algiers, Naples, Constantinople, Cairo. The last three were overpopulated: Constantinople was said to have a population of 700,000, that is double the size of Paris and four times the size of Venice. And to this list should be added the large number of minor towns that nevertheless took part in international exchanges, playing a role more important than the size of their population would suggest.[12]

In this most populous band of coastal cities, political power was concentrated in the hands of nobles, state functionaries, and large merchants, patrician or otherwise. Guilds or artisanal craft production organized along age hierarchies and master-servant relations predominated in most local workshops; the streets teemed with the petty commercial activity and production of storefronts, workshops, grocers, and others.

Transhumance and population shifts brought far-flung populations with strange customs into contact with the port cities around the Mediterranean basin in seasonal cycles for grazing livestock. Mountain villages and towns provided a source and sink of surplus populations for urban cycles of boom and bust in the littoral. In the mountain villages, "there was no tight urban network so no administration, no towns in the proper sense of the word, and no gendarmes," Braudel writes. "The hills were the refuge of liberty, democracy, and peasant 'republics.'"[13] Humans and animals lived under the same roofs in peasant huts of beaten clay; extra mouths were expelled to cities. Surplus populations from the hinterlands often made up the labor forces of the ports and galleons involved in the circulation of goods and, when necessary, were recruited to form mercenary armies for princes. Freshly arrived mountain dwellers were suspected, feared, and mocked in the coastal cities for their strange customs and costumes.[14]

Culture was necessarily syncretic in ports of trade along coastal routes that connected Orthodox, Catholic, and Moorish cities of the basin with the cities of northern Europe. Maritime labor was of an international sort and mixture; sailors were in high demand and had no loyalty to any particular city. Braudel relates how the dense urban network of the Mediterranean functioned to sustain the world of sea traffic; a large, disciplined, and imperial city was "indispensable with its supplies of yards, sail-cloth, rigging, pitch, ropes, and capital; a city with its tradesmen, shipping offices, insurance agents, and all other services an urban centre can provide."[15] But these forces of discipline were limited to the extent that the skilled labor of sailors was highly mobile, as Braudel observes:

> The attraction of the big cities is the more understandable in that sailors in the Mediterranean have always been wanderers ready to migrate. In 1461, the Venetian Senate expressed anxiety at the shortage of crews and cabin boys and asked for details: the sailors "go to Pisa . . . where they are well paid . . . to our loss and another's gain." Many of these sailors left because they had debts to pay or heavy fines imposed by the *Cinque Savii* or the *Signor de nocte*—the night police of Venice. As the result of a legal dispute in 1526, the accounts have survived of the ship *Santa Maria de Bogoña*, which sailed in the Atlantic, stayed for a while at Cadiz, and put in at Lisbon and the island of São Tomé before arriving at Santo Domingo with her cargo of Negro slaves. This takes us out of Mediterranean waters, but among the *marineros* and *grumetes* (cabin boys) on board her could be found sailors from Lipari, Sicily, Majorca, Genoa, Savona, some Greeks, and a man from Toulon—a real rendezvous for adventurers. At the Hague in 1532, there were similar complaints that the sailors, "always ready to move away," were leaving Holland and Zeeland for Lübeck. In 1604 a group of Venetian seamen, "being no longer able to live on the ships of the Signoria because of the low wages," fled to Florence and no doubt to Leghorn. These were daily occurrences of minor importance, but when circumstances lent a hand, they might become indices of large-scale change.[16]

For our purposes, these details of the everyday life of Mediterranean sailors *are* indices of a large-scale transformation of human sexuality brought about by a transient life at sea. Braudel stumbles across a document from the archives of the Venetian Senate suggesting that the city's crackdown on sodomy and other morals charges might have driven away able-

FIGURE 3.1. Antonio Vassilacchi, *Conquest of Tyre*, c. 1590, oil on canvas. Palazzo Ducale, Venice.

bodied sailors and cabin boys to more favorable cities. Sailors were a multi-ethnic, multicultural, and itinerant population able to move from port to port as conditions became more or less favorable, as moral crackdowns became more or less ferocious.

Arab Muslim cities of the eleventh through fifteenth centuries display similar social and economic patterns as the northern Italian cities that have been our focus so far. Until the Dutch began routing the spice trade around the Cape of Good Hope in the middle of the seventeenth century, spices still passed through Cairo, silk was brought over land through a network of cities from Iran, and, from Yemen, Cairo imported coffee that then traded throughout the Mediterranean world; cities of the Maghreb were the central nodes of trade in gold, ivory, and slaves from beyond the Sahara. The wealth of this immense trade network partly flowed into the coffers of the army and state bureaucracy and partly into the hands of merchants, manufacturers, and bankers. Cities were governed through a partnership between large merchants and higher ulema. Beneath the state edifice of palaces, the barracks, and the merchant elite stood a middle stratum of shopkeepers and a variety of tradesmen producing goods for the local market—textiles, pottery, leather goods, metalwork—and higher-quality goods such as fine textiles for a wider market.

Beyond this stratum of fixed occupations was a wide sea of informal, occasional, and itinerant labor.[17] As in northern Italian cities, women played only limited roles in the public economic life of markets and trade in Ottoman cities, and the extent to which women led a public life reflected the extent to which they were from poor families.[18] Whereas Spanish and Venetian power was in decline by the eighteenth century, continued population growth enabled the Ottoman Empire to increase the size of its armies and navies.[19]

Slavery persisted long after antiquity in the Mediterranean world in general and in Islamic and Moorish cities in particular. The preference of Mamluk elites in Egypt and Syria for non-Muslim boys, Turks, and Christians is well known. The Mamluks purchased boys as slaves, favoring the beautiful and the strong, converted them to Islam, trained them as soldiers and incorporated them into the ruling elite. Sexual relations between men and boys, and among boys, was a normal and inevitable part of such a state machine based upon housing subjects in sex-segregated barracks, removed from their families.[20] The poetic praise and satire of elite boy love went in and out of courtly and literary fashion, according to taste, but the political and social biases toward pederasty continued more or less unabated as the Mamluks were dissolved and incorporated into the Ottoman Empire.[21]

Although the sexual practices of the majority of the population, which is to say its poor and working classes, during this period are difficult to discern, contemporary travelers' anecdotes furnish some evidence that sexual relations between men structured by age and status hierarchies were as familiar to Ottoman society as they were elsewhere in the Mediterranean.

Future research in the archives of these cities may well uncover significant new evidence. To take the example of the Ottoman Empire at its apogee during the reign of Suleiman "the Magnificent," who ruled from 1520 to 1566: as part of his many legal reforms, the code pertaining to sexual behavior was modified to allow for progressive sliding scales of penalties and to eliminate

CHAPTER THREE

the lash, a transformation strikingly similar to that adopted in Florence. Perhaps future research in the archives of Arab Muslim cities of the Mediterranean will turn up records regarding actual rates or details of conviction under these new laws. Because the Qur'an does not explicitly refer to such offenses as a form of *zina*, or fornication, Islamic jurisprudence contains an uncertain framework for punishing sex between men and between men and boys, crimes referred to in Arabic as *liwat* or *amal qaum lut* (the deeds of Lot's people); punishments, however, do seem to have been customarily meted out by local authorities. Although considered abominable in juridical commentaries, sex between males was subject to heated disagreement in all schools of law.[22]

Suleiman's famous work of legal reform, the Kanun-i Osmani, promulgated between 1534 and 1545, opens with a chapter on fornication, proposing a sliding scale of fines as punishment for men found guilty of homosexual or heterosexual zina, chastisement for minors who yield to a pederast, and a fine for fathers.[23] Heads of households—ministers, grand viziers, provincial governors, commanders of the army, and high-level functionaries of the imperial palace—were largely responsible for the promulgation of the *kanun*. Considering the normalcy of pederasty among this elite group, it is likely that Suleiman's reforms provided an increased regulatory power over the homosexuality of the poorer populations of the Ottoman Empire, just as they did in Florence.[24]

What does the above perspective on the geographic and political-economic underpinnings of Mediterranean sexuality indicate about a longer view of human civilizations in the region? Since the rediscovery of ancient Greece by the West, modernity has for good reasons defined itself as radically other than antiquity, but the pictures we have of these ancient civilizations have gained complexity and depth with major advances in archaeology and philology. The project of humanism inaugurated by the Renaissance has resulted in a plural historical view of human societies and civilizations. What use are the ancient Greeks to us now?

The rediscovery of same-sex love in the classics of Greek literature played a central and sweeping role in transforming Christian views of the practice. For most of this history of "rediscovery," only a narrow substratum of elites had access to these texts and art in translation and even fewer had the ability to read and access them in their original language. It was not until the middle or late nineteenth century that the general level of education made these "classics" accessible to a wider popular audience of middle-class readers. Despite this limited circulation, commentary and discussion of the alternate sexual mores of seventh- and sixth-century Athens and ancient Rome once served as the only indicator, aside from anthropological accounts, of a world in which same-sex sexuality was not only tolerated but perhaps even celebrated as the foundation of cities and republics. More recently, such ancient texts have served as alibis for the contemporary gay rights movement's claims for nominal political equality and access to particular state institutions. Such mainstream appropriations of ancient Greece for political ends have purged much of what is historically particular about the same-sex sexuality of the ancient world and have sought to silence discussion of what is ethically uncomfortable—such as the love of adolescents. Much of queer theory and feminism have at least implicitly supported this censorship of the same-sex sexuality of the ancient world by adopting the view that pederasty was universally sexually abusive for the boy.

As the above discussion indicates, this is a politically and ethically fraught subject. These dilemmas needn't detain us here, for in what follows I advance an argument for why the same-sex sexuality of seventh- and sixth-century Athens is germane to a longue durée view of European sexuality. It illuminates (1) the origin and persistence of a same-sex sexuality structured by socioeconomic relations of dependency, or master-servant relations; (2) the origin and persistence of a same-sex sexuality structured by martial institutions for waging war, first among an aristocratic elite and later among semipopular armies; and (3) the demographic causes, motives, and effects of same-sex sexuality in a Mediterranean world with scarce resources.

The transformations following the Dorian invasions discussed in the previous chapter had profound effects on Greek society. Greece found a new function for money beyond its previously sacral role in the collection of taxes and debts. Once internal to a regime of gift, sacrifice, and redistribution, money became a means for separating the political and economic orders with an apparently neutral institution for circulating values. It could be used to defuse the class conflict over debt, to pay out wages in craft production, and to finance war and colonial expansion.

Beginning in the sixth and seventh centuries BCE, the relations of production and the patriarchal family form of the early modern Mediterranean world contributed to the near-universal homosexuality of its men.[25] Although many archaeologists now date specialized craft production for trade to the middle and late Bronze Age, there is little doubt that the discovery of iron transformed craft production. This form of labor, based on apprenticeship and relations of dependency, persisted long into the development of industrial capitalism. Craftsmen and servants of one kind or another made

CHAPTER THREE

up the majority of the working population of cities during the early modern period. Historians are in agreement that nearly 20 percent of the population lived in conditions of extreme poverty. Guilds and apprenticeships created demographic patterns of late marriage. The mode of production was, in this way, directly responsible for pederasty.[26] Sexual segregation of public and private spaces and the close guarding of women's virginity made pederasty and prostitution the only sexual outlet for young working men deprived of property and superfluous to agricultural production.

Master-servant relations were, so to speak, built into the technology of the means of circulating goods and waging wars. The architecture of the merchant ship and warship—essentially, a galley propelled by oars, with a large square sail mounted on a single mast—remained unchanged for nearly three millennia in the Mediterranean, from the merchant ships of the Phoenician empire of 1000 BCE (which were in turn modeled after the Egyptian war galleys) to the merchant ships of Venice and Florence in 1700. This technology was adapted to cabotage, or coast-hugging, which partially explains the need for slaves: Mediterranean commerce was powered by human labor rather than by wind. Globally, by 1000 CE, the sail had ousted the oar as the prime means of ship propulsion everywhere but the Mediterranean. Seagoing placed men of all ages and from many cultures and religious traditions into intimate, highly cooperative, and mostly sex-segregated labor processes. Same-sex sexual relations and bonds of fraternity and love were as inevitable in such milieus as they are in today's prisons. As for the same-sex sexuality of Mediterranean warrior cultures and the possible demographic motivations for institutionalized pederasty, it is illuminating to revisit Aristotle's discussion of the matter in *Politics*.

Aristotle's claim for the Mycenaean origins of institutionalized homosexuality, and its association with communal property relations in Sparta and Crete, is striking for being a plausible if ultimately unverifiable account of the origins of the Greek cult of masculinity and homoeroticism. Nevertheless, Aristotle and Plato considered the sexuality of their societies as quite central to the project of evaluating the proper political form for a polity.

Broadly speaking, Aristotle's disagreement with Plato's plan for communism in the *Republic* hinges on an antinomy in which "both the household and the state should be a unit, but they should not be so in every way. For in one way the state as its unification proceeds will cease to be a state, and in another way, though it continues a state, yet by coming near to ceasing to be one it will be a worse state, just as if one turned a harmony into unison or a rhythm into a single foot."[27] Central to the conflation of large household and state in Plato's *Republic* is Socrates's argument for a community of wives and children. Aristotle makes no moral argument of his own but merely indicates the bonds of love among a polity so ordered would be weak, as the meanings of proper nouns would weaken. Aristotle indicates the central contradiction of Plato's sexual schema: its ideal of a communal family is at variance with all customs of love and sexuality while assuming these very same customs of human interaction and community to be the basis of his city:

> Moreover it is not easy for those who institute this domestic commons to guard against such objectionable occurrences as outrage, involuntary and in some cases voluntary homicide, fights, abusive language; all of which are violations of piety when committed against fathers, mothers, and near relatives as if they were not relatives; but these are bound to occur more frequently when people do not know their relations than when they do, and also, when they do occur, if the offenders know their relationship it is possible for them to have the customary expiations performed, but for those who do not, no expiation is possible. Also it is curious that a theorist who makes the sons [υἱοὺς, *huious*] common property [κοινοὺς, *koinous*] only debars lovers [ἐρώντων, *eronton*] from sexual intercourse [συνεῖναι, *suneinai*] and does not prohibit erotic love [ἐρᾶν, *eran*], nor the other intimacies [χρήσεις, *chresis*], which between father and son or brother and brother are most unseemly, since even the fact of erotic love [ἐρᾶν, *eran*] between them is unseemly. And it is also strange that he deprives them of sexual intercourse [συνουσίαν, *sunousian*] for no other reason except because the pleasure [ἡδονῆς, *hedones*] is too powerful [ἰσχυρᾶς, *ischuras*]; and that he thinks it makes no difference that the parties are in the one case father or son and in the other case brothers of one another.[28]

The problem with Plato's *Republic*, according to Aristotle, is that it envisions education too narrowly, without considering the pedagogical importance of laws and customs; moreover, in addition to such sexual anarchy, Plato envisions a unity in the state that relies on racist subdivisions of its population into castes:

> For one will only be able to construct Plato's state by introducing its partitions and dividing up the community into common messes and also into brotherhoods and tribes. So that in the upshot no other regu-

lation will have been enacted except the exemption of the Guardians from the work of agriculture, which is a measure that even now the Spartans attempt to introduce.[29]

Relations of mastery, in other words, produce unstable polities, according to Aristotle, who apparently rejects Plato's necessity that there be a noble lie.[30] Contrary to Marx's insightful commentary in *Capital, Volume 1*, that Aristotle could not think the form of equivalency between a house and five beds because the labor of his society was performed by slaves, these passages indicate an awareness of the political-economic monstrosities generated by a society organized around slave labor.

Aristotle draws out the political-economic implications of the sexuality of warrior cultures, arguing that "all men of martial spirit appear to be attracted to the companionship either of male associates or of women," tending to produce either institutionalized homosexual arrangements or cults of the family unregulated by the laws of the city; those drawn to women, he argues, wind up establishing a state in which "wealth is held in honor," as women remain beyond the laws of the city and "live without restraint in respect of every sort of dissoluteness, and luxuriously."[31] Although Sparta is sometimes associated with the former political form of institutionalized homosexuality, Aristotle argues that the unregulated family cult in Sparta determined their drive to war and produced an unstable polity. Despite its cult of same-sex eroticism, Athens too reflected a mixed form of institutionalized homosexuality and unregulated family cults. In every case, the official sanction of the family cult, by excluding women from citizenship and participation in civic life, wound up producing class-polarized societies, cut through by political factions, organized to defend their interests against others.[32]

Although marginal with respect to the political economy of most Greek city-states, institutionalized same-sex eroticism was not free from the distortions produced by extremes of wealth and poverty, virtue and vice. Prior to a discussion of the role that sexual offenses played in the downfall of cities and constitutions,[33] Aristotle discusses how geography, class, and moral outrages form the greatest theaters for the play of political factions, the causes of which are often "small matters," and he cites the example of Syracuse, where

the constitution underwent a revolution as a result of a quarrel that arose between two young men, who belonged to the ruling class, about a love affair. While one of them was abroad the other who was his comrade won over the youth with whom he was in love, and the former in his anger against him retaliated by persuading his wife to come to him; owing to which they stirred up a party struggle among all the people in the state, enlisting them on their sides.[34]

In these passages Aristotle links the drive to accumulate wealth through conquest to a warrior cult of the family in which female whims and desires are unrestrained by the laws of the city because they are secluded from its spaces and subject only to the customs of households, which were at the master's whim. As we see in the above passage, the Greek culture of same-sex eroticism among the nobility was also responsible for kicking off internecine wars. This is not a misogynist or essentializing argument about women's nature or a phobic argument about same-sex passion, as it may appear at first glance; rather, Aristotle's argument is that the seclusion of women from public life and public institutions produces hideous distortions of both female and male desires and that the resulting family cult enshrines wealth as the supreme value of families.

Aristotle traces Sparta's attempts to found a more communist polity and institutionalize pederasty back to the Mycenaean culture of Crete and its culture of public mess-tables. "[I]n old days the Spartans called them not 'phiditia' but 'men's messes' as the Cretans do, which is a proof that they came from Crete."[35] The Cretan public mess tables were superior to Sparta's, Aristotle argues, because Crete fed all citizens with food from communal lands, whereas Sparta excluded the poor from participating in the communal meal with a poll tax:

> And the lawgiver has devised many wise measures to secure the benefit of moderation at table, and the segregation of the women in order that they may not bear many children, for which purpose he instituted manly sexual intercourse [τήν πρός τούς ἄρρενας ποιήσας ὁμιλίαν] as to which there will be another occasion to consider whether it was a bad thing or a good one.[36]

As to the goodness and badness of the thing, Aristotle never pronounces a judgment in *Politics*; Plato's Socrates, by contrast, remains somewhat wary and, at turns, terrified of anal sex in the *Republic* and the *Symposium*, and he endorses laws against sodomy in the *Laws*. Aristotle's term, however, "manly sexual intercourse [ἄρρενας ὁμιλίαν]," for all its strangeness, may be the first social scientific attempt to describe the phenomenon. Unlike Aristotle's preferred term for such "associations"— *suneinai* (συνεῖναι), a term used throughout the *Politics*—his word choice here indicates kinship, a mode of being together, communion, a private and public intercourse in addition to the sense of physical sexual intercourse. The word, which appears infrequently in the *Politics*, is used elsewhere to describe a customary mode of sexual conduct.[37]

Although verifying Aristotle's claim—tracing institutionalized homosexuality to Crete and to Sparta's attempt to replicate it—is beyond the scope of this project, it is worth noting, in passing, that archaeological research has achieved something of a consensus concerning the communal political-economic organization of Mycenaean civilization. Like the Mesopotamian civilization of the second and third millennia BCE and the pre-Columbian Incan Empire, the economy of the late Bronze Age Mycenaean kingdoms was mostly a nonmarket, nonmoney economy in which goods were largely appropriated through tax and tribute from the surrounding lands for a ruling elite, with large-scale craft production organized out of state-controlled workshops. Surpluses were indeed shared with the population in communal feasts, corroborating Aristotle's argument about the stabilizing function of communal meals.[38] In Mesopotamian and Incan civilizations, state-controlled handicraft production tended to employ surplus populations—widows, people with disabilities, and the sexually nonreproductive, among others. This admittedly fragmentary evidence could be marshalled to support the idea that this political-economic form tended to favor cultures of nonreproductive, same-sex sexuality. Unfortunately, the work of a comparative world-historical account of the dynamic between sexual cultures and political-economic forms is in its infancy.

THE MEDITERRANEAN WORLD under northern Italian hegemony was a transitional world whose geography, climate, and work rhythms allowed for a certain kind of public life that tended to be overwhelmingly male. These factors remained constant for the longue durée of the basin's history and, at least partially, account for the same-sex eroticism of the Mediterranean world. Streets were busiest during the time between the conclusion of the workday and sunset. The unity of the climate throughout the larger region established patterns of seasonal labor. The long, hot summers required clothing that more easily facilitated sexual encounters among men at land and by sea. Streets, markets, and squares were spaces of free association between men. They were "free" in a double sense, in that such spaces represented time away from work but also time free of both the master's domination in the workshop and the family structures of the home. In northern Africa, as in the cities of the northern Mediterranean, cafes and baths were the centers of the homosocial life of villages and towns. Mediterranean cultures of public bathing provided not only a same-sex space facilitating erotic encounters but also the sanitary conditions necessary for a sexually free body.

On the one hand, the sexual freedoms of this lifeworld were constrained by the relations of mastery essential to the functioning of these economies, which were based on direct domination in handicraft production and most other specialized trades, as well as on the loosely feudal ownership of land. On the other hand, dramatic new vistas of sexual freedom opened up as older relations based on domination and a family-centered model of peasant production were dissolved. These prebourgeois and preindustrial sexual constraints and freedoms are clearer in Mediterranean cities of the early modern period because they are more distant from us in time and their societies appear in starker relief than those of the period in which advances in the modes of production favored large middling classes in cities. Such a perspective of "early modern" Mediterranean sexuality perhaps illuminates some continuities and discontinuities with ancient civilizations in the region. What explains the eclipse of this Mediterranean world?

In addition to the political-economic history of a large-scale relocation of capital and power to the north and a period of war that drained the region of its wealth, there may be a geographic explanation for its end in the fifteenth century: the discovery of the New World and the outbreak of syphilis. This human geographic event threatens to explode out of the continuum of homogeneous time. Noting that syphilis "is ignored by the Nights," Burton assesses the difficulty of discussing the temporality of epidemic disease, as

> diseases do not begin except with the dawn of humanity; and their history, as far as we know, is simple enough. They are at first sporadic and comparatively non-lethal: at certain epochs which we can determine, and for reasons which as yet we cannot, they break out into epidemics raging with frightful violence: they then subside into the endemic state and lastly they return to the milder sporadic form. For instance, "English cholera" was known of old: in 1831 (Oct. 26) the Asiatic type took its place and now, after sundry violent epidemics, the disease is becoming endemic on the Northern seaboard of the Mediterranean, notably in Spain and Italy. So small-pox (Al-judrí, vol. i. 254) passed over from Central Africa to Arabia in the year of Mohammed's birth (A.D. 570) and thence overspread the civilized world, as an epidemic, an endemic and sporadic successively. The "greater Pox" has appeared in human

bones of pre-historic graves and Moses seems to mention gonorrhœa
(Levit. xv:12). Passing over allusions in Juvenal and Martial, we find
Eusebius relating that Galerius died (A.D. 302) of ulcers on the genitals
and other parts of his body; and, about a century afterwards, Bishop
Palladius records that one Hero, after conversation with a prosti-
tute, fell a victim to an abscess on the penis (phagedænic shanker?).
In 1347 the famous Joanna of Naples founded (æt. 23), in her town of
Avignon, a bordel whose inmates were to be medically inspected—a
measure to which England (proh pudor!) still objects. In her Statuts
du Lieu-publique d'Avignon, No. iv she expressly mentions the *Mal
vengut de paillardise*. Such houses, says Ricord who studied the subject
since 1832, were common in France after A.D. 1200; and sporadic ve-
nereals were known there. But in A.D. 1493–94 an epidemic broke out
with alarming intensity at Barcelona, as we learn from the "Tractado
lla-mado fructo de todos los Sanctos contra el mal serpentino, venido
de la Isla espanola," of Rodrigo Ruiz Días, the specialist. In Santo Domingo the disease was common under the names Hipas, Guaynaras
and Taynastizas: hence the opinion in Europe that it arose from the
mixture of European and "Indian" blood. Some attributed it to the
Gypsies who migrated to Western Europe in the 15th century: others
to the Moriscos expelled from Spain. But the pest got its popular name
after the violent outbreak at Naples in A.D. 1493–4, when Charles VIII.
of Anjou with a large army of mercenaries, Frenchmen, Spaniards, and
Germans, attacked Ferdinand II. Thence it became known as the Mal
de Naples and Morbus Gallicus—una gallica being still the popular
term in neo-Latin lands—and the "French disease" in England. As
early as July 1496 Marin Sanuto (Journal i. 171) describes with details
the "Mal Franzoso." The scientific "syphilis" dates from Fracastori's
poem (A.D. 1521) in which Syphilus the Shepherd is struck like Job, for
abusing the sun. After crippling a Pope (Sixtus IV.) and killing a King
(Francis I.) the Grosse Vérole began to abate its violence, under the
effects of mercury it is said; and became endemic, a stage still shown
at Scherlievo near Fiume, where legend says it was implanted by the
Napoleonic soldiery. The Aleppo and other "buttons" also belong apparently to the same grade. Elsewhere it settled as a sporadic and now
it appears to be dying out while gonorrhoea is on the increase.[39]

Burton's geographic and social history of syphilis was strikingly far in advance of its time, and is now confirmed by social history and genetic studies

alike.[40] His understanding of the epidemic outbreak of syphilis in Europe due to war and the conquest of the New World reflected an end to the period of geographic isolation of the disease, which in turn marked the beginning of more restrictive sexual mores.

William of Orange, or The Lower Decks

Around 1730, as Amsterdam's stock exchange shifted its capital from investment in trade on the Baltic to debt-financing mercantilist states' wars for hegemony over the Atlantic, the custodian of the Dom Church of Utrecht grew outraged at the scandalous and unnatural behavior of men he had observed in and around his charge, the tallest church tower in the Netherlands and symbolic center of Utrecht. The good parson brought charges against two soldiers whom city authorities had arrested, tortured, and secretly executed for what Immanuel Kant would call, at the end of the eighteenth century, the *crimina carnis contra naturam*, or *commercium sexuale* "with a person of the same sex."[41] The Enlightenment doyen's terms reflect a watershed moment for both the epistemological transformation of sexual categories and the sweeping transformation of individuals and societies by general market dependency.[42] Although residuals of the medieval paradigm remain in Kant's conceptualization—for instance, the grouping of same-sex sex with bestiality—the commodity form has transformed the essential coordinates of human sexuality.

The secret executions in Utrecht caused a tumult in the city that reached the English papers. On June 13, 1730, the *London Journal* reported that "Seven young Persons" who had been prosecuted for sodomy the weeks prior "were, after Conviction, publickly executed here, though if Money could have been of any Use to them, (I am sorry to say it) none would perhaps have been wanting to commute the Punishment." The seven were hanged, and, according to the report, two were burned and "the other Five carried to Scheveling, and thrown into the Sea."[43]

A week later, rumors circulated in Amsterdam of the secret executions. On June 17, 1730, London's *Daily Journal* reported "that 16 Coffins were carried from [Amsterdam's] City-House, or Guildhall, which Coffins were supposed to contain Bodies that had been privately executed for Sodomy, of the richer Sort of People; and that Morning about 29 Persons, of mean Extraction, were to have been publickly executed for the like Crime"—all of which caused a great tumult as "the Populace arising in Arms, and demanding publick Execution of the Rich as well as of the Poor, (there then being about

CHAPTER THREE

300 of all Ranks in Prison in that City, accused of that Crime, and some of them of great Note and Substance) the Magistrates were oblig'd to send to the Hague for Assistance to quell this Mob, which was very outrageous; upon which 1000 Soldiers were sent to their Assistance."[44] As merchant-class sodomites who had been accused fled the city to their country seats "to convince People of their being free from any Fear or Apprehension," riots broke out in other cities throughout the United Provinces, according to the report. "The same Cause had occasioned the like Tumults at the Hague, Rotterdam, &c." "We hear," the report concludes, "that, hoping to appease the People, the Magistrates promised a Number of Persons of Distinction should be publicly executed as Tomorrow, on which Day a Parson was to be burnt alive at Rotterdam."[45] A month later an unnamed Dutch diplomatic attaché in London demanded that the British government force retractions from the newspapers, to wit, the *London Journal* and the *Daily Journal*, which subsequently ran nearly identical statements "that this Affair has been very much misrepresented and magnified" and that the particulars of these stories were "calculated and designed to give a bad Impression of the Magistrates, and of the good Inhabitants of the principal Towns in Holland."[46]

Although the number of executions in these reports could have been exaggerated, the scope and scale of the Dutch problem of sodomy, and the controversy of class injustice in the cities, was not—despite the official denials and retractions printed in British papers. The confessions of two anonymous sodomites led to the arrest and interrogation of Zacharias Wilsma, a former soldier and valet whose sexual escapades, travels, and confessions uncovered a thick web of sodomitical connections, with central nodes in Amsterdam, The Hague, Haarlem, Delft, and Utrecht. The Dutch state's discovery and investigation of Wilsma's sexual network led to a historically unprecedented and coordinated series of arrests across the United Provinces.

Although historical anecdotes and demographic trends indicate that homosexual subcultures likely existed throughout the Dutch Golden Age, there is no comparable municipal crackdown on sodomites. Secret "Confession Books" hidden in an alderman's cabinet in city hall disclose the existence of a wide subcultural milieu of homosexuality with well-known haunts, styles of dress and slang, casual prostitution, and middle-class social clubs. Between Wilsma's confession in 1730 and the establishment of the Napoleonic Code decriminalizing sodomy in 1811, a little over 200 men stood trial for sodomy and related offenses: 115 men were sentenced in absentia to exile; 16 died on the scaffold; and of 28 men confined to prison, 12 died in their cells. In the entirety of the United Provinces, 94 cases of sodomy were punished by the death penalty between 1730 and 1732, suggesting that reports of secret executions were far from exaggerated.[47] By comparison, only 8 death sentences were executed in all of France during the eighteenth century. However historically unprecedented the recourse to capital punishment may have been, the eighteenth-century Dutch persecution of sodomy in the metropolis was never systematic and did not represent a significant proportion of overall criminal prosecutions. Nevertheless, the wave of prosecutions demonstrates both the class prejudices of these investigations and punishments in the United Provinces and the ambivalence of the gallows, or the tendency of such public executions to inflame the passions of the city against its ruling elites.

The small village of Faan in the northern province of Frisia, bordered to the north and west by estuaries of the North Sea, had experienced a long period of economic stagnation following the drop in North Sea trade and the decline of peat-cutting industries. Faan was the site of the "most notorious of these persecutions," according to historian Theo van der Meer: "On 24 September 1731, twenty-two boys and men from this and nearby other villages were executed by the country judge, Rudolf de Mepsche."[48] Demonstrating the presence of an emergent metropolitan conception of homosexuality in the United Provinces, a coordinated wave of homosexual persecutions in the great cities had become the concern of a *grietman* from the provinces. As Dutch military power and economic activities had proletarianized a significant proportion of rural labor, the countryside was in no way impervious to the economic shockwaves and panic about sodomy emanating from Amsterdam.

The trial in 1689 of four young men in Amsterdam provides an earlier, and perhaps far more telling, example of the Dutch "problem" of homosexuality, which was more often punished with vagrancy statutes. A roving gang of twenty-somethings had taken to the neighborhood surrounding the Bourse, cruising for the wealthy sons of merchants, who, by stepping on the boys' feet, indicated that they were interested in an erotic encounter. As these men signaled their interest, the boys were known to grab them by the crotch, demanding money and issuing threats. "Whatever else happened," the historian Dirk Jaap Noordam writes, "the gang always extorted money from the man." Whenever his pocket change was considered an insufficient sum, the boys "followed him to his home or another place where he could get more money for them. The gang consisted of a fluctuating number of youngsters because sometimes members left Amsterdam under the flag of the East Indies Company. The head of the gang was hanged, and the other

FIGURE 3.2. Lucas van Leyden, *Lot and His Daughters*, c. 1525, oil on wood. Musée du Louvre, Paris.

three . . . were sentenced to detention in the house of correction."[49] During the 1720s, other gangs of wild boys cruised the city's public lavatories—wooden structures erected in the eighteenth century beneath Amsterdam's many bridges—accosting upper-class men, showing even greater contempt for wealth and status than their predecessors had. "In 1735 they were finally brought to trial, and received the same sentences as the gang in 1689: the leader was hanged, his accomplices confined." Apparently similar gangs of youths emerged in The Hague, cruising the city's central woodland park where one Gabriel Du Bergé was arrested and sentenced to death.[50]

Although none of these men was charged with sodomy, their stories indicate that the persecution of sodomy was carried out for the sake of class interest rather than religious sentiment. Convicted sodomites were lower class, almost without exception. Although footmen implicated aristocrats and patricians, few were arrested or charged. Some members of the middle class were accused, but most escaped with the aid of legal counsel or fled the country.[51] As in the northern Italian city-states, the wave of persecutions reflected a secular economic crisis of capitalism: a floating mass of surplus labor appeared alongside surplus capital seeking speculative investments abroad and at home. The Dutch ruling classes' punishment of sodomites in the 1730s more closely resembled the cruel spectacles of Venice than the bookkeeping operation of Florence's Officers of the Night, although it seems to have involved some elements of both. Dutch *regenten* pursued sodomy to punish the poor and provide spectacles of cruelty during a period of economic and political decline.[52] The spectacles indicate something of the mythic power sodomy had accumulated in the bourgeois imaginary. Sodomy stood out from other crimes; its presence in public space represented a sort of return of the repressed, something profoundly filthy, an *excrementum* that could only be purged with water.

The ruling merchants of Amsterdam executed sodomites for active and passive anal intercourse along with other convicted criminals on a scaffold built for the occasion two or three times a year, always on a Saturday. The scaffold was fixed to the façade of city hall. Executions were attended by crowds, and gallows ceremonies lasted several days. Sodomy was most often punished by garroting—strangulation with a handheld ligature of rope or scarf—which in eighteenth-century Amsterdam was, according to historian Theo van der Meer, "a typical punishment for women": "The faces of two sodomites garroted in 1730 were scorched after their executions. Two others were drowned in a barrel on the scaffold, which according to a compiler of a list of persons executed in Amsterdam, was 'a surprisingly harder death' than garroting. While in the scorching a remnant of symbolic purification may be found, the drowning was meant to wash away the sins."[53]

As in the rest of Europe, in Amsterdam the bodies of executed criminals were normally exhibited to the public in a gallows field, as putrefying ornaments of state power, warnings to potential criminals and foreigners, demonstrating the rule of law in the city. However, the Dutch Edict of July 21, 1730, demanded that the corpses of executed sodomites be burned or tossed in the sea. In Amsterdam, "the executed sodomites were thrown into the deepest part of the River IJ."[54] Following execution, a final baptism was meant to symbolically purge the Protestant city of its *helsche boosheit*, and the body of the condemned sodomite was delivered unto the abyss.[55]

Amsterdam's "reformed" penal apparatus, which employed vagrants, whores, thieves, and others on loom and wheel, was established at the end of the sixteenth century as a solution to the problem of vagabondage. Concern for the moral progress of these unfortunates motivated a gentler way of punishing through imprisonment and forced labor. The spectacular executions of sodomites through drowning, by contrast, was a legacy of the Protestant Reformation: after 1578, Amsterdam punished offenses against the family and natural sexual order by purging the evil with water.

The ritual drowning and consignment of sodomites' bodies to the abyss was part of a moral geography associating political power with dominion over water, the reclamation of land, and immorality; losses of power were figured in narrative accounts of drowning, shipwrecks, and the oblivion of the deep.[56] The drowning of the sodomite produced signs of his foreignness, of his lack of control over his own appetites, his moral culpability. Consigning his body to the deep was a form of physical and spiritual exile. "Dutchness," writes Simon Schama in *The Embarrassment of Riches*, "was often equated with the transformation, under divine guidance, of catastrophe into good fortune, infirmity into strength, water into dry land, mud into gold." Explaining the rationality of these punishments, Schama writes: "The ordeal of water as a determinant of moral authenticity could, within the same cultural frame, be turned upside down to isolate the self-evidently alien. Any crime so abhorrent that its very perpetration announced the impossibility of Dutchness might be punished by a drowning from which no escape was possible."[57] The spectacular execution of sodomites in the city resonated with a political imaginary that emerged from the middle of the sixteenth through the middle of the seventeenth century in the United Provinces as the Dutch established a political identity of independence from the Spanish empire and the Catholic Church.

The Dutch authorities conceived of sodomy as a practice and habit that circulated—like commodities or contagions—between men. The sodomite was "corrupt, but only because someone else had corrupted him by initiating him into the techniques to which he had willfully consented. In his turn, he could pass those techniques on to others."[58] When the Dutch wave of persecutions reached its peak in July 1730, homosexuality received great publicity. Cheap poetry, theological treatises, gossip, pamphlets, and broadsheets shaped the public persona of sodomites as a debauched race with possibly foreign allegiances. They were held responsible for visiting all manner of catastrophe upon the Republic, were to blame for "commercial decline, rising unemployment, the demise of strict church practice, the rising influence of papism and, concomitant with papism, the overwhelming influence of French and Italian culture and *mores*."[59]

The circulation of homoeroticism and criminality in popular discourse, broadsides, and pamphlets (especially of a condemnatory tone) betrays multiple structures of feeling in addition to the affects of "fear" and "panic"; this literature generated far more ambivalent identifications among the men of the lower decks, who were the intended audiences of these didactic exempla. In fact, there is an ambiguity surrounding newspaper accounts detailing the blasphemies of the gallows, a proletarian celebration of lawlessness and rebellion that circulated as a structure of feeling within the very same ideologeme of the cautionary tale and exemplary punishment.[60]

ALTHOUGH THE FOUNDATIONS of imperialist capitalist expansion were laid by the seizure of land in the Americas, England, Ireland, and Africa, the expanding territorial power of mercantilist states was maintained through an extension of state power over the sea. The Dutch had long established a sophisticated military art of discipline, perfecting the art of training through drills, which kept soldiers constantly active and improved their performance. They attained an "obedient and efficient instrument of policy" in the 1630s that the United States would later achieve only with bureaucratic rationalization in the twentieth century.[61]

The military and naval prowess of the Dutch was demonstrated at the crucial strategic victory over the Spanish in the Eighty Years' War, a victory in which a Dutch naval blockade of the Scheldt River in 1585 cut off international trade with the Spanish-occupied city of Antwerp. The blockade effectively ended Antwerp's economic role as a center of textile manufacture and entrepôt of commodities from the east. Antwerp's loss was Amsterdam's gain, as 60,000 to 120,000 southern Dutch refugees fled north with capital and industrial and commercial skills.[62] In 1590, the Dutch States General declared its sovereignty and the state took shape as a ruling coalition of merchant-regents—who assumed advantageous fiscal positions and established autonomous naval power under the corporate, town-based system—and the *stadholders*, or landed gentry, whose power base was the army.[63]

By the conclusion of the Eighty Years' War with Spain at the Peace of Münster in 1648, the Dutch had established their hegemony over maritime trade with the East Indies by internalizing defense costs and establishing trade monopolies in key commodities through the Dutch East Indies Company, which had been established in 1602.[64] The East and West Indies Companies allowed Dutch metropolitan elite to create an international commercial and colonial system with the cities of the Netherlands as central entrepôts of the most valuable commodities in the world system. The Dutch commissioned privateers to pillage the rival merchant fleets of the Spanish. As other states began commissioning these privateers with letters of marque, banks provided the first credit swaps on perilous maritime trade routes, securitizing the risk of this system.

The Dutch were also involved in the construction of earthworks that dramatically increased agricultural productivity by expanding the area of arable land through reclamation. The process of state-building and the struggle against water were conjoined. Between 1590 and 1640, some two hundred thousand acres were recovered. By 1640, the labor of three thousand men and a thousand horses increased acreage by some 40 percent in the Noorderkwartier region north of Amsterdam.[65] These agricultural gains significantly expanded the power and population of Dutch cities, which together enabled an expansion of municipal bureaucracy and police activity. Amsterdam's population increased from about 11,000 at the beginning of the sixteenth century to about 60,000 a century later. By the second half of the seventeenth century, Amsterdam had over 200,000 inhabitants.[66]

As the city grew, the responsibility for maintaining safety shifted from a private responsibility to a public provision. Until the late sixteenth century, the only light came from candles shining before statues of saints on street corners after the "criminals' curfew" beginning at 9 PM. In 1579, taverns were required to have lighting on the street until 10 PM. In 1682, Amsterdam adopted Jan van der Heyden's design for streetlights running on beet oil. A total of 2,380 lampposts, which were manned by 134 lamplighters, were installed throughout the city and continued to be used to illuminate Amsterdam well into the nineteenth century. Van der Heyden's invention would also be adopted in Berlin, Leipzig, and Dresden.[67]

With the banishment of darkness and increased street activity at night, the gulf between middle-class sexual morality and that of the popular classes became socially visible. Municipal measures for public safety made the sodomy of Dutch cities vulnerable to interventions by state bureaucracies, even as these same bureaucracies provided infrastructure—such as public urinals installed beneath the bridges—which enabled the practice of sodomy. Lighting made the streets safer for movement at night. Perhaps the riots around the gallows in Amsterdam, The Hague, Rotterdam, Delft, and Utrecht convinced the ruling classes of these cities to scale back on their prosecutions of sodomy. Criminal prosecutions for sodomy appeared in waves in the 1730s, 1750s, and 1780s. The pattern reflects not only the contingent discoveries of networks of sodomy based on confessions of individuals; it may also reflect blowbacks. The gallows were risky in the heavily class-polarized world of the Netherlands at the end of the Dutch Golden Age and indicate the political problem of spectacular and violent executions for "offences against nature" in a class-polarized society.

Rich burghers had captured the infamously ramshackle and fragmented state by fusing elite patriarchal families and merchant capital with a locally grounded patrimonial state whose purview was war-making activities. Power was thus transmitted, via an elite cult of masculinity, through male scions whose sexual integrity had to be policed to ensure the maintenance of power from one generation to the next.[68] The capacity to father children was the sine qua non of elite manhood, extending, in Julia Adams's analysis, "beyond lineal reproduction to a more general sense of political husbandry and direction."[69] In fact,

> patrimonial offices served as a direct source of economic resources; from their privileged positions, the regent patriciate drew fixed rents and intermittent windfalls, such as the sheriff's (*schout*) percentage of the fines he imposed and the [Dutch East Indies Company] director's percentage take of cargo returns. The impressively increasing amounts bequeathed in regents' wills indicate that over time the merchant-regent elite was considerably enriched as well as empowered.[70]

Directorships in chartered companies became the exclusive property of families. Two-thirds of the directors of the Dutch East Indies Company in the Rotterdam chamber stood in relation to one another as son, father, or grandfather. Nine of the first seventeen mayors serving in independent Amsterdam from 1578 to 1590 were succeeded by sons or sons-in-law.

This intensely patrimonial structure of power turned the Dutch elite into a rentier class. Amsterdam's merchant elite invested only negligible revenues in state bonds in 1600; a century later, nearly half their wealth was invested in these instruments, mostly issued on the United Provinces public debt.[71] Adams writes that the family was essential to this patrimonial group: "For a man or his family, the successfully achieved social fiction of an unbroken line of honorable, preferably patrilineal, descent was what counted in establishing enduring claims to politico-economic privilege."[72] Such a *huwelijkspolitiek,* or "politics of marriage," was captured cynically by one seventeenth-century Dutch regent: "my little niece carries a place on the city council under her skirt."[73]

War and commerce were the motors of an accelerating demand for sailors. Between 1688 and 1697, the population of men at sea more than tripled from 12,714 to 44,743. The total number of ships at sea increased from around 1,500 in the first decades of the eighteenth century to around 2,500 by the 1730s. By 1770 over 4,000 ships took to the sea. These ships

> provided a setting in which large numbers of workers cooperated on complex and synchronized tasks, under slavish, hierarchical discipline in which human will was subordinated to mechanical equipment, all for a money wage. The work, cooperation, and discipline of the ship made it a prototype of the factory. Indeed, the very name *factory* evolved etymologically from *factor,* "a trading representative," and specifically one associated with West Africa, where factories were originally located.[74]

Those who governed ships feared desertion, insubordination, mutiny, and open rebellion, and they maintained discipline through the use of violence and terror. Men at sea were subject to the often capricious whims of captains, who had discretionary power to discipline their sailors as they saw fit. Sailors, and especially the pressed men of navies, were drawn from poor and ethnically diverse populations, making discipline all the more necessary as it made the ship "a forcing house of internationalism" if not a pressure cooker of revolutionary upheaval.[75]

This was a period of explosive urban growth largely driven by two forces: the growing administrative functions and offices of the state and the increasing significance of new and expanded maritime trade routes. Between 1600 and 1750 the capital cities of Europe—Berlin, Copenhagen, London, Madrid, Paris, Stockholm, The Hague, and Vienna—doubled in size. Whereas kings and courts provided the steadiest source of urban growth in capital cities, transatlantic trade brought prosperity to port towns in western Europe, attracting unskilled workers and new investment.[76] The Atlantic outstripped the Mediterranean as the quickest path to the best markets, and seaside towns with good harbors from Denmark to Spain gained new importance and experienced rapid growth. Bordeaux, Bristol, and Liverpool participated in trade organized around sugar and slaves. From these ports ships carried manufactured goods back to the Gold Coast of Africa, North America, and the Caribbean, bringing sugar, rum, cotton, and other colonial products back to European warehouses situated along the docks and quays. Amsterdam emerged as the primary entrepôt of world commerce by centralizing "the storage and exchange of what happened to be the most strategic supplies of European and world commerce at any given time."[77] Louis XIV developed four new towns—Brest, Lorient, Rochefort, and Toulon—as ports, dry docks, and naval bases under state patronage. The Danish Crown created Frederikssund and Frederikshavn.

In times of peace, when maritime labor was less in demand, sailors were discharged and formed landed communities outside the regimented discipline of ships. Seasonal patterns of employment were also prevalent among coastal merchant shippers. Winter months were seasons of unrest and ferment. The situation at the bustling port city of Hull is representative of other coastal towns during this period; the streets became, in the words of one contemporary, "crowded with boys, intended for the sea-service, who spend their time in open violation of decency, good order, and morality; there are often fifteen hundred seamen and boys, who arrive from the whale fishery, and often double that number of unemployed sailors, are left at leisure to exercise their dissolute manners on the inoffensive passenger in the public street."[78]

Within this new and expanding social world of port cities, sailors formed a population of flexible labor essential to the circulation of capital, commodities, and military power; however, they did not have the decency to simply disappear whenever capital or war no longer required their work. Much to the contrary, their superfluousness threatened social and political upheaval in the metropolitan core. The seaman's forced and often unruly leisure time on land sometimes confronted his previously expended labor time on opposite sides of the barricade. Thus, sodomy and threats of social instability arrived in port towns throughout the world system under Dutch and English hegemonies of merchant capitalism.

Records from the Dutch East Indies Company show that sodomy persecutions were five times higher in the Cape Colony, which was founded as a supply station in 1652, than in any Dutch city during this era. Sailors engaged in "dirty passions" across lines of class and race, raising the specter of those forms of solidarity that were utterly anathema to the government of ships, not to mention a slave trade based on the fiction that some humans were less than human. The concern for homosexuality cannot be due to those famously Protestant concerns for moral decency and uprightness, despite whatever pieties were pronounced around the gallows; prostitution existed at the Cape of Good Hope and was organized out of the Company's slave lodge; authorities seem to have encouraged such iniquities to guard against others.[79]

Although merchant and navy ships could not have been utopias for homosexuality, considering the harrowing realities of harsh discipline, spectacular executions, poor provisions, frequent disabling accidents, rampant epidemic disease, and long delays in the payment for wages, sodomy was likely common among the men of the lower decks. These practices likely conformed to patterns of age-hierarchy as ships employed both men and boys. If pleasure was had, it was won under working conditions that were slavish and hard; if sexual freedom was experienced, it was within lives that were brutish and short. It is far more likely that sodomy came to the attention of authorities and was punished sooner at sea than on the land. As the contemporary Samuel Johnson put it, "being in a ship is being in jail with the chance of being drowned."[80] The very same physical proximity and mixed live-work spaces that made sodomitical encounters possible on ships and in jails also lent it greater social visibility, making it more of a target for discipline and punishment. Young men had much more freedom, sexual and otherwise, aboard the ships of pirates, which explains why so many sailors of this period voluntarily joined such outlaw groups whenever their vessels were captured.

Trade across the Atlantic and around the Cape of Good Hope expanded the reach of merchant capital and commerce originating in the Mediterranean world. In doing so, it also expanded the stage for confrontations between merchants and pirates. The Dutch and English East Indies Companies consolidated their military power and economic rights to trade with the East by internalizing defense costs. East Indiamen grew in size, eventually outstripping the warships of the period. Many carried guns and military personnel. European penetration of the largest capital cities of the East (Beijing had the largest population of any city in the world in 1750) was extremely limited, and colonial outposts were restricted to the coastal cities—Canton in the Pearl River delta, Shanghai, Bombay, and Goa—and the resource-rich island chains of Java and Batavia and the Moluccas. An expansion of transoceanic shipping expanded the theater of operations for piracy, which became an enormous problem for merchant capitalists in the seventeenth and eighteenth centuries.

As the polar opposite of the highly regulated and brutal life onboard merchant and navy ships, pirate society was "a world turned upside down," as Peter Linebaugh and Marcus Rediker write, one "made so by the articles of agreement that established the rules and customs of the pirates' social order. . . . Pirates distributed justice, elected officers, divided loot equally, and established a different discipline. They limited the authority of the captain, resisted many of the practices of the capitalist merchant shipping industry, and maintained a multicultural, multiracial, multinational social order."[81] Having seized the means of production and circulation, pirates established societies according to their own rules, societies in which homosexuality not only was allowed but was an important form of comradery in these mostly male communities:

> These same freedoms, once recognized by the ruling class, would fuel a campaign of terror to eliminate the alternative way of life, whether at sea or, more dangerously, ashore. Some among the powerful worried that pirates might "set up a sort of Commonwealth" in areas where no power would be able "to dispute it with them." Colonial and metropolitan merchants and officials feared incipient separatism in Madagascar, Sierra Leone, Bermuda, North Carolina, the Bay of Campeche and Honduras. Colonel Benjamin Bennet wrote of pirates to the Council of Trade and Plantations in 1718: "I fear they will soon multiply for so many are willing to joyn with them when taken."[82]

Sailors were indeed "taken" with pirates. Following the War of Spanish Succession, working conditions deteriorated rapidly in the merchant shipping industry, and seamen joined pirate ships by the thousands, perversely "multiplying" like some strange new social and political species. Freebooter Bartholomew Roberts, whose pirate convoy raided ships full of gold and supplies to be traded for human flesh at ports of call along the Gold Coast, "struck a Pannick into the Traders," according to naval surgeon John Atkins. Roberts ultimately forced the hand of British merchants, who petitioned Parliament for relief in 1722, commissioning a naval squadron to defeat Roberts's men.[83]

Pirates, however, were not without their own variety of discipline. This grouping could not have threatened the mercantilist world order without its own regulation of sexuality, but this too was a "world turned upside down." The historian B. R. Burg writes,

> The volume of literature on piracy is concerned primarily with maritime depredations, but the few instances that survive to reveal the more human side of the buccaneers demonstrate a willingness on the part of at least some marauders to suffer torture, deprivation, and even death to protect their lovers. One such incident occurred aboard the ship commanded by Bartholomew Roberts when a crewman, having too much to drink, made the grave mistake of insulting the captain. Roberts demonstrated that his reputation for a quick temper and as a formidable adversary in individual combat was well deserved. He drew his sword and killed the fellow on the spot. When the dead sailor's partner, a man named Jones, learned of what had occurred, he sought out the captain and showered him with vituperation. The captain was no more willing to accept insults from Jones than from his mess mate. He again drew his sword and ran the man through. The second thrust was not as well aimed as the first, and Jones was only injured. Ignoring his wound, the enraged sailor grabbed Roberts, threw him over a gun and beat him soundly. Jones was later sentenced to receive two lashes from every man aboard for daring to attack the commander, a deed that no man would have attempted unless severely distressed.[84]

Adopting a remarkably regulative sensibility, Roberts's crew agreed to ban boys and women from their ships, as these presumably caused petty disputes and dissension in the ranks. Sex aboard their fleet could only be had with a coequal male compatriot operating under the articles of agreement. Far from eliminating erotic disputes, this policy effectively raised the stakes of homosexuality, producing a disciplined crew of impassioned warriors rather than a feuding gang of infatuated lovers.

Through an examination of newspaper reports during the period, the sociologist Charles Tilly has demonstrated that sailors played a crucial role in the popular debates and revolts of eighteenth-century England from the Seven Years' War of 1756–1763 until the Napoleonic wars:

> mutinies of pressed military men breaking windows of householders who failed to illuminate; collective seizures of food, often coupled with sacking the premises of the merchant; verbal and physical attacks

on malefactors seen in the street or displayed in the pillory; taking sides at public executions; workers marches to public authorities in trade disputes; ridicule and/or destruction of symbols, effigies, and/or property of public figures or moral offenders; pulling down and/or sacking of dangerous or offensive houses; donkeying or otherwise humiliating workers who violated collective agreements; breaking up of theaters at unsatisfactory performances; liberation of prisoners; fights between hunters and gamekeepers; battles between smugglers and royal officers.[85]

After this period of intensive "popular contention," which reached its height in the mutiny and blockade of London following the Nore and Spithead mutiny incidents, social movements began to conform to a model of institution-building (rather than sporadic outbursts of popular anger), with meetings, demonstrations, and organized agitation becoming prominent by the end of the Napoleonic wars.

Although the mutinies at Spithead and Nore in April and May 1797 were a direct response to the immediate concerns for better food and pay and objections to disciplinary rules, there is also evidence of Jacobin influence. The event was, according to E. P. Thompson's account in *The Making of the English Working Class*, "of world-wide significance." Thompson writes that "they show how precarious was the hold of the English ancien régime":

> For the British fleet—the most important instrument of European expansion, and the only shield between revolutionary France and her greatest rival—to proclaim that "the Age of Reason has at length revolved," was to threaten to subvert the whole edifice of world power. It is foolish to argue that, because the majority of the sailors had few clear political notions, this was a parochial affair of ship's biscuits and arrears of pay, and not a revolutionary movement. This is to mistake the nature of popular revolutionary crises, which arise from exactly this kind of conjunction between the grievances of the majority and the aspirations articulated by the politically conscious minority.[86]

There is evidence that the Napoleonic wars increased the social visibility of sodomy, as punishments for the crime became more harsh in the French and British navies. The court-martial aboard the *Africaine* illustrates the difficulty of punishing sodomy in an environment where it was a common practice. On February 1, 1816, Captain Edward Rodney of the *Africaine* hanged four members of the ship's crew for buggery. John Parsons received

200 lashes for "uncleanliness." One Jack Hubbard was given 170 lashes out of his sentence of 300 because the surgeon decided he could not take any more punishment without endangering his life.[87] The evidence of the affair centered around three individuals, Raphael Seraco, an Italian sailor; Frank Jean, hailing from Madeira; and Emanuel Cross, a Moor from Santo Domingo. Testimonies involved racial slurs against the men, and the willingness of the men to cooperate with prosecution may have involved ethnic prejudice. The historian A. N. Gilbert writes,

> Two of the seamen tried and hanged for sodomy were Italians, and the English had long believed this was a popular pastime in Italy. Buggery was known commonly as *le vice Italien*, and one eighteenth-century English writer referred to Italy as "the mother and nurse of sodomy" while eminent legal authorities such as Edmund Coke claimed "the Lombards had brought into the realm the shameful sin of sodomy."[88]

However, the testimonies of the crew uncovered far too many accusations for prosecution to take place in every case. Seraco alone accused twenty-three members of the crew of sodomy, and "the thought of 15 to 20 men hanging from the yardarm of the *Africaine* was too much for even the most ferocious moralist. The navy rarely hanged that many men for mutiny, a crime most officers admitted was more dangerous to the ongoing life of the service than buggery."[89]

The discourses surrounding the Dutch suppression of sodomy and the English suppression of mutiny and piracy merely followed the conventions of the wider northern European world in considering such behaviors to be social contagions rooted in an outlaw culture of *hostis humani generis*, as they were known under international law.[90] In the early eighteenth century, the pirate and the sodomite were ideological twins through which the ruling classes sought to understand and eliminate the social instability accompanying another global economic shift in the balances of power. Mutiny, piracy, and sodomy were, according to bourgeois conceptualizations, practices that threatened to spread in the international crews and wide-ranging geographic space opened up by commerce centered around the Atlantic. They threatened to spread through imitation or mimesis and multiply such practices like a new species or disease throughout the population of men necessary for capital accumulation, statecraft, and war but superfluous in times of peace, economic decline, and seasonal unemployment.

4

HOMOSEXUALITY AND BOURGEOIS HEGEMONY

Les Enfants de Sodome

"After wandering at random, strolling hither and thither absorbed in melancholy on the Champs-Elysées, I entered the jardin des Tuileries at the pont-tournant and shed tears for the situation of the Palace," wrote the anonymous author of a panorama of revolutionary Paris published in 1790. "I cannot help but indulge in the bitter reflections provoked by that pitiful sight":

> I no longer see this garden as it was under the reign of the voluptuous and shameless Louis XV, who presented a spectacle of dissolution to the Nation over which he exercised a tyrannical power: now I behold whores under the trees of the garden, turning the residence of our

kings into a public brothel, and on the adjacent side, my gaze was on some dozen occasions drawn to that infamous traffic of the children of Sodom [*enfants de sodome*], whose species abounds in France and who have established a nightly rendez-vous on the terrasse de Feuillants for conducting the most abominable orgies under the name, "The Path of Heavy Breathing" [*allé des Soupirs*]. . . . On this terrace and the adjacent lawns, one could thus behold one portion of Paris, rolling their eyes in imitation of the Satyrs that Ovid and Petronius painted for us with such force and intensity, introducing general license and depravity of morals, defiling purity, and transforming the most illustrious spot in the capital into a true receptacle of infamy.[1]

Perhaps the author of *Le nouveau tableau de Paris* wished to draw a contrast between the revolutionary scene and that relative decency displayed by the "great mass of common prostitutes" whom Louis-Sébastien Mercier observed—only a decade before, in his predecessor text *Le tableau de Paris*—"leaning in doorways, leering from windows, and otherwise displaying their charms in public places," and whom, he attested, "may be hired like hackney carriages at so much an hour."[2] The Revolution had begun to collapse these quaint boundaries between private acts and public space, as a portion of Paris moved their sexual activities out of rented rooms and other private spaces into the streets and parks. This movement initiated a struggle between proletarians and the bourgeoisie over the legitimate use and moral order of the urban fabric and generated a wholly new kind of libertine literature, one declaring the solidarity of all bodies pursuing sexual freedom outside middle-class norms.

Considered as a whole and situated within the context of the French Revolution, these sexual manifestos' political function was *not* to announce some new sexual identity, although this is how they might read in retrospect. If, according to historian François Furet's astute observation, "the Revolution allows everyone to look for filiations," whether Jacobin, royalist, anarchist, or liberal, "all those histories, which have bitterly fought each other for the last two hundred years in the name of the origins of their opposition, in fact share a common ground: they are histories in quest of identity."[3] Indeed, if the urge to find filiations between contemporary sexual identities and those of the French Revolution is set to one side, the politicized sexuality of the revolutionary period may be understood as an autonomous, unified political field, across which the bourgeoisie, aristocracy, and proletarians attempted to establish and contest the moral separation of private sexual acts from public space. These sexual activities and texts politicized a form of life, manifesting bodies whose pursuit of sexual freedom and pleasure remained at the limits of what was once considered "human," that of bodies exposed to the ravages of venereal diseases that two centuries of war and colonial conquest had spread throughout Europe.

By situating the "abominable orgies" of that "populous species" of sodomites in "the most illustrious spot in the capital," the anonymous author of *Le nouveau tableau de Paris* was not indulging a sentimental moralism. This description was eminently political, even alarmist. Although later admired by Romantics such as Baudelaire and Hugo, Mercier's panorama was criticized by his contemporaries for providing a handbook for police work. If this quality was barely suppressed in Mercier's *Tableau*, it is openly expressed in *Le nouveau tableau*. As described in the text, this gathering of sodomites was held on the northern edge of the Tuileries. Mostly sheltered from view from the garden, it was the route by which one entered the salle du Manège from the garden. As the largest indoor space in Paris, the Manège had been the meeting place of the National Assembly since November 9, 1789. The Manège was entered from the Tuileries by the narrow alley of the Feuillants monastery along the southern part of the rue de Castiglione, which opened upon the garden after skirting the monastery on the rue Saint-Honoré.

The author of *Le nouveau tableau* denounces as "loyal partisans of this rendez-vous of buggery" some prominent members of the National Assembly, including l'Abbé de Montesquiou, deputy (and previously president) of the Assembly, the infamous sodomite Marquis de Villette, and Bazard, prévôt-général des Monnaies.[4] The explicit political function of this discourse on sodomy, as denunciation or calumny, is typical of the period, however deadly it may have been for those named. Other pamphlets denounced members of the clergy and the royal camp, including Marie Antoinette, for same-sex proclivities.[5] This kind of calumny was historically continuous with the denunciations in Renaissance Florence, in the sense that sodomy accusations could humiliate political rivals and foment popular opinion against members of the ruling class. However, what was once considered a normal sexual behavior among Florentine men, albeit one perhaps associated in political discourse with injustice and the abuse of power, had by the time of the French Revolution become coupled with a new quasi-scientific discourse of monstrous sexual abnormality. The shift is an indication of how much the bourgeoisie had begun to fashion the Enlightenment epistemology of sex into a weapon in the struggle against both the popular classes and the nobility, and of how extensively the pseudoscientific discourses of race had penetrated the Enlightenment mind.

Police records from the period demonstrate that the spatial centrality of public sex between men and prostitution in the gardens of the royal camp was not the stylistic flourish of a depressed feuilletonist. These gardens were the center of a public culture of sex between men and of traffic in women.[6] Castle parks made their first appearance in mid-seventeenth-century France, spreading rapidly throughout Europe along with other fashions, architectures, and tastes of the French court. As Jürgen Habermas describes it,

> The castle park permitted a courtly life sealed off from the outside world. However, the basic pattern of the representative publicness not only survived but became more prominent. Mademoiselle de Scudéry reported in her *Conversations* the stress of the grand festivities; these served less the pleasure of the participants than a desire to demonstrate the grandeur of the host and guests. The common people, content to look on, had the most fun. Thus even here the people were not completely excluded; they were ever present in the streets.[7]

Following the well-known events of the first year of the Revolution—the storming of the Bastille, the Tennis Court Oath, and the march of women to Versailles with demands for bread—prostitutes and pederasts appropriated the Tuileries, the jardin du Luxembourg, and the Palais-Royal for their erotic displays and pursuits. These spaces were opened to the public, frequented by all classes, and formed the center of civic life in Paris; during the Revolution, they became theaters of sexuality and political freemasonry of every stripe.

By appropriating the property of the noble classes for subversive political and sexual encounters, the pederasts and prostitutes of Paris sullied the prize of the bourgeoisie's victory over the rights and privileges of the ancien régime. These scraps of green space were symbolically important. Similarly, a century later, the development of the Ringstrasse on the former military glacis surrounding Vienna's city center would provide the most socially visible and culturally significant indicator of liberalism's triumph over the institutions and political structures of the Habsburg Empire.[8] The transformation of Paris by Georges-Eugène Haussmann and others announced, on an equally monumental scale, the triumph of the bourgeois culture of the Second Empire.[9] The opening up of castle parks to the citizens of Paris during the French Revolution thus formed an important prelude to such later transformations of urban space as would follow on the heels of the revolutions of 1848.

The dedicatory poem to *Le nouveau tableau de Paris* declares that this "frightful panorama" of revolutionary Paris had revealed "a criminal and savage Nation."[10] These pithy lines betray a new political rationality for the policing of sodomy, a rationality that would unfold over the course of the century to follow, animating all subsequent attempts to establish bourgeois hegemony over urban space through police intervention. The sobriquet of the "criminal and savage Nation" signals a wide-ranging transformation of historical discourse. In his lectures at the Collège de France in 1976, Foucault characterized this transformation as the moment in which the historical discourse of nations and wars, once the purview of nobiliary reaction, became dialectical in the hands of the bourgeoisie. War no longer plays the role of constituting history by legitimating public right, but instead is henceforth conceived as a means

> to protect and preserve society; war is no longer a condition of existence for society and political relations, but the precondition for its survival in its political relations. At this point, we see the emergence of the idea of an internal war that defends society against threats born of and in its own body. The idea of social war makes, if you like, a great retreat from the historical to the biological, from the constituent to the medical.[11]

Within the edifice of the French absolutist state, the monstrous sexuality of noble blood—particularly that of its military class, or *noblesse d'épée*—was understood by both the juridical class, or *noblesse de robe*, and the middle classes to be a sign of its tyranny. Publicizing this monstrous sexuality was thus a weapon of class struggle both within the ruling class of the old regime and between the old regime and an emergent bourgeoisie. The coupling of tyrannical power with monstrous sexuality in *Le nouveau tableau de Paris* enjoyed a wide circulation in the pamphlet literature of revolutionary Paris, particularly among the Jacobins.[12] The institutional apparatus for handling sodomy accusations was nowhere near as developed as that of Florence; everyday police operations in Paris were mostly concerned, as in Florence, with the sexual unruliness of the popular classes rather than the sexual escapades of nobles. Sexually transmitted diseases such as syphilis, or *le mal de Naples*, and a virulent but rare strain of gonorrhea, or *cristaline*—both termed "antisocial diseases"—came to be used as medical justification for the policing and regulation of prostitution and pederasty in the national interest. The influence of the nobility in the early legislation of the revolutionary period, including the quiet removal of sodomy laws from the criminal code, likely contributed to whatever degree of leniency there was toward the "antisocial" sexualities of prostitutes and pederasts from the lower classes.

Le nouveau tableau de Paris is remarkable for regarding sodomites as a "species," a biological threat to the social order, and for inscribing homosexuality at the center of a wide reworking of the political concept of the nation. The Revolution politicized sex, and homosexuality formed a unified field for advancing bourgeois claims to represent the morally legitimate core or estate of the nation. Against the norms of middle-class family formation and intimacy, necessary for the stable transmission of property and class status from one generation to the next, the alternate sexualities of the popular classes and nobility appeared abnormal and were thought to have monstrous consequences for the health of the nation. This transformation signaled a new political function of the discourse on same-sex sexuality: the practice provided an important moral basis for the struggle of the bourgeoisie against both the libertinage of the ancien régime *and* the sexual publicness of the lower classes. From the pamphlets that survive the revolutionary period, it is possible to identify this major shift in the politicization of sex—from a calumnious and perhaps humorous denunciation of nobles and *lumières* to a contestation of the public sexuality of the lower classes, from a weapon wielded initially against the aristocracy to one mobilized against prostitutes and pederasts—over the course of the nineteenth century.

Another anonymous text of 1790, *Les enfants de sodome*, and a whole series of pamphlets responding to it together form a sort of comedic antidote to the spirit of bourgeois reaction announced by *Le nouveau tableau de Paris*. It provides a remarkably similar description of the orgies of the *allé des Soupirs*, reimagining the gathering of buggers as a political assembly and declaring the Tuileries to be the "*jardin de l'Amitié.*"[13] The pamphlet is a tongue-in-cheek manifesto of abnormal sexuality. Mocking both the solemn Jacobin invocations of the ancient virtues of Rome and Greece and the political assemblies of chambermaids and tailor apprentices gathering throughout the public squares and bridges of capital, the text declares its solidarity with the new sexual freedoms of Paris and marvels at the bravery of those who would participate in such orgies given the risks. *Les enfants de sodome* thus appropriates and inverts the Jacobin hierarchy of masculine virtue by valorizing receptive anal intercourse as the height of courage. Moreover, it elevates the practice for men and women alike. The appeal to

Greek and Roman antiquity was merely customary; in truth, these cultures' economies and sexualities were based on the subjugation of one human being to another. Their poets rarely valorized the receptive or passive sexual role.

The pamphlets in response to *Les enfants de sodome* submit the cause of homosexual men and women of all ages and classes to the growing list of grievances against the ancien régime—staging a special assembly of the "most zealous partisans of buggery" in the Tuileries on the terrasse des Feuillants to approve a list of demands[14]—deliver a complaint on behalf of prostitutes and other women against the activities of homosexual men,[15] and provide a statement of tribade, or lesbian, solidarity with the pederasts against the complaint of heterosexual women.[16] The pamphlets imagine that reactionaries will mobilize the National Assembly to step up police operations against homosexual men in order to protect the moral interests of heterosexual women and the economic interests of heterosexual female prostitutes. A speech put in the mouth of Mademoiselle Raucourt, a well-known actress famous for her libertine salons, is staged on the floor of the Comédie-Française in the Palais-Royal, declaring tribade solidarity with the cause of buggers against the demands of straight women for increased policing, and arguing for a kind of embodied solidarity among those who have "renounced fucking in its ordinary fashions."[17]

The first of this comical cluster of pamphlets, *Les enfants de sodome*, describes the formation of a special political faction—the Ordre de la Manchette, or "Order of the Cuff"—for making demands on the floor of the National Assembly, which met only a few hundred yards away. The speech of one participant announces the revolutionary platform: "In the future, antiphysics [*l'anti-physique*], derisively called buggery by its detractors, considered, even to this very day, an illicit game of lust due to centuries of ignorance, and named *bestiality* by men of law, shall be a science known and taught in every class of society."[18] *Les enfants de sodome* proposes a seven-point manifesto for this new partisan coalition, formulating the right of each of its members "to make use of his person, to give or receive, as he sees fit," in the public spaces of the Tuileries, the Panthéon, and the Luxembourg gardens "without anyone making an obstacle to such pursuits."[19] It demands treatment for the "antisocial diseases" and research into a cure, blaming prostitutes for the spread of these diseases among antiphysicals. A list of membership appended to the demands outs over 150 individuals for having unnatural sexual inclinations and behaviors, many of whom would be guillotined for one thing or another by the end of the Revolution.

These libertine tracts—the term "pornography" doesn't exactly do them justice—signal a shift in sexual discourse, from satires on the sexual escapades of court life, or perhaps even anatomies of its pleasures, to political satire on the bourgeois class's concern for the sexuality of the popular classes during the Revolution.[20] In other words, there is a shift among political alliances. It indicates a far-reaching transformation of the concept and political function of the nation, in which the bourgeoisie begins to call upon the state to police and regulate the sexuality of the popular classes, to politically neutralize the antagonism of an alternate moral order in the streets and public spaces of Paris. The material reasons for this class alliance between noble libertinage and proletarian sexuality are not difficult to imagine. It is worth recalling that the Bicêtre and other prisons held both libertines and vagabonds, often for the very same crimes against public decency. Police practices justified themselves in terms of concern for medical safety and security as well as for the protection the decency and morals of women. Each aspect of this emergent bourgeois political rationality is humorously caricatured and viciously attacked in its turn. The texts suggest that alongside the Jacobin project of promoting austere republican virtues, there was a position from which to appreciate the new sexual freedoms unleashed by the Revolution.

L'amour Antiphysique and Enlightenment Thought

Although the medical distinction between sodomy "as an act" and pederasty "as a criminal desire" would appear in 1819 with the publication of the sixty-volume *Dictionnaire des sciences médicales*, the police dossier and Enlightenment philosophes make it clear that this distinction in French thought, between pederasty as desire and sodomy as an act, had been in operation and circulation for well over half a century, if not longer.[21]

In the language of Enlightenment philosophers, homosexuality was the *goût* or *amour antiphysique*, the taste or love against nature. The terms were in circulation from at least the mid-eighteenth century; "antiphysique" was first published in an obscene epigram attributed to the infamous *littéraire* Jean-Baptiste Rousseau in 1741.[22] The concept appears in the work of Diderot and Voltaire. Whereas Diderot seems to admit that the "antiphysical taste" could perhaps result from natural causes, or from some combination of nature and culture, both Voltaire and Montaigne follow Jean-Jacques Rousseau, more or less, in conceiving of the crime against nature as the product of a corrupt civilization and bad education, something to be corrected by laws and pedagogy more in conformity with "Reason." Boarding schools loom large in the account of both philosophers as examples of the way civilization hideously distorts man's original state of nature in the moral education of youths. Broadly speaking, this Enlightenment disagreement represents the earliest manifestation of the antinomy between the apparent naturalness or the cultural construction of human sexuality.

Amid commentary on the barbarism of the Spanish conquest of the New World and the discovery of the antiphysical taste among Americans, Diderot formulated a typically eccentric theory of its prevalence in a text first published in 1772. Discounting the idea that the practice resulted from some congenital physical weakness of the American races, Diderot writes,

> I believe that the cause must be located in the hot climate, contempt for the weaker sex, the dullness of pleasure in the embraces of a woman exhausted by hard labor, the variability of taste—that peculiarity that drives everyone towards uncommon jouissances—the search for delights more easily perceived than honestly explained. The cause is perhaps in the natural disposition of the organs [*conformation d'organes*] which may have established a greater harmony between American men than between an American man and an American woman. Such disharmony might have developed the Americans' disgust for their women just as it cultivated their taste for Europeans. Besides must not these hunts, which occasionally separated men from women for months at a time, have had the tendency of drawing man closer to man? Everything else is but the consequence of a general and violent passion [*d'une passion générale et violente*] found in civilized histories too, for which nothing is sacred—neither honor nor virtue, decency nor integrity, laws of blood nor patriotic feeling. For Nature, which has ordained everything for the survival of the species, has little to do with the perpetuation of individuals; it preserves the species without accounting for the meaning of those activities to which civilized peoples have, with reason, attached ideas of morality completely foreign to the savages.[23]

It is clear from the condemnation Diderot heaps upon "the stupid barbarism" of the Spanish government—"which approved of such horrors" as the systematic killing of native Americans and "which would employ dogs

CHAPTER FOUR

trained to hunt and devour men"—that his source for the life and customs of the "berdaches" and the Spanish atrocities committed against them was Pietro Martire d'Anghiera's *De rebus oceanicis et orbe novo, decades tres* (1533), in which Balboa is said to have murdered some forty effeminate male members of Panamanian king Quaraca's harem by siccing mastiff hounds on them. The European imaginary had come to associate the New World's goût antiphysique with its other taste, for human flesh, since these first accounts of the Spanish conquest.[24]

Diderot's vision of a polymorphous natural world posited an experimental philosophical praxis that could make such diverse natural processes intelligible to human thought: "Everything in nature is neither against nature nor outside nature, I exclude neither chastity nor voluntary continence."[25] This vision could, as the above indicates, admit of a sexual taste outside European norms with a multitude of causal factors, a kind of antipodal if not exactly antinatural sexuality. The comparative perspective of this speculative anthropology does not lead Diderot to question European sexual norms from the perspective of some more perfect or noble state of nature, as he considers the morality foreign to "savages" to be a product of a superior reason. The sexual division of labor in hunter-gatherer societies looms as large in his anthropology of sex as the possible anatomical incompatibility of American Indian men and women. However, if these men's sexual taste for one another is "against nature," for Diderot it is in the strictly limited sense of it being an individual, however widely shared, variation of taste that does not alter or contribute to the overarching natural process of species reproduction.

The thesis of Voltaire's article on the *amour dit socratique* in the *Dictionnaire philosophique portatif* grapples with the same antinomy from a different angle: "Socratic love was never an infamous love," he writes. It was a military institution in some Greek cities, and a respected pedagogic institution. It was not infamous, as it was in conformity with the laws, and he cites Laius and Sextus Empiricus as his authorities on the point. He argues, like Diderot, that it would destroy the race if exclusively pederastic behavior were universal, and he poses the following antinomy: if Socratic love is thus "against nature," how could it have been "so natural" among the ancients?[26] He responds that it is apparently a "disorder" from childhood. Voltaire writes:

> If young males of our species are raised together, feeling this force that nature begins to grow in them, and never find the natural object of their instinct, they abandon themselves upon that which resembles

this object. Often a young man with a freshness of complexion, radiance of character, and sweetness of eyes, resembles, for two or three years, a beautiful girl; if one loves him, it is because nature is mistaken, we pay homage to the sex in being attracted to that which is beautiful in it, and when age has dissolved these resemblances the error is finished.[27]

Pederasty would be, according to Voltaire, a primitive or residual homoerotic fixation from childhood, in which same-sex environments force the substitution of pretty boys for "*l'objet naturel*"; it is not exactly against nature, as pederasts are attracted to the likeness of nature. Civilization, Voltaire argues, has distorted nature by producing situations in which the semblances of nature deceive boys into substituting young men for women in the fulfillment of natural sexual inclinations.

Montesquieu and Cesare Beccaria, on the other hand, were attuned to the political dangers of laws criminalizing pederasty. They argue that the example of the ancients proves that laws against the practice were easily subject to tyranny, opening the door to calumny. The "crime against nature," Montesquieu asserts in *The Spirit of the Laws* (1748), "will not make much progress in a society unless the people are also inclined to it by some custom."[28] "Do not clear the way for this crime," Montesquieu writes, with institutions such as the naked exercises of the Greeks or the boarding schools of his own time in mind; "let it be proscribed by an exact police, as are all the violations of mores, and one will immediately see nature either defend her rights or take them back." Nature, he argues, "has scattered pleasures with a liberal hand; and by overwhelming us with delights, she prepares us with our children through whom we are born again, as it were, for satisfactions greater even than those delights."[29]

Reflecting his proximity to the social and sexual life of the Mediterranean world, Cesare Beccaria blames the institution of master-servant relations for having produced a pederastic form of same-sex sexuality. He thus modifies the popular Enlightenment criticism of civilization to attack the socioeconomic institution of mastery, establishing a sexual-political continuum between the slavery and sexual forms of the ancients and the relations of dependency underpinning the sexuality and economy of his own day. "Pederasty," Beccaria writes,

is founded less upon the needs of the isolated and free man than upon the passions of the sociable and enslaved man. It draws its strength not so much from a surfeit of pleasures as from the sort of education that begins by making men useless to themselves in order to make them useful to others. It is the result of those institutions where hot-blooded youth is confined and where there is an insurmountable barrier to every other sort of relationship; all developing natural vigor is wasted in a way that is useless to humanity and that brings on premature old age.[30]

Beccaria makes the argument that punishments for pederasty must be considered unjust so long as a nation has not attempted to "prevent that crime" through a liquidation of these relations of mastery that confine youth and distort its sexual behaviors. Moreover, he says, pederasty and adultery "are crimes difficult to prove, are the ones that, according to accepted principles, admit of tyrannical presumptions, of quasi-proofs and semi-proofs." They are crimes "in which torture exercises its cruel sway over the person of the accused, over the witnesses, and even over the whole family of a poor wretch."[31] Far from addressing the root of the problem in the lack of laws guaranteeing men's freedom, far from liquidating relations of mastery, laws against pederasty, he argues, actively contribute to tyranny.

The execution of two infamous sodomites, one Jacques Chausson, called "des Étangs," and one Jacques-Saunié, called "Fabri," in December 1661 stands as an example of the tyranny of such an older rationality. In the account of the lawyer Mathieu Marais, the two were "condemned to make honorable amends before Notre-Dame, led to the Grève to be bound at the stake, their tongues to be ripped out and to be both burned alive with the trial records." With body and text "reduced to ashes, cast to the wind," the punishment stipulated that "sixteen hundred livres in damages [be paid,] one part to l'Hôpital-Général, the other to the Hôtel-Dieu plus eight hundred livres in damages to the Châtelet. The remainder of their property [was] to be seized by the King, and so declared against several persons of status and others."[32]

The punishment largely conforms to the pattern established by Foucault, as a raw confrontation between the power of the crime and the power of the king, of crime as an offense against the rights of the king.[33] However, in Marais's description we may already see the glimmerings of an Enlightenment rationality at work in the dispensations for the institutions of criminal justice system. As described, the public execution was still invested in a medieval cosmology of punishment: sovereign power confronted the body of the condemned with an overwhelming display of force. In the tearing out of tongues, a residue of the medieval paradigm associating sodomy with heresy remains.

The word "bugger"—derived from the Latin *bulgarus*, or "Bulgaria"—was originally a name given to a sect of heretics from the region in the eleventh century, and thereafter to all "heretics" associated with "abominable practices." This medieval paradigm, present only in a kind of ghostly form in the spectacular execution of Chausson and Jacques-Saunié, was at odds with that governing principles of police work in Paris during the eighteenth century. The absolutist state almost never executed sodomites for sodomy as such. Only seven men were convicted of sodomy and condemned to be burned at the stake in eighteenth-century Paris; extant records of the final executions for the crime demonstrate that most of these men were punished for monstrous abuses of power—clergy who made sexual assaults on boys, nobles who kidnapped and murdered boys or sold them as sex slaves to other aristocrats. Sodomy had to be compounded by other more monstrous crimes to be punished with the stake.[34]

The paradigm of these final executions was residual to the medieval episteme: it could never have served the purpose of terrorizing Parisian sodomites, as executions were rare and those executed tended to be so spectacularly corrupt. The paradigm, which associated monstrous sexuality with a tyrannical abuse of power, drew its last gasp in the late eighteenth century; in its final incarnation, it had lost its teeth: what was once considered a capital crime when associated with abuse of power had become a subject of gossip and character assassination.

There is one notable exception to the above pattern, if such a small number of executions can be said to provide the basis for any kind of pattern: the punishment of two very young workmen, Bruno Lenoir and Jean Diot, a joiner apprentice and a butcher by trade, eighteen and twenty years old. The two were caught one night while drunk and engaged in the act of sodomy on the rue Montorgueil and were publicly burned in the place de Grève on July 6, 1750. According to one contemporary, the lawyer Edmond Jean-François Barbier, their sentence was exceptional, "as these two workers had no relations with persons of distinction, either at court or in the city, and made no accusations against anyone else."[35] They had not calumnied anyone. Despite claiming that their execution "was done to make an example, especially since it is said that the crime is becoming very commonplace, and there are many men in the Bicêtre for the deed," Barbier indicates that their sentence was not announced publicly by a crier, "apparently to spare everyone the name and nature of the crime."[36]

Only a trace of the medieval cosmology remains in the punishment. Far from being an anachronism, the execution of Lenoir and Diot in 1750 il-

CHAPTER FOUR

lustrates the emergence of a new paradigm operating within the ancient punitive apparatus of public executions. Concern about the infamy of the crime had short-circuited the scaffold. Barbier's description articulates a political contradiction between the old imperative to make an example of these workers who engaged in sex with one another so publicly and a new and overriding concern that publicizing their crime would simply repeat it. The revolt of the crime was met by a mute exercise of force. The ritual recitation of the crime was apparently abandoned in view of public decency, but there were likely other reasons. Far from serving as a deterrent to the crime, it was feared that publicizing it might multiply the offense. The fact that these men were workers and not corrupt aristocrats doubtlessly made the execution problematic; the fact that the crime, as Barbier is careful to mention, was "becoming very commonplace" implies that announcing the crime could have risked triggering the popular anger of the crowds who attended the spectacle.[37]

In any case, the example of these two executions, separated by little over a century, signals a political shift. The 1750 punishment announced a new struggle over the moral and sexual order of public spaces that would rage for well over a century. The bourgeoisie would over the course of this struggle call upon the institutions of medicine and law to constitute a knowledge and regulatory power over the public sexual relations between men and with prostitutes. These working-class men and women announced a freedom to express and publicly take pleasure in their desires that mirrored the libertinage of the noble classes—but with a difference. If the libertines had troubled bourgeois distinctions between private acts and public spaces, they did so in word or gesture alone; the proletarians troubled this boundary in act. If the libertines enjoyed this freedom on the basis of their privileged status in the absolutist state and in the relative seclusion of palaces, private gardens, and interior rooms, proletarians enjoyed it as the fruit of a struggle over the use of public space.[38] Unlike libertine texts, the circulation of which was in any case always very limited to elite literary cliques, this new figure of sexual publicness could not be censored or suppressed. This new species of sexual freedom necessitated the intervention of armed bodies of men.

The texts considered above are notable for sitting at the hinge of an older discourse, denouncing the libertinage of the nobles, and an absolutely new struggle for power in civic life, a struggle launched by the bourgeoisie and aimed at repressing the sexuality of the popular classes during the revolutionary period. With *Le nouveau tableau de Paris*, we observe the bourgeois reading his political legitimacy off the external world of social relations, positing his moral right to govern over and against these public spectacles of sex, which are themselves, according to this perspective, symptoms of the decline of the ancien régime to which a later generation of scientists of race would refer as the "society of sick men."[39] In fact, this perspective is only the false consciousness of the revolutionary bourgeoisie, for, as campaigns to suppress the sexuality of the popular classes would demonstrate over the long nineteenth century, the social phenomenon in question was historically new.

If ribald texts publicizing the sexual antics of the court under Louis XV and Louis XVI had whittled away at such a boundary between private act and public space, this took place only in coterie-limited pamphlets and gossip, within a narrow—though no less symbolically significant—economy of representations and gestures connected to the political function of publicness under the ancien régime.[40] These sexual freedoms and gestures were still imprisoned within that old social form, restricted by what Jürgen Habermas has identified in *The Structural Transformation of the Public Sphere* as the order of "representative publicness." Of eighteenth-century court life, which achieved its apogee in the ceremonial etiquette of Versailles under Louis XIV, Habermas writes:

> Only after national and territorial power states had arisen on the basis of the early capitalist commercial economy and shattered the feudal foundations of power could this court nobility develop the framework of a sociability—highly individuated, in spite of its comprehensive etiquette—into that peculiarly free-floating but clearly demarcated sphere of "good society" in the eighteenth century. The final form of the representative publicness, reduced to the monarch's court and at the same time receiving greater emphasis, was already an enclave within a society separating itself from the state. Now for the first time private and public spheres became separate in a specifically modern sense.[41]

This historical separation of the state from society, the private from the public spheres, was the necessary precondition for a politicization of sex beyond character assassination and calumny. To be sure, these old modes for politicizing sex would find new traction in the first modern democracies. The public sexuality of court life, however sociable or mannered, was vulnerable to moral and political attacks due to its discontinuity with the family-centered social life, property relations, and mores of the emergent bourgeois society.[42] This sexual publicness was tightly linked to the bourgeois sense of royal and nobiliary corruption during the French Revolution; libertinage was one among many grievances animating the bourgeois struggle. The sexual license of the nobility was doubtless taken as an avatar of representative publicness in its final form in Western societies.

The humorous profanity of the erotic discourse on royal and noble bodies is an indicator of the gulf separating this latter doubling of the royal body from that of the medieval funeral processions that Ernst Kantorowicz has so memorably explicated with the juridical doctrine of "the king's two bodies." Those processions, Kantorowicz writes, presented "the uncanny juxtaposition of a decaying corpse and an immortal Dignity as displayed by the sepulchral monuments, or the sharp dichotomy of the lugubrious funeral train surrounding the corpse and the triumphant float of an effigy-dummy wrapped in regalia," a doubleness that reflected the same intellectual world as the solemn discourse of jurists concerning the divine right of kings.[43] Whereas the effigy and the corpse of the funeral procession crystallized the contradiction between a God-made mortal body and a man-made immortal office, libertine texts exhibited an erotic body—equally subject to exquisite pleasure and decay, a subject enslaved to his or her sexual appetites—as the double of governmental power. The juxtaposition is no less uncanny; except where the royal corpse once elicited solemn reflections on the body politic, the erotic body provoked only laughter. This peal of laughter at the sexuality of blue bloods also emerged from the same intellectual world of sentiment and thought that compelled men to cut off the head of their king.[44] The noble body exhibited in flagrante delicto appeared alongside the mortal indignity of the office.

With respect to both aristocratic libertinage and the bourgeois family, pederasts represented a new species of exemplary act and sexual personality. Their rank was drawn from the very same popular classes as the sans culottes: craftsmen, service laborers, apprentices, domestics, and other more informal laborers. In one historian's analysis of police records from 1770 to 1780, officers mostly arrested workers in the formal and informal economic sectors between fifteen and thirty-five years old for sodomy; almost all of those arrested were infamous street personalities. At issue was not merely open solicitation on the street, which had been a more or less constant feature of life in Paris and a concern for police authority since its establishment in the mid-seventeenth century. Instead, buggers and prostitutes had begun engaging in sexual acts en plein air, with flagrant disregard for bourgeois notions of public decency, in the centers of the civic life of Paris. Pederasts were antisocial in this limited sense. They made and flaunted theatrical sexual personas on the streets, taking titles such as La Baronne, La Comtesse, La Tante, and Le Môme, cultivating a camp sensibility and attracting a rotating audience of fans and onlookers. It was this theatrical and publicly visible culture of sex that was the subject of a wide literature of pamphlets in reaction to and in solidarity with these men and women in the first year of the Revolution.

The Champ de Mars

The procession of the Fête de la Fédération began at dawn on the first anniversary of the storming of the Bastille, July 14, 1790. Some half a million soldiers and citizens assembled on the Champ de Mars to swear a public oath of national unity. One hundred and fifty thousand soldiers, sailors, cavalrymen, grenadiers, and veterans were selected as official delegates from local districts from all departments of France. Local festivals were organized in the provinces to take the same oath as those assembled in Paris at noon. Marquis de Lafayette, general of the national guard, stood upon an altar constructed for the occasion and led those assembled on the Champ de Mars in the oath "to remain united with all the French by the indissoluble bonds of fraternity."

Cannons fired a salute as the thousands assembled declared, "I swear."[45] "After the oath," according to the account of the journalist Camille Desmoulins, "there was a touching spectacle of soldier-citizens throwing themselves into one another's arms."[46] Thus, the revolutionary army was ordained with an exuberant oath of fraternity, that rallying cry of the Jacobins and others, and the knightly tradition of a brotherhood in arms was adapted to the newly democratic citizen army as a symbol of the passage of the ancien régime.[47]

Under the old regime, the royal army had consisted of some 280,000 men; the officer corps was the exclusive purview of the aristocracy. The size of the army nearly doubled as 100,000 men enlisted in 1791 and another 150,000 joined in 1793. Following the seizure of the Tuileries and the fall of the monarchy on August 10, 1792, most of the aristocratic leadership of the national guard had fled or been ousted. Many of the hired mercenaries had left the army, as wages were irregular during the Revolution. The reforms of 1793 established a common uniform and equalized pay brackets. Officers were promoted based on merit, talent, and experience from a corps of subofficers and NCOs, with a full third of these positions elected by popular vote.[48] With the levée en masse of 1793, military service was restricted to bachelors between the ages of eighteen and twenty-five, and over 300,000 peasants, laborers, artisans, clergy, and petit bourgeois were conscripted into military service.

This explosive growth of a citizen army of bachelors was not without certain sexual consequences. "With news of the oath of federation," provincial women complain in a ribald pamphlet from 1791, "we had some hope for tranquility. We said in our hearts, 'The pledge that will allow our husbands to have nothing to do with the soldiering of France will intimidate the aristocracy; they will desist from their manoeuvres, happiness and joy will be reborn for us.' But alas, how we were wrong!"[49] The pamphlet continues:

> They use another ploy; they pay to ship the scoundrels to the brothels of Paris, where they fuck the women who are in the vile trade of courtesans. They have given them all the pox, and these spoiled girls carry about in all of the public spaces, on all the promenades, and places that have been prepared for fêting them.[50]

Mademoiselle Sophie, "president of the brothels," responds to the complaint of these women from the provinces by proclaiming, "It's true, and here's our hardship, as good patriots we are all too easily drawn to the defenders of the fatherland. Since the Revolution, the victors of the Bastille, those old French guard and friends of liberty who left their regiments to join with us, have inspired such an enthusiasm in us that each of us desires to repay their bravery, like the Lacedaemonian women, by sharing out the charms with which nature has endowed us with them and the bourgeoisie."[51]

Consideration of the French Revolutionary wars opens up a comparative perspective on how war transformed French and English societies' exercise of sexual hegemony. If Paris was the seat of a new kind of political modernity, a break from the old regime, London was the seat of a new economic order centered around advances in the mode of production. As the revolutionary state effected a new, democratic culture of war-making, so too it required a new politicization of sexuality. Libertinage represents the final incarnation of an older mode of representative publicness attached to a warrior class. The democratization of war expanded the scope and scale of a libertine culture just as it expanded the reach of sexually transmitted diseases. In fact, these three processes— the mobilization for war followed by the politicization of sex and the spread of syphilis and gonorrhea—would go hand in hand for the two hundred years that followed.

Richard Jennings, or The Epistemology of the Monkey Closet

In 1841, Paris made history by installing the first standardized public urinals along its busy thoroughfares. Named after the comte de Rambuteau, the pioneering civil engineer and hygienist who began many of the modernization projects for which Haussmann often receives credit, the urinals were incredibly phallic structures, towering twelve feet above the street, capped with a round glans-like finial. An alcove cut out from the cylindrical column provided a discrete space for the fulfillment of the bodily function in question.

However, this municipal provision of sanitary conveniences couldn't break Parisian men's habit of relieving themselves wherever they saw fit, and the number of columns erected could never satisfy the demand. In April 1843, the *Gazette Municipale* reported that men continued pissing en plein air on the streets; bourgeois women and children could no longer look out their windows or leave their houses without suffering "outrages against morals," for "public decency is too deeply and too frequently damaged by these ignoble spectacles for which the authorities provide neither surveillance nor serious repression."[52] Even where men did use the Rambuteau columns, women could still catch glimpse of a penis from the street, and they demanded partitions erected around the columns to cut off all lines of sight.

These were primitive provisions of sanitary convenience—essentially, iron slabs with no drainage. Structures were erected throughout Europe during the mid-nineteenth century on more or less the same architectural principle, outside pubs, in alleyways and parks. James Wright's seminal 1891 text for sanitary engineers, titled *Plumbing Practice*, describes the bourgeois affect of disgust regarding such urinals in London:

> On entering one of these places the person's eyes begin to run with tears, and the pain of the nostrils is similar to that just before a fit of sneezing, so strong are the ammoniacal vapours. Although these places are for the use of the public, a great many of them are private property. When they become so bad as to be a public nuisance, they sometimes get washed down and a coat of lime-white may be laid on the walls. A few days afterwards these white walls are invariably found to be covered with disgusting literature and quack doctors' hand-bills. The sooner the sanitary authorities seek out these places and have them removed the better it will be for those unfortunate people who reside near them, and those who, from sheer necessity, must make use of them.[53]

These two rather typical primary sources articulate the kind of outrage these municipal conveniences provoked from nineteenth-century publics. There was a virtual flood, so to speak, of middle-class discourse, predominantly female, about the placement of urinals in large cities throughout Great Britain and northern Europe. While urinating in the street apparently caused an "outrage against morals," the provision of urinals could cause a "public nuisance," which ran the gamut from the handbills, stench, and sexual latrinalia detailed by Wright, to the loitering, cruising, masturbation, and sex between men of concern to the police of major cities throughout Europe at the time.

To state the policy problem facing these mid-nineteenth-century sanitary reformers as clearly as possible: middle-class women considered the sight of men's penises and urethral functions to be an "outrage against decency" and demanded that municipal authorities contain or enclose such activities within an architecture that would shield them from view; however, the new architecture of enclosure concentrated the exercise of such bodily functions around a few nodal points along busy thoroughfares and erotically intensified the experience of urination in public by providing a semiprivate, same-sex urban space. These were, to put it figuratively, temples of urethral eroticism. The subjective responses of bourgeois women and working-class men to the architectural enclosure of public urination were part of a new political struggle over the presence of the phallus in public space, and they reveal a lot about the great divide in psychosexual subjectivity between the bourgeoisie and the working class, between men and women, and the differing notions of sexual freedom that were mutually exclusive and in competition with one another.

This nineteenth-century sexual struggle over the phallus can be sketched in broad strokes thus: the entry and influence of middle-class women into the public sphere is the decisive factor in changing norms of urban policing around public displays of sexuality—namely, prostitution and homosexuality. Middle-class women extended the domestic norms of sexual consent—consent to copresence with sexual acts—from their own households into the public spaces they circulated within. For the nineteenth and much of the early twentieth century, working-class men and women did not enjoy any kind of "privacy" in their own homes, as they lived crammed five or more to a room in boardinghouses or with relatives. The only privacy working-class people had was, paradoxically, to be had in public. As middle-class women extended such domestic norms into public spaces, the previously male-dominated public sphere was, over the course of the nineteenth century, domesticated. The material history of urinals and the social history of their placement in urban space demonstrates the growing influence of concerned middle-class women. As the example of Manchester indicates, women called for the construction of urinals to prevent "public indecency" and then pushed them out of neighborhoods when they become centers of homosexual activity.

During the nineteenth century, urinal design shifted from a kind of primitive communism of the open trough, or slab without drainage, to an individuating architecture of partitioned spaces, enameled basins, and drains for making the urine, along with its offensive ammoniacal vapors, disappear. George Jennings's design for what he called "monkey closets" popularized this new architecture. His urinals were first installed at the Crystal Palace at the World's Fair of 1851, and they were the highlight of the fair for many contemporaries. His designs were installed throughout Europe and were imitated by municipal authorities and other plumbing companies around the world.

This shift in plumbing practice coincides with the mid-nineteenth-century shift toward a feminized public sphere and with the psychological definition of homosexuality by forensic medicine in France and Germany. The architectural shift, toward partitions and individuated troughs, gave each man his own sex and anxiety about that of the man whose sex he could not see. His bodily fluids no longer mingled with those of other men and now disappeared down a drain. Urinal design during this period reflects new kinds of anxieties about homosexual activity in pissoirs. The example of George Jennings's popular design could be considered an architectural expression of the contradictory sexual regulations and the new sexual pleasures spawned by bourgeois senses of propriety.

It would be interesting to consider this proprietary technology as a precursor to later commercial architectures of homosexual sex like bathhouses, video arcades, and now mobile apps like Grindr and Scruff. But a look at the engravings from George Jennings's patent book, considered with reference to Johanna Drucker's concept of "visual epistemology," brings the concerns of Jennings's contemporaries into greater focus. Drucker argues that engravings and prints mediated scientific knowledge production by serving "as a site for focused inter-subjective exchanges among professionals—contributing to the creation of a scientific community."[54] The scientific status of these images fails to mask the contradictory drives motivating the bourgeois reformers of public space. Considering how these images were used to market urinals—should the homoerotic content of these images be considered to be unconscious? Or is the homoeroticism of the monkey closet

CHAPTER FOUR

precisely one of the attractions for urban reformers? The juxtaposition of text—detailing some of the struggles, between reformers and shopkeepers and others concerned with offenses against decency, around the placement of a urinal on Tottenham Court Road in the St. Pancras area—with image, one showing a gentleman hailing a stagecoach while families with women and children all stroll by paying no heed to the structure on the sidewalk beside it, raises a number of questions.

What was this image meant to communicate? Is it the inoffensive presence of the urinal in public space? Why are there men loitering outside it? And what's going on inside this space? The engraving gives us a glimpse of a male figure on the right-hand side of the structure, just inside the entrance, with his back turned to us, elbows out, as if he is holding his member or unbuckling his pants, yet the architectural plan for the structure shows that the nearest urinal is in the opposite direction, or ten feet away. Are we reading homoeroticism into these images, or is this precisely how they were appreciated at the time? If this content is unconscious in these images, did that add to the appeal of the design?

European Sexuality in the Longue Durée

Such images sit at the nexus of a partially obsolete sexuality, characteristic of the transition to capitalist wage relations in the metropoles of world empire, and a more modern one, familiar to us today. But they shed light on a contradictory process, one whose outlines the preceding sections have begun to sketch. Still, many questions about the mechanism of this process remain. How did capitalist development dissolve and reconstitute the organic family structures of feudal Europe? What role does this dissolution/reconstitution of the family play in the reproduction of capitalist social relations? Did this development favor cultures of homosexuality during the modern period, and, if so, why and how?

The value of such historical approaches is considered at greater length in the following chapter, but suffice it to say that a truly comparative approach to economic development and sexuality becomes possible only with a theoretical approach foregrounding the combined and uneven development of the capitalist world system. Developments in one sector of the world economic system, such as the early development of large-scale manufacture and machinofacture in the English textile towns of the mid-eighteenth century, along with corresponding sexual forms, are not generalizable to other development contexts.

Most importantly, most perspectives fail to account for the agrarian origins of the capitalist system. In my approach, property relations are understood as they are defined by Robert Brenner, as "the relationships of the direct producers to the means of production and to one another which *allow them to reproduce themselves as they were.* By this account, what distinguishes pre-capitalist property relations—asiatic, antique, feudal—is that they provided the direct producers with the full means of reproduction."[55] Peasants as "communities of cultivators" could preserve themselves as owners of the means of production, but they could not invest in the further development of their productive forces beyond a certain maximum. Societies characterized by this kind of property relations are determined by cycles of scarcity and plenty. England's early transition to capitalist property relations had to do with its class structure, one in which lords cooperated with the absolutist state to liquidate the old rights of peasants and managed to invest in the means of production on large estates.

The situation was different on the continent, where urban populations (above all, in Paris) responded to scarcity by directly confronting the state as a political force. In France, the absolutist monarchy worked to undermine the powers of the noblesse oblige, appointing members of the bourgeoisie to administrative positions, expanding the ranks of the bureaucracy, and directly taxing the peasantry to pay for this enormous state edifice. Such an economic interest explains why the French Crown supported the traditional rights and privileges of small landholding peasants against lordly encroachment for so long: peasants represented a major source of revenue. This combined model of property ownership forestalled the transformation of the French peasantry into a wage-dependent urban proletariat for a long time in France, while intensifying the political confrontation between the third estate and the king.

Although the above is neither a complete nor an uncontroversial account of the transition from feudalism to capitalism, it does begin to account for why the British and French experiences are exceptional. The essential thing to grasp about feudal property relations is that peasants did not have to "rent land or seek waged employment to survive" because they could reproduce themselves directly as communities of cultivators.[56] Two further things bear noting about this social relation: first, the ownership of the means of production could only be reproduced within family units. Thus, property ownership was directly reproduced through biological procreation, and this took place under conditions of high infant and child mortality rates, at least compared to those of the advanced capitalist societies of the early twentieth century. Second, rulers could only maintain themselves by appropriating a surplus through extra-economic coercion, by force. Politics was an extra-economic confrontation between lordly communities of force and peasant communities of cultivators who maintained themselves through small-scale craft production and agriculture involving all members of the family.

As Wally Seccombe points out in *A Millennium of Family Change*, human sexuality was limited by feudal property relations because population increases necessarily implied a subdivision of landholdings below subsistence level. In the transition to capitalism, an extractive extra-economic political power based on peasant proprietorship was slowly replaced by a productive political-economic power that, by limiting the traditional rights of peasants, installed a new system of wage-dependent social relations, which were the necessary precondition of capital investment in the land. Before this advent of capitalist social relations, one's membership in a family-centered community mediated one's life options. Thus, the lordly power to extract a surplus is based in turn on a kind of parasitism of the family unit upon the productive powers of its individual members, a feudal version of the ancient *patria potestas*. The family mediated political power. In the same way that the development of the forces of production was held back by small-scale peasant ownership, the development of the free individual was held back by the rigidity of kinship structures. Capitalism, on the other hand, is predicated on a separation of families from their means of reproduction; it reproduces humanity through impersonal, socially mediated interactions in the market. This system intervened where the community (and family) receded.

The above account of property relations shifts focus away from a deterministic account, one in which an increasing division of labor drove technological advances and urbanization, by bringing to light some of the contingent features of the transition to capitalism. It casts light on the functional coherence and ultimate limitations of family-based and community-reproduced property ownership. Market expansion and increasing divisions of labor could not then, according to this view, be the primary driver of a history of sexuality because peasant production was never primarily about exchange. In any case, a transformation of property relations was necessary before an expansion of national market economies could take place according to a mercantilist model.

Alternate or queer sexualities—primarily homosexuality and prostitution—emerged within the interstices of transformed property relations, through population displacements from the countryside and the subsequent concentration of those workers who were superfluous to agrarian production in urban centers, as well as within the institutions that attempted to manage or capture these surplus populations—factories, workhouses, standing armies, policing and punitive apparatuses, naval and merchant fleets, and colonial territories.

Peasant communities in Europe reproduced conservative sexual norms from generation to generation for nearly one thousand years, but they reproduced them in an uneven fashion, with many practices—incest, sodomy, bestiality, bastardy—prevailing outside of norms and very little power to prohibit such practices except by discovery and ostracism from the community. Communities of cultivators likely tolerated these aberrations within nearly universal patterns of family formation, which were economically necessary for most people.

Although the Protestant ethic probably had much to do with the birth of a new sexual morality, one centered around the family romance, among the middling and ruling classes of northern Europe, a longue durée perspective on this north-south split in sexual practices may be ventured. Slaves in the Roman Empire were overwhelmingly male, by a factor of two or perhaps even three, and agrarian labor was strictly sex-segregated, with male slaves working in gangs under intense supervision and housed in barracks. The slave system was bad at reproducing itself sexually and required constant wars to maintain.[57] Whereas the *patria potestas* prevailed in the south, the power of women seems to have been more determinant among the semipastoral Germanic tribes to the north. These German tribes traced their relations through the female line for certain purposes, valued female chastity in marriage, punished adultery in wives harshly, maintained polygynous norms, and gave women higher status within the household economy.[58]

Peasant women married much later in the north, probably in their early twenties, than in the Roman south, the latter of whom placed teenage girls under the hand of adult husbands. In *Germania*, Tacitus writes that German women played crucial roles on the field of battle

> as the witnesses whom each man reverences most highly, whose praise he most desires. It is to their mothers and wives that they go to have their wounds treated, and the women are not afraid to count and compare the gashes. . . . It stands on record that armies already wavering and on the point of collapse have been rallied by the women, pleading heroically with their men, thrusting forward their bared bosoms, and making them realize the imminent prospect of enslavement—a fate which the Germans fear more desperately for their women than for

themselves. Indeed, you can secure a surer hold on these nations if you compel them to include among a consignment of hostages some girls of noble family. More than this, they believe that there resides in women an element of holiness and a gift of prophecy; and they do not scorn to ask their advice, or lightly disregard their replies.[59]

The combination of these two worlds is responsible for the resulting feudal peasant family structure which prevailed for nearly a millennium among the class of dependent peasant cultivators. Through this family form,

> members secured access to the means of production and subsistence. Inheritance for peasants did not normally extend beyond the next of kin, and an eligible heir had to be produced on each holding or there was a risk of reversion to the lord. The feudal mode of production was thus characterized by a strong linkage of landholding to marriage and marriage to procreation. Those without land could not easily marry, and those with land had to marry and produce offspring to keep the holding productive and in the family. Only legitimate offspring (i.e. those sanctified by wedlock) could succeed to a holding, and marriage was the principal social regulator of fertility. The land-poor therefore tended to marry later than well-established peasants, and to raise fewer children. The poorest stratum did not reproduce their own numbers in most periods. The population grew by means of a molecular process of downward mobility engendered within peasant families. Those young adults who were not favored by inheritance and lost out in the scramble for established village holdings became the mass labor force of the system's extensive growth, moving to the periphery and clearing new land.[60]

Given this structure, some of the earliest Malthusian attempts to curb the growth of populations by restricting marriage in the countryside, a phenomenon noted throughout continental Europe in the 1830s and earlier in England, probably represents one way in which the regulation of marriage was mobilized to break the backs of peasant proprietorship.

Sexuality is, as I have articulated above, an absolutely crucial dimension of the primitive accumulation of capital, for proletarianization decouples biological reproduction from the reproduction of ownership of the means of production. This decoupling occurred very early in the Mediterranean world as a direct precondition to the capital surpluses generated by early merchant traffic.

FIGURE 4.1. Francisco Goya, *Summer, or The Harvest*, 1786, oil on canvas. Museo del Prado, Madrid.

The growth of markets and an increasing division of labor and bureaucratic rationality can only partially account for the conditions of possibility of homosexuality or any other "sexual freedom." The production of a propertyless condition is the decisive factor in the transition from economic production centered around mastery, reproductive marriage, and agricultural community to one based on impersonal market-mediated relations in towns and cities. The compulsion to produce for an employer or for the market is a form of life that produces surpluses, leading to the further development of the forces of production. It is a form of life that emerged on the periphery of peasant proprietorship, a population superfluous with respect to inheritance and land. This kind of population and these social relations emerged alongside the first large-scale textile industries, for reasons that have been discussed above, and specifically in the Mediterranean world, which remained at variance with the wider sociodemographic pattern of family formation in the rest of Europe.

Mediterranean sexuality was a transitional form between that of feudalism and capitalism, combining elements of the old and new, and this sexuality really was at variance with demographic patterns of family formation within the agrarian societies of the western European peasantry. The stark contrast demonstrates how this world's social form—maritime commerce and relations of mastery and direct domination—formed one of

CHAPTER FOUR

the necessary preconditions of a homosexual way of life. The longue durée has allowed us to see how a combination of factors—a pastoral way of life based on transhumance, a piratical kind of political-economic activity at sea, a specific climate, the urban dominance over surrounding populations, and a strict social hierarchy based on blood relations—form the necessary preconditions for this earlier form of homosexuality. The eclipse of Mediterranean homosexuality or, rather, its transformation in the context of a new world system centered around the Atlantic is, at its outer limit, marked by the geopolitical decline of its hegemony and cultural influence, exposure to syphilis, population decline, and out-migration.

A residual form of this Mediterranean social and sexual formation persists in later Dutch and English capitalist hegemony and even well into the twentieth century in the immigrant communities of North and South America. Mediterranean sailors were still in high demand in the maritime world, and the sexuality of Mediterranean emigrant men was considered ambiguous and suspicious by the Protestants of the north. This is due not only to the out-migration of Mediterranean populations, but this factor is worth considering. The Protestant north understood homosexuality according to a model of contagion, as a foreign influence having spread from the Mediterranean south. Here there was within this new social formation the symbolic conflation of a new disease, syphilis, with "unnatural" sexual appetites. Panics concerning the discovery of homosexual networks in northern cities doubtless reflect an increasing anxiety about a transformation of the morals and sexuality of urban populations resulting from economic cycles of boom and bust and the unevenness of economic development.

The most striking residue of the older Mediterranean form was the institution of domestic service under Dutch and British hegemony. Servitude was much more common as a basis for nonnormative sexualities in northern Europe. Although this labor was thoroughly feminized, and though male workers only ever accounted for a small fraction of the total population of domestics, a concern over menservants reflected an increasing anxiety about the homosexual character of the institution. Menservants, and especially valets, are associated with luxury, as the labor of men was dearer than that of women and the institution and role of the manservant had an archaic, aristocratic quality. They were heavily taxed in London in the early nineteenth century, and they appear in popular diatribes against the rich. Female domestic servants are, by comparison, an enormous workforce and a major institution of both the United Provinces' and Britain's middle classes.

The Development of Sexual Modernity

Urban male homosexuality was a culture of cross-class and intraclass sexual contact. Before the industrialization of this urban world, skilled labor processes were organized according to a guild or apprentice model, and norms of late marriage, bachelordom, and casual sex with other men were common, especially during periods of political, economic and social upheaval. Men entering skilled artisanal trades left their families to live and work in the house and workshop of an older man. The large towns of the early modern period therefore tended to favor homosexuality as they combined urban artisanal labor with maritime trade, and slave and servant labor with merchant capital. Military and maritime worlds reflected similar sociodemographic patterns as urban employment in handicraft production: hierarchies structured by age and class, all-male milieus, and relations of mastery. The cities of this period also supported a family-centered mode of production for less-skilled crafts and feminized labor, producing goods for merchants on the putting-out system.

While this structure, favoring sex between men along pederastic lines, prevailed during the early modern period in the populous port cities of the Mediterranean and northern Europe, the vast majority of the human populations of Europe was still enmeshed in feudal property relations. They existed socially within a family-centered, agrarian mode of production for everyday needs and produced little surpluses beyond these needs. Population in excess of that required for subsistence—disinherited peasants, for example—became servants on other families' land and in other household economies. Even as traditional peasant ownership of the land was liquidated by a capitalist model, the agricultural labor of tenant farmers still required a family-centered mode of production. Among tenant farmers, labor-intensive seasons of planting and harvesting required the labor of every family member who could toss seed, heave a scythe, or direct a plow.

The rapid growth of populations and cities, the expansion and intensification of agricultural activity, the creation of large standing armies and navies, and the development of large-scale manufacture in western Europe from the mid-eighteenth to mid-nineteenth centuries were mutually reinforcing dynamics that profoundly transformed human sexuality, as the capitalist social form liquidated precapitalist communities of primary peasant producers and as more efficient agricultural production displaced tenant farmers, reducing the proportion of the population required for food production.

Patterns of late marriage, bachelorhood, births out of wedlock, casual sex between men, and casual prostitution prevailed in cities during periods of economic recession, when wages were too low to support a family, work too infrequent or too itinerant, and rent too high for any kind of privacy or nuclear family structure. It wasn't until major outlays of capital for sanitation reform, housing redevelopment, and wage increases at the close of the nineteenth century and in the early twentieth century that the poor and working classes began to develop stable family patterns and sexual mores like those of the middle classes. This process of family normalization occurred first at the core of the capitalist system, in Victorian England, where bourgeois reformers and working-class mobilization achieved higher standards of living for the working class, who supported the policing of prostitution and homosexuality to gain moral respect. A decline in mortality rates and epidemic disease, another precondition of free sexuality, obtains throughout Europe and the United States by the turn of the century.

Fordism extended the package of middle-class commodities—such as cars, appliances, housing—and their corresponding forms of life to greater swaths of the population in the United States, Europe, Japan, and Australia following World War II. The mass production of penicillin, first developed for soldiers, released humankind from a host of bacterial pathogens, sexual or otherwise. The postwar mass production of birth control technologies transformed women's basic relation to their biological capacity to reproduce human life. These conjunctural and structural forces led to the development of the nearly universal norm of nuclear family types and companionate marriage throughout advanced capitalist countries and the establishment of middle-class norms of sexual freedom through sexual consent. These same forces also paved the way for a whole variety of sexual lifestyles outside this norm, including homosexuality. Homosexual enclaves of the postwar era tended to coincide with settlement patterns of demobilized soldiers and sailors in the port cities that had been significant in the World Wars.

Following the transition to industrial capitalism, the "development of modern sexuality" is nonlinear: sudden jolts forward, backward, or laterally into entirely different sexual norms seem to be the rule. Although there is no straight path to capitalist sexual modernity, crucial structural and conjunctural forces may be discerned. Structurally, the combined and uneven path of socioeconomic development has tended to magnify the social visibility of homosexuality and prostitution in "backward" sectors of the world economic system; this "backwardness" has also been magnified in such sectors during periods of political, economic, and public health "crisis." Key inflection points here for the politicization of sexuality would be the outbreak of large-scale civilian wars, beginning roughly with the French Revolutionary wars, the American Civil War, and the Franco-Prussian War, and continuing through the First and Second World Wars and the subsequent wars in Asia. The periods following such warfare, in which governments sought to renormalize societies, is sometimes marked by freer sexuality—as at the end of the Napoleonic wars and in the period between World Wars—and sometimes marked by deep anxiety about social instability and mass hysteria concerning sexual deviants, as in the period following World War II, during the Red Scare. These vacillations conform less to a predictable pattern than to contingent circumstances. Ambiguous homosexual relations and prostitution were perceived as threatening to municipal governments and the army, navy, and merchant marine during periods of social and political upheaval, as well as during periods of mobilization for war and afterward.

Toward the end of the nineteenth century, male homosexuality and female sex work became problematic when and where previously anarchic proletarian sexualities were subsumed through the extension of bourgeois norms to greater swaths of the working-class population. In such places and times, urban elites understood this sexual behavior as deviant and mobilized forces of social control, although never total in their reach, for its repression. These campaigns of repression tended to shore up the political support of urban middle classes. In this respect, socioeconomic progress is directly to blame for a wider basis for sexual repression. Thus the massive American economic boom of consumer society following the Second World War extended middle-class sexual norms to ever more Americans and led to the most extensive policing of homosexuality in any period of history.

A social movement of homosexuals, understood as a defined political grouping seeking rights from the state, did not force the public recognition of homosexuality. What movements did exist in the late nineteenth century sought modest reforms of the penal code, such as the repeal of sodomy statutes, and promoted scientific understandings of sexuality. Actually existing homosexuality was rarely criminalized by such statutes, which often required confirmation of the act. Homosexuality was more frequently criminalized by vagrancy statutes, which sufficiently establishes the class basis of this kind of persecution.

Although there were other candidates for the primary figure of "unnatural" sexuality in the period from the nineteenth to the twentieth centuries, none of them played as central a role in marking out the field of sexual cate-

CHAPTER FOUR

gories and identifications as homosexuality. With respect to social power, however, the disciplining and regulation of female sexuality and the policing of the moral limits of acceptable female sexual expression was far more important to the regulation of human sexuality than policing the boundaries of some emergent category of homosexuality. Our epistemological account of male homosexuality remains not only incomplete but essentially damaged to the extent that it does not grasp how women's entry into public spaces and institutions has transformed the basic coordinates of male homosexuality and homosociality. Homosexuality can only be considered central to the epistemology of unnatural or abnormal sexuality; the regulation of the sexuality of women, by contrast, and women's movements for emancipation played a far more central role in the historical deployment of social power over sexuality as such. There exists a historical dialectic between women's emancipation and homosexuality that remains to be explored.

Despite Foucault's emphasis in *The History of Sexuality, Volume 1*, sexual science was *not* the decisive force in the formation of social power over homosexuality or sexuality as such, as we have seen. An epistemology of homosexuality existed long before the phenomena in question were given that name. It emerged and circulated with merchant ships and capitals, in military hierarchies and barracks, in navies and port cities. As a mirror of princes in the Renaissance, homosexuality reflected back how norms of domination and subjugation were functioning or malfunctioning, where age and status hierarchies provided for the continuity of social life or where affinities of the lower strata of men threatened to burst forth in a riotous struggle. As an apparently normal feature of everyday life for men of all classes, homosexuality provided a stage for a morality play between classes. Whether or not the discrepancies between northern and southern sexualities may be explained by the rise of a Protestant ethic, the ruling classes of the hegemonic Dutch and English capitalist lifeworlds were no less decadent than their southern antecedents. Perhaps what explains the strange moral chill on discourses concerning the vice and the willingness of these ruling classes to look the other way is less some religious sentiment than a secular economic development. Perhaps the chorus of the middle classes who stepped on the stage of this sexual morality play sometime around the middle of the eighteenth century in northern Europe explains the apparent silence on the subject of homosexuality. These classes preserved the family form as a spiritual good, over and against the rapaciousness of the noble classes and anarchic sexuality of the poor and working classes, and economic development, print culture, and republican political experiments all favored their perspective. In the slow liquidation of the ancien régime, alternate sexual mores became a central signifier of the class division between bourgeois and proletarian.

Over the course of the twentieth century, economic development established the normality of family life and companionate marriage by extending the moral hegemony of the bourgeoisie over the working classes. Sexual science merely codified the earlier sexual typologies of the earliest forensic science of France and Italy. In fact, the earliest scientific knowledge of homosexuality in nineteenth-century Paris or early twentieth-century New York or Chicago had nothing to do with psychological types or subjective desires. These early scientific "discoveries" of homosexuality resulted from inquiries into female prostitution and sexually transmitted diseases in these cities. The discovery of subcultures of male homosexuality thus resulted from a concern for female sexuality, from bourgeois women's concern for public morality and decency, and from men's concern for decency of women in the public sphere. This tangle of middle-class identities and moral interests drove the policing of male homosexuality in nineteenth- and twentieth-century cities.

Just as the earlier close guarding of women's chastity and virginity, the relations of socioeconomic dependency in work and life, the seclusion of female bodies from public view, and cultures of male violence drove many men toward intensely affective and sexual relations with boys and other men, so the spectacular entry of bourgeois women into the public sphere began to transform and exert a civilizing influence on the violent sexual excesses of a male-dominated world, driving this culture outward toward the liminal spaces of immigrant and working-class neighborhoods and into the frontiers that had opened up in the New World and Australia. The nineteenth century is at the center of this transformation.

homosexuality and the desire for history

5

This much will probably be thought enough: if more proofs were necessary, it were easy to collect materials enough to fill a huge, a tedious, and a very disgusting volume. —JEREMY BENTHAM on the history of pederasty in "Offences against One's Self," 1785

HISTORICIZING THE
HISTORY OF SEXUALITY

Homosexuality as Human Freedom

Did a homosexual ever exist? And if such a thing as a homosexual existed in the past, does he still? Perhaps it's too soon to pose Jean-Paul Sartre's question from *Saint Genet* in the past tense; after all, there are still some men around who identify with the word, however unfashionable or camp it's become. Alternatively, Sartre's question may strike today's readers, especially a younger, queerer generation, with greater profundity than it did his audiences in the 1960s: "Does a homosexual exist? Does he think? Does he judge, does he judge us, does he see us?" What would count as his being then or now? From what standpoint could it even be determined?

This way of posing the question of homosexuality, which has long been a familiar trope of modernist literature, defamiliarizes these accumulated meanings and associations. It removes the question from an epistemological register of the homo/hetero binary, one apparently originating in nineteenth-century sexual science, and reframes it as a problem of historical ontology. How a homosexual subject once antagonized a particular form of bourgeois society could be what counts as his existence, rather than how bourgeois society and its institutions reacted to this antagonism or sought to classify his behavior and desire scientifically. This shift is a significant one, with wide-ranging consequences for how the subject of inquiry is defined, from the political considerations of which class perspective is emphasized to the empirical considerations of the conditions of possibility for an imagined community of homosexuality in the capitalist world system. Significantly, it requires parting ways with a cherished piece of Foucauldian doxa: namely, that homosexuality was discursively produced by sexual science. In fact, however, social antagonisms and intellectual understandings existed prior to sexual science, which sexual science and other institutions sought to subsume under the term "homosexual." Sexual scientific epistemologies, initially circulated among elite professional classes, would require an immense military-bureaucratic apparatus, greater rates of profit, higher standards of living, general literacy, and the establishment of normalized family units among working classes to achieve any kind of hegemony outside the historically bourgeois community of letters. Psychological understandings of homosexuality achieved intellectual hegemony outside Europe and among the popular classes of Europe only after the First and Second World Wars.

Sartre's question—Does a homosexual exist?—isn't as paradoxical or ironical as it may seem in a book about Jean Genet. Nor did he ask after the existence of a homosexual from some phobic standpoint, denying the fact of same-sex desires, behaviors, or sexual subcultures among men. Far from it. It's not a question about "sexuality" per se, as we've come to understand this phenomenon in terms of an expression of or identification with sexual object choice, erotic feelings or behaviors, or familiar tropes of beauty.

For Sartre, it was a matter of establishing whether or not some homosexual subject presented a standpoint of human freedom. He was deeply dissatisfied with the view favored by the prominent homosexual littéraires Marcel Proust and André Gide, who held that homosexuals are the way they are as the result of a natural compulsion, pathological or otherwise. Whether this compulsion is thought to be inborn or culturally constructed would have made no difference to Sartre. According to both paradigms, the being of the homosexual is figured as an inert, passive self-identity. Neither can account for homosexuality as a being-for-itself, a consciousness that ap-

CHAPTER FIVE

proves and chooses itself by actively transforming itself. "Does a homosexual exist?"—this is to ask if a homosexual life is different from other forms of life in the sense that it could be freely chosen as a conscious negation of social and cultural givens rather than an expression or identification with some compulsion, however natural or culturally constructed. "If he does exist," Sartre writes, "everything changes: if homosexuality is the choice of a mind, it becomes a human possibility."

Consider the internal monologue of Genet's antihero Querelle as an exemplary description of the homosexual freedom that Sartre attributed to Genet. This primal scene, from *Querelle de Brest*, stages historiographic problems that are the focus of the analysis that follows. Prior to the scene in question, the handsome sailor Querelle is led back to his superior officer Lieutenant Seblon's quarters to retrieve a borrowed, grease-stained handkerchief, reversing the power dynamic of an earlier encounter on the ship's deck in which Lt. Seblon reprimanded and threatened to punish Querelle for cocking his standard-issue red beret at an angle "to look thuggish [*d'avoir l'air voyou*]":

> "Faggot?" [Querelle] thought, "what's that? What could a faggot [*pédé*] be?" The corners of his lips were gently drawing his mouth into a contemptuous smirk. A thought softened the expression into a hazy sluggishness: "I'm a punk-ass faggot [*enculé*] too." That probably made him look bad, if it didn't outrage him, but then he felt sad about it and noticed he was clenching his butt so much—or so it seemed to him— that his cheeks were no longer touching the canvas of his pants.[1]

This scene of recognition and embodiment raises problems of translation and interpretation not limited to the difficulty translating the two insults— *pédé* and *enculé*—from one idiom to another. To be sure, such insults interpellate the two men from different classes into an imagined sexual community, where codes understood only by the initiated (or the paranoid) govern what is knowable about erotic possibility between men and its repression. The themes of how this knowledge therefore implicates individuals, sustaining relationships of power, are familiar tropes of twentieth-century homosexual literature and its reconstruction by queer literary criticism, following Eve Kosofsky Sedgwick's *Epistemology of the Closet*.

That tradition of literary criticism was ultimately torn between the idea that the sexual subjectivity in question was primarily produced by an identification with abjection—which opens up certain possibilities of self-transformation, inversion, and the transvaluation of values—and the idea that it was produced primarily as a recoil to sexual science and psychology, making its sensibility, however subversive, essentially reactionary. Although individual works stand out as thematic explorations of one or the other interpretive paradigm, the formation has largely vacillated between the two poles of abjection and pathologization with a characteristic undecidability. The tradition has richly developed this tropological opposition: the dialectic of abjection between law and transgression, on the one side, and the dialectic of pathologization between the norm and subversion, on the other. Whether it is philosophically useful to keep these two dialectics analytically separate or to collapse them into some common dynamic—perhaps recalling the analogous case of the ancient sophistic opposition between *nomos* and *physis*, the customary and natural orders of things—is beyond the scope of the present inquiry.

My own sense, briefly stated, is that this interpretive ambivalence concerning homosexual literature reflects a deeper ontological prevarication concerning the naturalness and constructedness of homosexuality at the precise moment when such problems were considered settled by queer theory and therefore beyond the pale of critical inquiry. In a truly perverse return of the repressed, Foucault's historical opposition between the normal and abnormal individual—or, more abstractly, the "normative" and "queer"—became a cipher that allowed the queer theory formation to reintroduce a naturalism or essentialism concerning sexuality by way of his critique of the "repressive hypothesis." Thus some of the most resolutely anti-essentialist writing of the intellectual formation—say, Judith Butler's *Gender Trouble*—must yet posit something extracitational in subversively self-reflexive performances of gender, a surplus that always slips away from power's grasp.

Queer theory generally downplayed the class relations at the center of literary scenes of sexual encounter, recognition, and ideological interpellation such as the one described above between Querelle and Lt. Seblon. This is partially due to the obvious class bias of literary sources; however, it is also due to a theoretical reduction of ideology and ideological effects to discourses or texts—rather than social struggles—and a spontaneous assumption that homosexuals have more or less existed among all classes during all periods of time.

Of course, discourse is itself material and has material effects, but when interpellation is reduced to a function of language, or performative utterance, our analysis of ideology can account for neither how Querelle's particular position in a division of labor might have made him into a sexual subject or object, nor what conditions required punishment for such small infractions as a coquettish tilt of a hat, nor how his sexual consciousness might differ from that of his superior officer. These intertextual considerations require some supplementary social theory or historical discourse to become intelligible. As queer theory was never "just" a reading of literary sources, and in fact produced a sophisticated theoretical frame for taxonomizing the cultural production of sexual dominants more generally, it is perhaps better read as a metahistory—that is, as a theorization of gay history in its generic register or form of appearance. One of the subjective modes in which this history appeared was the homosexual novel, which the intellectual formation of queer theory has rigorously theorized. The other subjective mode—and the one considered at length in this chapter—is gay historians' experience of the archive of state bureaucracies. Perhaps due to the strength of queer theory's ability to perform an analysis of the artifacts of a now-dead bourgeois culture, the plebeian public sphere discovered by gay historians could not appear in their metahistory as the dramatic scene of modern homosexuality.

One needn't share Sartre's existentialist philosophy—or his preference for the male personal pronoun—to appreciate the significance of his framing of the question. The problem eschews the great dispute among postmodernists concerning the essentialism or cultural construction of sexual binaries, for both nominalist and essentialist responses to the question would prove wholly insufficient. To frame the question in this way is to move away from a history of deviant sexual behaviors and identities, their purely negative relation to some law or norm, and to ask instead about the transformative and emancipatory possibilities of love and intimacy outside the institutions of family, state, and the couple form. These creative possibilities could be universal, given certain conditions, and not strictly limited to same-sex object choice. Didier Eribon finds a particular resonance of this Sartrean vision of freedom in post–World War II gay male culture, writing, "Even if the mental structures of shame and domination cannot be fully grasped within the terms of a philosophy of consciousness, we must nonetheless leave open a place for an individual decision at the foundation of freedom and emancipation—even if it is clear that this individual choice is only made possible (save in a few very exceptional cases) by the existence of . . . 'gay culture' and by the possibility of a kind of countersocialization that that culture enables."[2]

This more expansive conceptualization of counterhegemonic sexual subjectivity, one leaving open a place for individual decision, could be approached from another angle by considering what Adrienne Rich terms "the lesbian continuum" in her classic essay "Compulsory Heterosexuality and Lesbian Existence." Rich expands the category of lesbian existence beyond a genitally organized sexual attraction oriented toward women in order to "embrace many more forms of primary intensity between and among women, including the sharing of a rich inner life, the bonding against male tyranny, the giving and receiving of practical and political support."[3] If heterosexuality marked a compulsory experience of intimacy and life possibilities, then some lesbian alternative had to provide room for various kinds of choice. Seeking out other aspects of woman-identified experience provided a principle of intelligibility for understanding forms as diverse as that of the Beguines in medieval towns of the twelfth to fifteenth centuries, Chinese marriage-resisters who organized women's strikes in silk mills during the Cultural Revolution, suffragettes, Emily Dickinson, Sappho, and others. It remains an important paradigm for feminist studies of lesbian and women's history.

This analytic tactic provides lesbians and other women-identified women with a cultural and political existence neither limited to some genitally organized sexuality nor subsumed by sexual scientific epistemology as some female variant of male homosexuality. Rich writes:

> I perceive the lesbian experience as being, like motherhood, a profoundly female experience, with particular oppressions, meanings, and potentialities we cannot comprehend as long as we simply bracket it with other sexually stigmatized existences. Just as the term "parenting" serves to conceal the particular and significant reality of being a parent who is actually a mother, the term "gay" serves the purpose of blurring the very outlines we need to discern, which are of crucial value for feminism and for the freedom of women as a group.[4]

Rich confronts us with another paradox of sexual hegemony: the extension, by analogy, of an epistemology of male homosexuality to women-identified women erases their unique political existence and history. Politically, however, this elision has made possible new forms of solidarity between gay men and lesbians for the achievement of formal equality, same-sex marriage, and the radical politicization of AIDS. Political mobilization around AIDS drew upon feminists' crucial experience in making women's health issues visible to medical bureaucracies. Feminist affinity with male homosexuality often involved solidarity with gender-variant types and with oppressed axes of class, racial, and sexual identity from which the mainstream movement for gay rights sought to distance itself. Although the feminist tradition con-

CHAPTER FIVE

tinues to emphasize the vital importance of particularity in understanding experiences and histories of oppression, the price of legal recognition for gays and lesbians as a class involved glossing over such particulars.

How one defines homosexual subjectivity and its particular forms of group belonging is not a neutral or unproblematic affair. Even the most sophisticated historical and theoretical framings of this problem are full of conflicting and contradictory understandings. A critical theoretical account might reconceptualize "homosexuality" as an immanently social category of thought, marking a set of contradictions that inhere to historical processes in which older, partially socialized relations for the seemingly organic reproduction of family life were wholly or partly dissolved to allow for the expansion of capitalist social relations. Such specific contradictions, as indexed by the category of "homosexuality," have to do with the persistence of "archaic" understandings of sexual acts between men as structured by social hierarchy alongside and within "modern" understandings of these acts as free expressions of a subjectively interior desire. The contradictions are indexed further by conflictual senses of propriety between male and female moral sensibilities and gendered experiences of social space, by the struggle between a plebeian and bourgeois public sphere, and by antagonistic understandings of the integrity of the body and senses of its violation. Each of the above contradictions brings into a different focus the central contradiction connected with homosexuality—and, by extension, with the category of heterosexuality and social power more generally—which is that of consent. A comparative historical presentation of the category of homosexuality provides an analytic for understanding the way various societies have understood consent as the basis of the exercise of power more generally.

Rejecting the qualification of prisoners' and soldiers' sexuality as "situational" as opposed to some "true" homosexuality found elsewhere, the socialist historian Jonathan Ned Katz radicalizes the social constructivist claim into a social contradiction: "All homosexuality is situational, influenced and given meaning and character by its location in time and social space."[5] Indeed, the problem of situationality and consent, especially as they obtain in sometimes violent cultures of sex between men, has historically formed the ideological inflection point around which a whole politics of homosexuality has turned. To the extent that same-sex desire in the past made bourgeois men vulnerable to proletarian roughnecks, whether by blackmail or robbery, to the extent that it made boys from popular classes prey to men of status and power, to the extent that it provided spectacles of shame or, alternately, infamy, and to the extent that it ultimately provided a way of regulating stranger intimacy between men, subjecting it to greater surveillance and control, breaking apart solidarities and conflicts within classes and between classes of men through the establishment of normal family units, it has been a switch point for relations of force and a theater for struggle over the basic coordinates of public and private life.

My focus on conjunctural crises does not attempt to resolve the historiographic tension between the disjuncture and the continuity of homosexual culture in favor of one or the other. Rather, analysis of the relations of force at play during periods of crisis indicates an actually contradictory historical process in which outcomes resulting from conflicts between social forces could have been otherwise. If "homosexuality" represents an actually existing contradiction, no just-so story in favor of either a model of continuity or discontinuity could do justice to this history. Only a dialectical treatment of the historical materials restores their specificity by removing the question of homosexuality from the purview of ready-made theoretical paradigms for the study of episodic sexual panics or phobias, paradigms that all too easily assume the dimension of timeless natural forces awaiting the right moment and conditions to break out.

Gay History and/as Rights Discourse

The revolutions throughout Europe in 1848 generated an intellectual formation of professionals, reformers, and civil servants, loosely in dialogue with one another, who were concerned with phenomena that came by the century's end to be collected under the label of "homosexuality." The national differences and the progressive and conservative tendencies within these intellectual formations are all important. Although they were both concerned with establishing the naturalness of homosexuality, the German formation understood homosexuality as a medical or psychological pathology, while the French formation produced what was essentially a forensic medical science of deviancy and racial degeneration, one most concerned with more effectively monitoring places of overt homosexual behavior, prostitution, and theft. Auguste Ambroise Tardieu's *La Pédérastie* (1857), Louis Canler's *Mémoires* (1862), and François Carlier's *La Prostitution antiphysique* (1887) all reflect the French ruling classes' efforts—following the uprisings of 1848 and the defeat of the Paris Commune—to consolidate physical control over the urban space of Paris and impose a moral order that would buffer any further shock waves emanating from the working classes. These medical-forensic treatises explicitly link the highly public working-class street culture of prostitution and pederasty with the threat of revolt from those classes involved in barricade fighting.

The relative absence of any analogous revolutionary working-class sub-jectivity or centralized state in the German context produced a medical sci-ence that was largely abstracted from such social considerations. Whereas Johann Ludwig Casper's *Praktisches Handbuch der gerichtlichen Medizin, nach eigenen Erfahrungen* (1858) was circumspect about Tardieu's claim concerning the naturalness of homosexuality, the wider formation of Karl-Heinrich Ulrichs, Carl Westphal, and Richard von Krafft-Ebing were con-cerned with establishing the natural pathology of same-sex desire as the basis for reforms of the penal code in anticipation of a unified German state in which Prussia's antisodomy law would become law throughout the Ger-man Confederation.[6] Ulrichs's impassioned appeals to the antiquity of ho-mosexuality in the 1860s, like the views expressed by Oscar Wilde in his trial at the end of the century, do not reflect a consciousness of the historicity of sexual mores and cultures. These understandings never went beyond an affirmative recognition of the existence of same-sex sex acts and love in the past; they therefore reflected a limited consciousness of the past in which citations of antiquity authorized modern homosexuality by precedent. In keeping with the progressive liberal tradition, this historical consciousness opposed civilizational custom to laws perceived as unjust. The elimination of sodomy laws from the Napoleonic Code was understood by German lib-erals to be a mark of France's enlightened, civilized legal system. Homosexu-als in both countries, however, were still largely criminalized with vagrancy and public indecency statutes, an outcome reflecting the false consciousness, or bourgeois idealism, of these early liberal reformers.

As liberal values entered a period of crisis in the late nineteenth and early twentieth centuries due to the political mobilization of working classes and the social destabilizations of war, a new intellectual formation crystallized around sexuality. In the last decade of the nineteenth century, Germany's apparently "backward" sodomy statute—section 175 of the German penal code, a legal product of unification—birthed a democratic socialist move-ment for its abolition. The history of homosexuality in its various cultural contexts began to play a more determinant role in swaying public opinion among the middle classes.[7] The beginnings of a historical understanding of homosexuality originated in the sexual science of Magnus Hirschfeld and Havelock Ellis as comparative histories establishing the universality of homosexual practices in different cultures and epochs. This comparative historiographic work—predicated upon the British empire's expansion of the sphere of European hegemony over ever larger geographic spaces—was largely based on ethnographic observation of non-European cultures.[8] Thus, by the late nineteenth century, "homosexuality" provided a unifying category for an enormously heterogeneous field of behaviors, subsuming practices and self-understandings of working-class populations of Europe and colonial subalterns within a single scientific frame. The political legitimacy of the category of homosexuality rested upon its claims to universality, a concept that had entered the first of its own many crises of legitimacy.[9]

The homosexual desire for history is itself historical, the product of a specific social valorization of historical knowledge in the nineteenth century, the emergence of a dominant bourgeois class presenting its demands as universal, and a supposed opposition between the "timeless" sexual cultures of traditional peoples and the "historical" ones of metropoles and settler societies. The presence of same-sex sexual behaviors in the former served as proof of the legitimacy, naturalness, and universality of the latter. A reactionary bourgeois racial science of degeneration equated colonized subjects and European working-class populations alike as sexual primitives, residual elements from a time before civilization. Bénédict Morel's *Traité des dégénérescences* (1857), Cesare Lombroso's *L'uomo delinquente* (1878), and Max Nordau's *Entartung* (1892) were all attempts to establish the naturalness of various deviant social and psychological phenomena, including homosexuality.[10] Sigmund Freud was very much a man of his time in retaining this civilizational hierarchy of desires in his notion of a primary repression of homosexuality and his appeal to ethnographic materials. The liberal reformist citation of ancient Greek and Roman homosexuality in the nineteenth and early twentieth centuries was an ideological attempt to counteract racist pseudoscience by establishing it as a time-honored custom of Western civilization.

Although social sciences and histories of this kind continued to be written in the twentieth century after the defeat of fascism—which itself perversely fused universal, classical homoerotic tropes with scientific racism—the history of homosexuality was transformed by the intellectual turn toward new social history after the 1960s.[11] This turn in homosexual history has been strongly associated with Foucault and with social constructivism, but the new social history of homosexuality, including Foucault's work, merged a poststructural emphasis on language with a long-standing sociological paradigm for studying periodic moral panics, one in which this or that figure of social deviance, or "folk devil," is imagined to pose a threat to the social order and catalyzes forces of repression. Social crises with obscure causes provoke a politics of scapegoating in the public sphere, mobilizing irrational fear and anger into a morally regulative force and resulting in the elaboration of new techniques of discipline and social repression.[12]

The paradigms of deviance and moral panic propose a problematic of the permitted and the forbidden that, from Émile Durkheim to Lévi-Strauss and from Freud to Jacques Lacan, has been a familiar rubric for social scientific inquiry. The distinction between permitted and forbidden acts permits a relativistic sort of cross-cultural analysis in which diachronic and synchronic features of culture and subjectivity come into focus. If the law creates desire, transgression would only ever be the fulfillment of the law, that which justifies the authority of the rule, as Durkheim's *Le suicide* (1897) sought to prove. Perhaps due to the influence of Kant's deontological ethics in German and French social science or perhaps for other reasons, the distinction between what is permitted and what is forbidden has provided the default paradigm for considering how homosexuality was problematized at various moments of its history. The moral reaction to homosexuality during the AIDS epidemic invested this theory with the explanatory power to describe past and present politicizations of homosexuality and to establish apparent historical continuity and intelligibility between historically episodic panics. This paradigm, however, is itself historical and ultimately results in elevating a liberal bourgeois theory of the state into the constitutive principle of human desire and all other cultural formations.

Foucault's Contradiction

Michel Foucault questioned the objectivity of historical knowledge with a historically grounded philosophical argument for how an eighteenth-century legal paradigm of the permitted and forbidden continued to determine the political thought of his own day. As he writes:

> The bourgeoisie and the monarchy succeeded little by little at establishing, from the end of the Middle Ages up to the 18th century, a form of power representing itself as language, a form of power which gave itself—as discourse—the vocabulary of rights. And, when the bourgeoisie had finally disposed of monarchical power, it did so precisely by using this juridical discourse—which had more or less been that of the monarchy—which it turned against the monarchy itself. . . . It appears to me, in fact, that if we analyze power by privileging the State apparatus, if we analyze power by regarding it as a mechanism

of preservation, if we regard power as a juridical superstructure, we will basically do no more than take up the classical theme of bourgeois thought, for it essentially conceives of power as a juridical fact.[13]

Foucault's critique of the so-called repressive hypothesis was not only an attempt to free sexuality from the old structuralist paradigm of permitted and forbidden; it was also an attempt to free power from certain forms of thought that emerged out of the revolutionary struggle of the bourgeoisie against the ancien régime. Whereas Foucault historicized sexuality according to a strict nominalism, he historicized power with the metanarrative of class struggle, the only historical paradigm that historicizes itself.

Both sides of this apparent contradiction are articulated in his critique of the repressive hypothesis. Foucault spends the greater part of the first volume of *The History of Sexuality* detailing how sexual science produced the cardinal points of modern sexuality—the child, the woman, the family, and the sexual pervert. He then attempts to demonstrate how these cardinal points of sexual identity functioned as targets for a historically unprecedented extension of power over sex, a power whose function was to stimulate sex and transform sex into discourse rather than repress it. There were periodic panics surrounding child masturbators, the effects of frigidity or hysteria on the family unit, and so on. The story is now so familiar, across so many disciplines and so many volumes of microhistory, that its repetition has become a commonplace. Two of his paradigmatic figures—the pervert and the masturbating child—are produced by a distinction between the permitted and forbidden, the "no" of the father and the juridical superstructure; however, the relative absence of a consciousness of class in such examples indicates a lapse back into the very model of social theory that Foucault criticizes.

Foucault's familiar narrative belies another significant contradiction. The volume begins by adopting a disabused stance toward the "repressive hypothesis" of sexual liberation, asserting that the sex talk of Foucault's contemporaries was strikingly similar to that of the much-maligned Victorians who served as their foil.[14] He singles out both a generalized compulsion to put sex into speech and a belief that sex contains the secret truth of an individual's identity as common to both periods' sexualities. For the Victorians and us, Foucault argues, sex has become a measure of man, offering more or less illusory promises of freedom and health.[15] Moreover, just as the nineteenth-century inheritors of the Enlightenment project historicized *homosexuality* on the basis of its universality, so the postmodern critics of that project learned to historicize *homosexualities* on the basis of their particularity.

Perhaps homosexuality provides the unarticulated standpoint of this critique of the politics of sexual liberation: Foucault's pessimism concerning the apparent revolutionary potential of its "liberation," or at least a certain dialectical ambivalence about it, is at the heart of his more prescient formulations in *La volonté de savoir*. Foucault's generational position within this developing subculture—he was fifty years old at the time of the publication of this work—and his experience of a period in which homosexuality was not as open or freely articulated lent him a more critical perspective on this emergent youth-obsessed subculture and its will to knowledge. Doubt about the emancipatory potential of a growing social acceptance of homosexuality, an understanding of how homosexuality had begun to be incorporated in highly productive circuits of consumer society, and a critical perspective on its thoughtless reproduction of predictable, time-honored canons of male beauty may all have led him to question any such liberatory potential with regard to any other sexualities.

Paradoxically, the final section of the book argues that all those apparently laughable scientific inquiries into sex were not chasing chimeras after all, for sex did contain the truth of a new human subjectivity—what contemporaries called "population"—which formed the material substrate of modern political-economic power, from labor power to the atom bomb.[16] If Foucault derived his general theory of power from Bentham and Marx, as he admitted to an audience of students at the Federal University of Bahia in 1976, then with his concept of "biopower" he ontologized the most controversial thesis in Marx's *Capital*: the tendency for capitalism to produce a population in excess of its industrial capacity to employ this human mass, or the so-called absolute general law of capital accumulation.[17] The thesis was dismissed by generations of Marxists as the "immiseration thesis."[18] However, during the late 1970s, when the structural crisis of late capitalism had become clear to some on the New Left, Foucault distanced himself from the Weberian leanings of the Frankfurt School by making the contradictory logic of capital accumulation, rather than its diverse institutional forms, central to his account of the emergence of capitalism out of the dissolution of the peasantry and its possible end in the dissolution of the welfare state.[19]

Although it is unfortunate that this thought remained imprisoned in a language so easily subject to demagogic abuse, a fact that Foucault acknowledged toward the end of his lectures on "The Birth of Biopolitics," it is to his credit that he stages the contradiction of the welfare state in such sweeping world-historical terms: sex is not the source of truth we hold it to be; sex is the ultimate source of truth for us moderns. Sexual discourse is both a frivolous, perfunctory activity and the linchpin of a totalizing "anatomo-politics of the human body" and "biopolitics of the population."[20] Biological interventions constitute "a society's 'threshold of biological modernity'" in which the power of the levy, symbolized by the sword or taxman, is no longer the basis of sovereign right. Instead, the basis of modern productive power is the power to guarantee life or disallow it.[21] If sex historically played such a role in the constitution of this sweeping power over life, it remains to be seen whether it will continue to be so central to the function of power as welfare states roll back their safety nets, as families and intimates are once again necessary to guaranteeing a minimum level of assurances.

A great dam of intellectual production was built upon the spring of this small book's historical insight. Foucault's remains the most influential genealogy of modern power over sexuality despite whatever quibbles scholars have had with his empirical data and narrative scope. His account of biopower gained currency far outside the specialty of sexuality studies. Such enthusiastic receptions give one reason enough to be circumspect about Foucault's clever criticism of the "repressive hypothesis."

Despite one's sympathy with his assault on one of advanced capitalist society's most cherished myths—that we are sexually repressed and unleashing sexuality contains seeds of some form of human freedom—and despite whatever respect one might have for the man who had the courage to make it in the heyday of sexual liberation, there is something clearly ironic about it. If sex talk is how we are dominated, why continue to engage it at all? Isn't our continued intellectual interest in its past, present, and future just grist for the biopolitical mill? What makes all those apparently sophisticated studies of the social construction of sexuality any different from the tomes whose titles wink and leer from the shelves beside them? Following Foucault's metaphor, is our current intellectual formation any less prurient than the sex manuals and pseudoscientific studies of the Victorians?

Absent a comparative historical engagement with the problem of sexual freedom, the Foucauldian paradigm gives rise to logical and historical fallacies. The tendency to attribute all too strong an agential role to forms of knowledge, such as sexual science, is a profound problem. Perhaps due to his professed Kantian leanings, Foucault cultivated an indifference toward dedifferentiating the ontological from the epistemic, reducing being to the historical limits and forms of knowledge. He avoids ontological questions with a nominalism where convenient (as with homosexuality and mad-

CHAPTER FIVE

ness) and stages ontologies with vague metaphorics (as with the concept of a "technology of power") where convenient. Whether this philosophical back-and-forth indicates a heterodox sense of practicality or weak thought is for others to decide.

Foucault posits a hegemonic sexual scientific understanding of sexuality in the West without accounting for how it achieved such hegemony.[22] This gives the impression that a formation of discourse spontaneously generated sexual subjects "through a network of interconnecting mechanisms, the proliferation of specific pleasures, and the multiplication of disparate sexualities."[23] In the rare places where he is explicit about his own inspiration, beyond such technological atmospherics and occasional slippages back into the paradigm of the permitted and forbidden, Foucault historicized power in terms of a metanarrative of class struggle. However, the narrative unfolding of a sexual scientific epistemology in the first volume of *The History of Sexuality* fails to account for the entry of women and children into industrial lines of production in the mid- to late nineteenth century; subsequent labor struggles over the working day defined these "other Victorians" according to categories of age and sex. These considerations are limited to a footnote to relevant chapters in Marx's *Capital, Volume 1*. Such a concealment of the origins of his own thought and a scant attention to working-class history are responsible for a dematerialization of what Foucault understood by the term "discourse" in subsequent theories and theoretically informed histories of sexuality.

Foucault makes the point, almost as a rhetorical aside, that sexuality was at its inception a bourgeois science, a concern for bourgeois bodies, and was only later (and with great difficulty) extended to the proletariat. He is flippant about the mechanisms for this deployment in *The History of Sexuality I*, and in a single paragraph of periodization he sketches that history in the broadest of strokes.

> Granted that one of the most primordial forms of class consciousness is the assertion of the body—at least, this was the case for the bourgeoisie throughout the eighteenth century—the bourgeoisie exchanged the blue blood of nobles for a fit organism and a healthy sexuality; it will be understood why it took so long and required overcoming such great reluctances for the bourgeoisie to award a body and a sex to the other classes—precisely to those whom it was exploiting. The living conditions dealt to the proletariat, particularly during the first half of the nineteenth century, demonstrate little worry over its body and its

sex, far from it: it was no matter whether those people lived or died, anyway it was reproducing itself on its own. Conflicts were necessary for the proletariat to be given a body and a sexuality, for its health, sex, and reproduction to become problems; conflicts over urban space were necessary, conflicts over cohabitation, proximity, contamination, epidemics like the outbreak of cholera in 1832, conflicts over prostitution and venereal diseases were all absolutely crucial. Economic emergencies were necessary—the development of heavy machinery requiring stable and competent workforces, the necessity of controlling the flow of populations and attaining particular demographic compositions. Lastly, it was necessary to establish a whole technology of control for maintaining supervision over this body and this sex for which they were finally recognized: schooling, housing projects, public hygiene, assistance and insurance agencies, the general medicalization of populations. In short, an administrative and technical apparatus allowed the *dispositif* of sexuality to be imported into the exploited class without danger; sexuality no longer risked affirming this class opposite the bourgeoisie; it remained the instrument of its hegemony. Hence the reluctance of the proletariat to accept this *dispositif*; hence its tendency to say that all this sexuality is a bourgeois affair and of no concern to it.[24]

Foucault is in agreement with Gramsci in considering sexuality as absolutely essential to bourgeois hegemony over the working class. However, his account of "modern sexuality" is completely lopsided to the extent that it emphasizes a late period in the development of modern sexuality and does not consider the other, proletarian side of the Victorian sexual formation in any detail beyond the parenthetical formulation quoted above. Tracing that history would have been a much more difficult project and one engaging with very different archives and source materials. The resulting theory of the emergence of modern sexual categories proceeds by assuming bourgeois sexuality to be hegemonic rather than rigorously accounting for how it came to be so.

David Halperin's programmatic statement of the social construction of homosexuality in *One Hundred Years of Homosexuality* is exemplary of the wider social constructivist formation inspired by Foucault. According to Halperin, the social constructivist hypothesis posits "a plurality of only partly overlapping social and conceptual territories, a series of cultural formations that shift as their constituents change, combine in different sequences and patterns." It is less a history of gay people than "a history written from the perspective of contemporary gay interests."[25] Thus, the postmodern conviction that categories construct their objects leads Halperin to the hypothesis that it is only in the last hundred years that persons seeking sex with other persons of the same sex "have been homosexuals." Halperin's muddle of tectonic cultural formation "shift," and cultural recombinations of "different sequences and patterns," like the Foucauldian language he inherits, proves to be a conceptual model of history with weak explanatory power.

Homosexuality and heterosexuality, as we currently understand them, are modern, Western, bourgeois productions. Nothing resembling them can be found in classical antiquity. A certain identification of the self with the sexual self began in late antiquity; it was strengthened by the Christian confessional. Only in the high middle ages did certain kinds of sexual acts start to get identified with certain specifically sexual types of person: the term "sodomite" begins to name not merely the person who commits an act of sodomy but one distinguished by a certain type of specifically sexual subjectivity that inclines them to commit those acts; sodomy remains, nonetheless, a sinful act that any person, given sufficient temptation, may be induced to commit. In London and Paris, in the seventeenth and eighteenth centuries, there appear—evidently for the first time, and in conjunction with the rise of companionate marriage—social gathering places for persons of the same sex with the same socially deviant attitudes to sex and gender who wish to socialize and to have sex with one another. In London, these are the so-called molly-houses, where men dress as women and assume women's names. This phenomenon contributes to what Halperin calls the great nineteenth-century experience of "sexual inversion," or sex-role reversal, in which some forms of sexual deviance are interpreted as, or conflated with, gender deviance. The emergence of homosexuality out of inversion, or the formation of a sexual orientation independent of relative degrees of masculinity and femininity, takes place during the latter part of the nineteenth century and comes into its own only in the twentieth. Its end point is the "straight-acting and -appearing gay male," a man distinct from other men in absolutely no other respect than that of his "sexuality."[26]

Both Foucault's and Halperin's language invokes complexity and historicity; however, as Eve Kosofsky Sedgwick has pointed out, "each is a unidirectional narrative of supersession."[27] Halperin's unidirectional model of cultural evolution takes Patroklos and Achilles as its zero point and the straight-acting gay man, or clone, as its "highest expression"—with a troublesome gender transitive interlude in between. The cultural shifts that Halperin tracks above are sealed off from the historical developments that have generated them. Epochs are invoked alongside one-dimensional cutouts of periods and places. Pseudoevents, like "the great nineteenth-century experience of 'sexual inversion,'" mark apparently major changes in the sequential development of a cultural formation.

There is nothing overlapping or plural about the conceptual territories Halperin maps. His response in *How to Do the History of Homosexuality* to the criticisms of this model merely spatialized the temporal contradiction with a metaphorics of geological time. In his words, modern homosexuality is the "cumulative effect of a long process of historical overlay and accretion," but he fails to account for whether or how subjects move through these sedimented layers of compressed space-time.[28] Presumably the accumulated weight of newer social formations compresses the bottom layers of earlier formations, according to the metaphor: a thick social layer of hypermasculine muscle queens would then rest atop the sexual formations among the Guyakí of the Amazon River basin and the customs of the mountain highlands of Papua New Guinea. The problem with both a simplistic timeline and a geological metaphorics of sexual subjectivity is that neither can account for why some past subjectivities resonate with present ones, why some are liquidated or continue to coexist with others. The one presents history as a nondynamic succession of gay heritage, and the other freezes this narrative succession over into static layers.

I don't share Sedgwick's suspicion of narrative history, but her critique of Foucault's and Halperin's unidirectional narrative signals the crucial importance of a dialectical grasp of contradiction for historical thinking. A historical materialist understanding of cultural artifacts requires dialectical ways of thinking the relationship between and simultaneity of residual and emergent social and sexual forms—which phenomena cannot be incorporated by either a model emphasizing radical breaks and discontinuities or simplistic models of succession and accretion.[29] Contradiction, according to this conception, is a narrative strategy for representing events, institutions, and cultural formations over which multiple forces have struggled to achieve certain outcomes; recognizing this contingency, often apparent only in evental disruptions of the status quo or dramatic reversals of fortune, as when winners lose and losers win, opens up a perspective on how struggles and contestation drive a historical process that would otherwise appear unilinear or geologically static.[30]

Halperin's narrative emphasis (like Sedgwick's critique of narrative history) says a lot about the "gay interests" of the early 1990s and about the distance of these interests from those of an earlier generation of intellectuals whose formative political experience was in the radical feminist, socialist, and civil rights movements of the 1960s and for whom Marxism was still a living tradition. Although history played the role of morally and politically legitimizing gay culture at a conjuncture of crisis, the politically decisive representational battles—establishing the recency of discriminatory laws against homosexuals—had already been fought. The homo/hetero binary, which social constructivism sought to historicize and which queer theory hoped to transcend, turned out to be crucial to the state recognition of homosexuals as a group suffering from historical forms of discrimination.[31] Whereas Halperin was still seeking civilizational legitimacy for same-sex love in ancient Greece (or vouchsafing the nominalist hypothesis of Foucault), semiotic theory played down the importance of historical knowledge and narrative for the queer theory formation represented by Sedgwick. What mattered more to the latter was how affects of panic and terror were transmitted and exchanged along semiotic cultural circuits to reproduce homophobia as a legitimate response to AIDS—as well as the possibility of the reversal of or resistance to such dynamics. Halperin's hagiography of Foucault illustrates both tendencies.

The Constructivist Account of Homosexuality and Capitalism

Historians of homosexuality have tended to narrate capitalist transformations of sexuality with a progressivist story of the increasing division and rationalization of labor, which favored ever more diverse forms of life. Homosexual desire would be one among many new desires that the general expansion of production beyond a subsistence base—in other words, production for the market—makes possible. Production for the market creates wage-dependency for broader swaths of the population, unseating the family as the primary economic unit of self-reproduction, and opens up sexual and life options outside its restrictive form. This narrative of capitalism as an institutional succession of modes of production is shared by many Marxists and sociologists.

In their historical assessments of the sexuality particular to market-based societies, social constructivists have tended to emphasize the freedoms accompanying a greater division of labor while considering the ways in which a Protestant work ethic accompanies such divisions, devaluing the pursuit of pleasure and stigmatizing groups organized around its pursuit. According to David Greenberg and Marcia Bystryn's thesis:

[H]omosexuality was highly stigmatized in nineteenth century France, as well as England and the United States, where the law remained more rigorous. The new capitalist order contributed to this stigmatization by intensifying competition among men, by fostering an ethos of self-restraint antagonistic to sexual expression, by sharpening the sexual division of labor and strengthening the ideology of the family, and by giving rise to an ideology which reinterpreted deviance in medical terms.[32]

Thus, Greenberg and Bystryn invoke the ethos of hard work and "competition among men" to explain why the capitalism of the late nineteenth century "stigmatized" homosexuality, which is equated with a kind of self-expression.

Emphasizing the transition away from a household economy, the universalization of wage labor, and the growing state bureaucracies of mid-nineteenth-century Europe and North America, John D'Emilio argues that

as wage labor spread and production became socialized, then, it became possible to release sexuality from the "imperative" to procreate. Ideologically, heterosexual expression came to be a means of establishing intimacy, promoting happiness, and experiencing pleasure. In divesting the household of its economic independence and fostering the separation of sexuality from procreation, capitalism has created conditions that allow some men and women to organize a personal life around their erotic/emotional attraction to their own sex. It has made possible the formation of urban communities of lesbians and gay men and, more recently, of a politics based on a sexual identity.[33]

Neither D'Emilio nor Greenberg and Bystryn discuss the social consequences of the unprecedented feminization of labor brought on by large-scale machinery in the textile industry during the nineteenth century. We know from subsequent historical work, largely conducted by feminist historians, that the rise and fall of fortunes in the textile industries directly impacted the lives and sexualities of the many women who worked within them.[34] Politicized by numerous late Victorian factory and housing inspectors, and famously by August Bebel's *Woman under Socialism* (1878), casual and occasional prostitution was often the only option for women living in garment districts when factories closed or laid off workers.[35] Just as the flexible accumulation model of our own period has relativized sexual morality, so the birth of industrial capitalism and the adoption of machinofacture

CHAPTER FIVE

abolished and reconstituted agrarian families and urban working-class families, leading to the irregularities of work, housing, and sexuality that had profound effects on the lives of people living through such transformations.

D'Emilio's argument and Jonathan Ned Katz's well-known thesis in "The Invention of Homosexuality," first published by the *Socialist Review* in 1990, were cited in the U.S. Supreme Court's majority opinion in the 2003 decision to overturn state sodomy laws in *Lawrence v. Texas*. According to Katz's argument, the term "heterosexual" is a late nineteenth-century invention, appearing after that of the term "homosexual"; the psychological and social experience marked by the term "heterosexuality" could only appear as problematic or historical in a world in which homosexuality is posed as problematic or historical. Katz's thesis, however politically useful to legal argumentation, merely begs the question: how was homosexuality invented if not from some stable unmarked category of normal heterosexual family life? How did it appear distinct to people who had no such conception? Homosexuality could only appear as problematic against the backdrop of a historical consolidation and normalization of working-class families, implying that the prior "invention" of some quasi-universal heterosexuality was the necessary precondition for a perception of homosexuality as abnormal. It cannot be the case that this distinction was invented out of whole cloth by sexual science. These dilemmas begin to indicate the limitations of a nominalist approach.

Neither Katz, nor D'Emilio, nor Greenberg and Bystryn consider how industry, industrial working conditions, pollution, toxicity, disease, sanitation, and crowded urban housing conditions destroyed workers' bodies and contributed to a net drain on human populations in Britain and continental Europe during the nineteenth century.[36] Surely these factors had something to do with the possibilities of the experience of a sexually "free" body among the working classes of industrialized Europe. Neither D'Emilio nor Greenberg considers the special case of the United States, whose frontier geography during the course of the nineteenth century supported a striking diversity of lifeworlds. A consideration of forms of life outside the strictures of middle-class morality within North America, South America, and Australia's various resource frontiers—ranching, sailing, fur trades, mining, logging, and other resource extraction—opens up a perspective on the sexuality and sexual mores produced by itinerant labor more generally.[37]

Such omissions and blind spots in the only systematic attempts to provide a synthetic account of the concern for homosexuality in capitalist societies are largely due to these historians' adoption of an ideal-typical analysis that is anathema to more complex models of development. Greenberg's thesis is clearly indebted to the perspectives of Adam Smith and Max Weber, in which a Protestant ethic of self-restraint, the competitive division of labor, and the institutions of marriage and medicine play crucial roles in the "stigmatization" of male homosexuality. This thesis cannot account for the ways in which capitalism destroyed and reconstituted the family structure of working classes, and its emphasis on a (modern) universal stigma attached to homosexuality is historically unfounded.

D'Emilio is closer to the mark in considering the crucial role played by the transition away from a mode of production centered around the family sometime around the middle of the nineteenth century, during the intensive phase of the first Industrial Revolution, and he is correct in his emphasis on the Second World War as the moment of a major transformation of sexuality throughout the societies affected by the war. He seems to assume that family-centered production prevented any sort of nonprocreative sexuality. It is also hard to square his portrait of the households of workers of the mid-nineteenth century—as happy, intimate centers of pleasure—with the reports of housing and factory inspectors in London from the same period.[38] Perhaps many of the reports emphasizing the sexual irregularities of the working classes were exaggerated, but it is far from certain that middle-class sexual morality was at all widely held by the poor and working classes of nineteenth-century Europe.

The above accounts by social constructivist historians were immensely productive despite certain limitations and omissions. They are the most widely cited accounts of the link between homosexuality and capitalism. The social constructivist formation has been criticized for proposing models that, despite their seemingly radical potential, fall victim to a certain antinomy, endemic to liberal social thought, between individual voluntarism and social determinism.[39] Within this liberal vacillation there is a tendency, on the one hand, to push for some more expansive, multi-axial explanatory framework through an additive logic; and, on the other, a tendency to push for a framework that leaves more room for subjective agency, one in which people are less the puppets of mechanically conceived social forces and more the complex intersection of forces and desires that they are presumed to be. "While [constructionism] asserts that people are social products," Steven Epstein writes, "it has no way of explaining how it is that social meanings come to resonate with the core of who people are."[40] Hence the deep rift between an intellectual formation lacking concrete political strategies and a popular movement for gay rights affirming the very sexual binary that is, according to social constructivists, the source of its oppression.

Although the initial wave of new social histories tended to project a historically specific concept of homosexuality as a persecuted minority over a vast expanse of historical time, the formation demonstrated the historicity of sexual mores, filled in crucial gaps in our knowledge of past sexual cultures, and indicated even wider chasms of unanswered, perhaps unanswerable, questions pertaining to subaltern sexualities. By emphasizing a distinction between sexual acts and sexual identities as the historical threshold for modern homosexuality, the social constructivist formation tended to downplay the significance of forms of homosexuality less compatible with a postwar gay identity.[41] The distinction, however, turns out to have been politically crucial to historical arguments in favor of gay rights, for it refuted the commonplace assumption that antihomosexual sentiments were some timeless prejudice of Western societies. The claim that a highly politicized gay and lesbian group identity, similar to an ethnicity, formed in response to completely unprecedented forces of repression in the middle of the twentieth century successfully troubled commonsense arguments about the incompatibility of homosexuality and American values by demonstrating the historicity of that very perspective. But if it was good at historicizing homophobia, the formation was less adept at historicizing homosexuality, which would have required accounting for how its own concept of gay identity and its peculiar desire for a history of prejudice were themselves outcomes of a historical struggle by middle-class gay people over the essential definition and understanding of sexuality. Historical knowledge was not only key to a sense of group belonging; it also conveyed legitimacy upon a political formation struggling for recognition.

The Homosexual Desire for History

Bolder propositions have tended to be advanced at the margins of gay history, buried in endnotes or writing not published in the historian's lifetime. To wit: "The assumption that there is such a thing as 'homosexual history' or a 'history of same-sex intimacy' should be carefully examined," one gay historian reflected in unpublished notes from around 1978. "The assumption that time and change are essential aspects of 'intimate same-sex' or 'homosexual' relationships, and the empirical research work designed to demonstrate this historicity, are themselves historical, part of a basic, present, ongoing reconceptualization of 'homosexuality' and 'same-sex intimacy' being undertaken by and initiated under the pressure of politically organized 'homosexuals' and feminist women."[42]

Another historian of some renown humorously wrote under a borrowed name that the politicization of homosexuality in France and the United States had taken the form of an Anglo-Saxon religious revival: "According to the logic inherent to every dissident religious movement, it was necessary to establish good relations with the authorities in order to be able to practice the cult. But it was equally necessary to receive the tolerance of society. Hence, the undeterred will—and very antitheses of the actual movement—to gain tolerance for homosexuality from families. Consequently, it would perhaps be naive to reproach it for conservatism: seeing as it's in the very nature of such a movement to desire tolerance for homosexuality from the powers that be and entry into the establishment."[43] Just as a political formation exerted pressure over intellectuals to give homosexuality a history, generating particular kinds of identifications with the past, so the historian's circumspection about playing consort to that political project was confined to the margins of his intellectual activity for political reasons.

Perhaps now that the urgency of this project has begun to ease up and the pressure has broken apart, we may finally subject this homosexual desire for history to criticism. The notes are those of Jonathan Ned Katz, whose monographs and essays on the history of homosexuality were, along with those of Jeffrey Weeks, George Chauncey, John D'Emilio, Allan Bérubé, and others, groundbreaking for the sheer volume of historical materials they unearthed, the sophistication of analysis, and the political importance of their respective projects. For all their originality, these projects were all indebted, in one way or another, to Foucault. He made it possible to pose new questions and lent sexuality the intellectual halo of French philosophy's *trente glorieuses*. Whereas queer theory largely followed Guy Hocquenghem in developing a philosophy and ethics of nonnormative desires and antihomophobia,[44] gay history eschewed Hocquenghem's ethical-political concerns (with notable exceptions) or entertained them with the agnosticism peculiar to their discipline. In neither intellectual formation was the homosexual desire for history itself historicized. These forays nonetheless generated a rich field of scholarship that makes a new historical-theoretical synthesis possible.

If George Chauncey's work shattered the myth of the closet by historicizing postwar gay identity and uncovering a rich "gay world" in early twentieth-century New York, his work and that of the wider formation seemed to confirm the existence of a closet of another sort.[45] The closet stands, in other words, as a spatial metaphor for bourgeois sexual epistemology itself, marking the representational limitations of a literary archive or reading practice—"novel gazing," as Sedgwick's pun would have it. Working-class homosexuals existed outside family structures that organically transmitted traditions and memories from one generation to another, either via oral tradition or via historical and literary discourses that constructed a national, historical identity. The oblivion faced by working-class homosexuals was an oblivion of historical memory; by contrast, their elite counterparts left behind a labyrinthine wardrobe of tortured interiority, self-involvement, and coded references in which subsequent generations of queer readers have wandered. That elite literary archive achieved hegemony within the imagined community of homosexuals precisely at its moment of intensive politicization in the 1960s and 1970s.

But this is not merely a matter of the metaphorics. As the AIDS epidemic took its enormous toll in the 1980s and 1990s, some of the papers, belongings, and memories of the dead were snapped up and preserved in archives—but most were lost irretrievably. Extraordinary lives exhumed from boxes buried deep in closets and storage spaces—such as the life story of tattoo artist and *salonière* Samuel Seward—stand out as visible remnants of an immense, deeply submerged mass of life stories that have sunk into gloomy historical oblivion.[46] Rather than preserving and presenting disinterested, scientific snapshots of the homosexual past for all eternity, these stories relate a particular subjective experience of that homosexual past in its moment of danger. Just as the continued existence of homosexual culture seemed threatened, its historical memory threatened to, once again, become "hidden from history" beneath the wreckage churned up in the gay plague's wake. Homosexual historical consciousness exploded like a flash, assembling together and connecting up a diverse constellation of places, times, and practices hitherto foreign to historical reflection, strengthening the conviction that homosexual history was not only vital to current political struggles and senses of self but was at risk of sinking into further oblivion.

Despite strong commitments to a historical nominalism, the intellectual formation wound up producing a remarkable and completely unprecedented social history of homosexual cultures whose very principle of unity and historical intelligibility was collective sexual behaviors and highly socialized sexual encounters between men, rather than some shared sense of psychological interiority or sexual identity marked with a particular term. Deaths from AIDS did not only lend these histories a political impetus and an urgency; death made socially explicit the material basis of male homosexuality in a shared set of sexual behaviors, comportments, and milieus. Whatever cultural continuities could be established between epochs were less the result of some organic reproduction of memory and tradition from one generation to the next, less the product of some stable consumer identity mediated by markets or print culture, than the consequence of codes, behaviors, and affects transmitted from body to body within a population, much like the virus itself.

A shared grammar of sexual possibility and availability produced by practices of cruising public spaces gave these particular codes their continuity or legibility across time and place. Homosexuality was reconceptualized as an active, counterhegemonic appropriation of urban space generating unique forms of sociality and culture centered around stranger intimacy. The very behaviors, structures of feeling, and types of recognition through which a homosexual culture was shared and shaped, and around which its sense of belonging congealed, had become vectors for HIV infection. Perversely, then, the cultural identification of homosexuality with the virus generated a new form of homosexual self-consciousness in retrospect: AIDS not only catalyzed a new kind of gay historical consciousness; it seemed to manifest the very semiotic structuring of subjectivity posited by poststructuralist thought.[47]

The above reflections situate the production of homosexual history from the 1980s and 1990s within a conjunctural crisis in which a new kind of historical reflection became possible. Of course, other preconditions were necessary: among other things, professional legitimacy for such questions, institutional support for the research, and the groundwork already laid by feminism and women's history. Nevertheless, a non-identitarian understanding of sexual activity was central both to public health interventions into the HIV/AIDS epidemic and to reconstructions of past sexual communities of men by the new social history. This mutually constitutive relationship, between new kinds of historical reflection and the political subjectivity and social visibility of men who have sex with men—"MSMS" in the bureaucratese of epidemiology and public health authorities—had important precedents in the nineteenth century. Biological, economic, and political crises have played determinant roles in shaping and reshaping the sexual categories of previous intellectual formations (with greater or lesser hegemonic influence) for state bureaucracies' responses to the "problem" of homosexuality.

6

The crises of libertinism have been many: every historical epoch has one. In order to achieve a new adaptation to the new mode of work, pressure is exerted over the whole social sphere, a puritan ideology develops which gives to the intrinsic brutal coercion the external form of persuasion and consent. Once the result has been to some extent achieved, the pressure breaks up . . . and is followed by the crisis of libertinism.—ANTONIO GRAMSCI, *Prison Notebooks*

HOMOSEXUALITY AS A CATEGORY OF BOURGEOIS SOCIETY

Industrialization and the Bourgeois Dominant

Two problems raised by the introduction require further elucidation with regard to the twentieth century's anomalous persecution and politicization of homosexuality. Posing these problems in their complexity provides a way of preliminarily concluding questions of methodology and historiography broached by the preceding chapter and the introduction. First, how did an apparently morally retrograde nation like the United States, whose history has been punctuated by periodic religious revivals of puritan ideology, generate homosexual forms of life and freedom with broad international appeal? Second, to what extent has a normative dissolution of the social and economic orders of postwar capitalism laid the groundwork for a more permissive sexual morality and the achievement of gay rights? In both instances, a comparison with the sexual transformations of the interwar period proves illuminating.

As hegemony is a notoriously slippery concept, it is important to specify what is at stake in these two problems. By the time of the Second World War, the social conditions for both a gay identity and the persecution of homosexuality in cities were shared by all of the major combatants, which had each achieved similar levels of economic and bureaucratic development. To ask how the American gay formation achieved cultural hegemony within this international sphere of influence is to determine whether a singularly American conception of sexual expression and liberation—a struggle over the publicness, public display, and social legitimacy of sexual perversions— came to define the essential coordinates of sexual identity for other national and cultural contexts. This pedagogical function of the American gay formation generated an international political movement with unified goals and expectations for certain rights and forms of state recognition.

In large American cities, the Christian Temperance movement and the first flowering of the "gay world," as we now know it, more or less coexisted. In fact, the YMCA was a crucial nodal point both for networks of homosexual activity and for the spread of Christian values throughout these cities in the early twentieth century.[1] How did a morally conservative Christian organization carve out a place for homosexuality in America's cities? One could similarly ask of the late twentieth century whether the apparently conservative fundamentalist Christian revival and the radical counterculture of free love weren't perhaps two faces of the same spiritual awakening, each intensifying the discursive status of sex by endowing it with profoundly transformative powers. In either case, how did moral or religious beliefs and sentiments respond to the conditions of possibility of a particular conjuncture, and what political effects did they have? How to tell the difference between the transitory phenomena of moral panic or sex fashion and the deep structural transformations of a given society? What is at stake in the difference between the two?

From a comparative perspective, the apparent contradiction between the Christian ideology of the YMCA and its tendency to foster intimate friendships and erotic attachments between men is no contradiction at all. From the late nineteenth century through the First World War, homoerotic sociality arose wherever young men were removed from their families and concentrated in more or less hierarchical same-sex milieus. This tendency was in keeping with a general propensity of early twentieth-century youth movements—movements essential to a variety of national and political formations, from nationalist projects to Zionist, socialist, communist, and Fascist projects—to foster erotic friendship and attachments between boys and youths in sex-segregated milieus.[2]

The archconservative anti-Semite Hans Blüher, an early German champion of Freud's theories, caused a scandal in 1910 when the second volume of his study of the Wandervogel analyzed the German youth movement as an erotic phenomenon, emphasizing the virtues of erotic associations between boys and men, or *Männerbund*. Blüher contrasted these positive, creative free associations of men with the family, which he considered to be a socially destructive force.[3] As the German youth movement was primarily a bourgeois affair, one understood as crucial to the molding of a future ruling class, Blüher's book forced the question of homosexuality upon a national formation that had become sensitive to the issue following the Eulenburg affair. The scandal around Blüher's study of the Wandervogel made youths and youth leaders conscious of the erotic nature of male friendship in new ways. Only a few years prior, the journalist Maximilian Harden had accused several prominent members of Kaiser Wilhelm II's cabinet of homosexual relations, an event that precipitated more accusations, libel suits, and counteraccusations. The Eulenburg affair was, according to some historians, directly responsible for the declining influence of moderate voices in the Kaiser's foreign policy circle and—following the embarrassing death of a certain chief of the military cabinet, Dietrich von Hülsen-Haeseler, who suffered a heart attack while dancing for the Kaiser in a tutu at a hunting retreat in November 1908—the increasing calls for a more bellicose German national manhood.[4] From the most innocent youth organizations to the heights of the German imperium, homosexuality signaled a crisis of the liberal (male) ego. In elite English boarding schools, a remarkably similar cult of homosexuality formed, shaping the experiences of ruling-class men who went on to hold prominent positions in the imperial bureaucracy and suffer like embarrassments.[5]

The massive mobilization of elite and popular youth throughout the industrialized world sexualized youth culture in new ways—not as the expression, according to some hydraulic Freudian theory of the drives, of a timeless, underlying erotic urge, but by intensifying intimate bonds outside the family and mobilizing these attachments in the various political projects that shaped the twentieth century. Youth sexuality became socially visible to state and national interests in a new way due to its institutional concentration and organization. Broadly speaking, nationalist mobilizations of youth culture at once created new possibilities for same-sex intimacy and erotic attachments and at the same time generated new epistemological frameworks through which it would be understood as a threat to national projects. In the ideological ferment bubbling up from the political and economic crises that brought an end to British hegemony, homosexuality figured as a symptom of political decline and sapped national vitality within discourses of degeneration and the various moral purity campaigns that targeted vice.

Gramsci understood America's moral campaigns against alcohol, prostitution, and gambling as the necessary complement of new techniques of production requiring greater concentration and skill. A moral ideology of restraint lent the coercive process of forced adaptation to a new labor process the outward form of consent and persuasion. This combination of Taylorism and "puritanism" was, according to Gramsci, "the biggest collective effort [ever made] to create, with unprecedented speed and a consciousness of purpose unique in history, a new type of worker and man."[6] It is worth considering, for a moment, why "man" was the target of this great collective effort and why organizations such as the YMCA sought to diminish the bad influences of cities by encouraging athletics and providing dormitory facilities for young men. These were not merely charitable enterprises.

As women entered the workforce in greater numbers during the Great War and afterward, taking on work that had been previously performed by men, the problem of reining in socially irresponsible male behaviors appeared in starker relief. Women, rather than religious ideologues, lent prohibition its moral and political force, as they endured the consequences of male excess and proved themselves to be a highly capable, reliable workforce during the war; women's entry en masse into the workforce demonstrated to industrialists the gains in productivity to be had from a sober, disciplined workforce. They mobilized this power to reshape society by seeking to improve the conditions of the working classes. In addition to the central issues of combating alcohol and tobacco use, the Woman's Christian Temperance movement advocated for penal reform, an eight-hour workday, and higher wages.[7] The pressure to form stable family units and to curb male excesses was also exerted through the labor market, where increasingly rationalized and detail-oriented labor practices required greater focus and precision. These jobs commanded higher wages, which risked enabling irresponsible male consumption but incentivized temperance with a breadwinner's wage.

The Great War had demonstrated the dangers of male sexual excesses to the health of the nation; physicians across Germany and France reported increasing rates of gonorrhea and chlamydia, diseases spread via brothels at train supply depots along men's routes home from the front. Cases among provincial women from geographically remote areas were on the rise, and physicians became increasingly concerned—after such great losses of human life in the trenches—about venereal disease's degenerative effects on their nations' reproductive capacities.[8] In the United States, then–Secretary of the Navy Franklin D. Roosevelt uncovered a network of homosexual activity after a sweep of the brothels at the naval base in Newport, Rhode Island.[9] In September 1913, the California newspaper magnate William Randolph Hearst led a front-page campaign in the *San Francisco Examiner* against San Francisco's infamous Barbary Coast district and its brothels.[10] Prostitution and homosexuality, both products of the socially disruptive mobilization for war, figured as central threats to the bourgeois project of ensuring national vitality for work and war. These were not merely moral considerations, as STIs were among the primary causes of soldiers' medical leave; most other battlefield injuries were fatal. The rate of transmission for venereal disease peaked in the British armed forces in 1895 at 52.2 percent for those stationed in India and 21.2 percent for those stationed at home or in Europe. The Contagious Diseases Act of 1864 had failed to reduce incidence rates, which were eventually brought under control by boosting the morale of troops with recreation facilities, drills, and other distractions.[11] The sheer social scale of the mobilization for two global wars unleashed these scourges on populations at levels unmatched since the Napoleonic wars—although figures for this earlier period are largely anecdotal. Where market pressures and moralizing failed, the state and extrajuridical forces stepped in with force to curb male excess, shuttering brothels, razing whole urban districts catering to certain popular forms of leisure, and increasing the regulation and surveillance of women.

The necessity of rationalizing the production process demanded a normalization of family life following the upheavals of the First World War. Concerns for workers' welfare were indistinguishable from attempts to create a disciplined labor force for new lines of production that promised to be immensely more profitable and efficient. The family provided a powerful regulatory instrument for reproducing a reliable, regimented laboring population. It was, as Gramsci writes, "in the industrialists' interest to put together a stable, skilled workforce, a permanently attuned industrial ensemble, because the human ensemble is also a machine that cannot be dismantled too often and renewed cog by cog without serious losses."[12] Hence, what might appear—to, say, a liberal or libertarian perspective—as America's moral backwardness vis-à-vis Europe's sexual open-mindedness and tolerance during the interwar period is nothing other than a transformation of the productive process requiring a reciprocal transformation of the worker's sexuality and appetites, for "excitement of the passions does not go with the timed movement of machines of productive human motions."[13]

Labor historians with access to archives have corroborated Gramsci's speculations from the confines of his prison cell. Ford's "Five-Dollar Day" program was initially proposed to counteract the high turnover of labor in Ford's factories. Difficulties with the complicated production process initially posed enormous obstacles to securing a regular working force. The use of foremen to harass workers in an attempt to extract more surplus value from their bodies proved anathema to the more demanding labor process and the expectations of workers. Only the promotion of stable family life and a rising standard of living could transform the ethnic immigrants of Detroit into proper "Ford men."[14] Thus Ford's Department of Sociology was created to investigate the living arrangements of workers' homes, noting the presence of renters; bachelors were excluded from the profit-sharing scheme; bank accounts were checked for regular deposits; workers' wives were advised on proper housekeeping and hygiene, and children's attendance at school was monitored. Ford factories innovated a disciplinary regime targeting areas of housing and family life that had historically been sources of trouble and irregularities for labor power. What had previously been a matter of indifference to the concrete production process came increasingly to matter over the course of the twentieth century, as the complexity and capitalization of the labor process increased apace and as these rational and technological advances were adopted across many lines of production.

In short, human sexuality is not only malleable and historical; indeed, at certain points in history, such transformations of human nature were central to the forces of production and to certain objectives of statecraft. The problem of sexual hegemony is both a question of establishing whether same-sex attraction, solidarity, and erotic attachments as such presented particular relations of force with an antagonism that required neutralization; and a question of what relations of force in a particular conjuncture enabled the repression of same-sex attraction, solidarity, and erotic attachments or, conversely, allowed them to exist unperturbed. These considerations have less to do with instances of "phobia" or "panic," taken without regard to political and institutional context, and more to do with uneven processes of development in which dominant groups, who viewed sexual regulation and repression as in their own best interests, intervened in these relations of force to effect such transformations. In the case of Ford's para-

digmatic sociology department, the forced adaptation to a more demanding labor process and to normative family life was coupled with material
rewards guaranteeing workers' consent.

The promotion of regular family units as the basis for predictable patterns of production and consumption was essential to the establishment of
this distinctly American form of bourgeois hegemony in the period following World War II. The investment of capital into a highly disciplined and
rationalized laboring body normalized the reproduction of labor power
within family units, allowing for the adoption of technologies that made
the production process far more efficient. A transformation of man formed
the material basis of a new global cycle of capital accumulation. Today, the
present ongoing decomposition of this nexus tying capital to labor, the defeat of antisystemic struggles, and the structural transition to an uncertain
new order of the world system all allow for a consideration of the dynamics
of partial liberation that have generated both promising counterhegemonic
tendencies and dreary forces of reaction.

Morbid Forms of Normative Dissolution

Gays and lesbians got a shot at dreams of the good life precisely at the moment of its political-economic liquidation. The disintegration of the normal
was a crucial condition of possibility for the gay and lesbian rights movement's struggle for recognition and for gains in formal equality. Before the
oil price shocks and recession of the mid-1970s, Dennis Altman's classic
tract *Homosexual: Oppression and Liberation* (1971) argued that gay liberation emerged in the United States due to particular social and technological
preconditions and then spread to other countries with a similar sociopolitical basis. In the United States, the increasing militancy of black and other
nonwhite populations, in addition to the youth opposition to the Vietnam
War, exploded into a mass countercultural opposition to the status quo
eroding the shared cultural assumptions on which an elite hegemony had
been based. Altman writes,

> Over the last ten years, the cultural hegemony dominating America
> has begun to erode as different segments of the population have come
> to see that America has been exclusively defined according to the
> needs and desires of ruling elite, white, middle-aged male heterosexu-
> als. In turn, blacks, the young, women, and homosexuals have chal-
> lenged this hegemony and as a result America is more fragmented,

more divided, and yet freer than ever before in its history. The cultural hegemony of the elite has begun to collapse, and out of this dissolution of the American identity emerge both some of its most hopeful characteristics and a growing degree of violence and repression.[15]

Reflecting upon Hannah Arendt's essay *On Violence*, Altman concludes, "It is when authority, based on common cultural assumptions, begins to crumble that authorities need to resort even more to force and repression."[16] As this dissolution of the normal within postmodernity and its socioeconomic causes were, to varying degrees, shared by nations with similar social and technological levels of development, so the gains of this counterhegemonic movement have been global, an index of the hegemony of American culture.

The achievement of homosexual rights in such places resulted as much from a depoliticization of sex, one contingent upon a dedifferentiation of vertical class structures, as from a successful politicization of homosexuality. A contingent repoliticization of homosexuality during the first two decades of the AIDS crisis obscured this structural transformation in ways that caught even the most radical political activists off guard. A much wider-ranging collapse of the hegemony of the normal enabled a dramatic cultural redefinition of marriage and sexuality in the space of a few decades, despite substantial moral backlash.

It is fascinating the degree to which intellectuals are willing to attribute such sweeping transformative ideological powers to television shows—such as *Will and Grace* or *Queer Eye for the Straight Guy*—as "groundbreaking" moments of "cultural visibility," without any evidence that such shows demythologized homosexuality or generated more tolerant views. By comparison, the mass distribution of videos depicting hardcore gay anal sex receives short shrift or no mention at all alongside these saccharine cultural confections, which, after all, never depict the thing itself.[17] A similar argument could be made about the cult of homosexuality in the English novel, which some have taken to be emblematic of a wider epistemological formation. The key would be to demonstrate how such forms of cultural visibility could have the power to transform affective responses to homosexuality, whose affective response they transformed, and how they could do it on such a scale; empirical analyses of distribution, a strong claim regarding whether and how culture mirrors social developments or propels them forward, and a material history of censorship and its effects would all be necessary for such an argument. Even a rigorous, historically informed analysis, accounting for how homosexuality has been made culturally explicit and for the changing styles of this exposition, would have to take into account the structural transformations that have made political breakthroughs possible.

The waning of sexual affect—the vanishing sensorium of titillation, shock, and intolerance toward differences of sexual taste—is by no means limited to the American experience; it is not simply a matter of what is called "cultural visibility." This waning of sexual affect is a distinctive feature of postmodernity, whatever causes one wishes to attribute it to: the ubiquity of hardcore pornography, the end of high bourgeois culture, digital cultures of over-sharing, the decline of the nuclear family, the dedifferentiation of public and private, and so on. The disappearance of shock and titillation at previously subversive or deviant sex acts and perversions has less to do with cultural representations of "queeny" behavior on television and a lot more to do with the historically unprecedented availability of pornography, the intensity of youth sexual hook-up cultures, the increasing feminization of culture, the prolongation of sexuality into old age with hormone therapies and erectile dysfunction pharmaceuticals, and the ways in which cybernetic technology is replacing the family in transmitting sexual norms and information to younger generations. Familiar countercultural psychedelics and newer designer drugs, heightening states of empathy and bliss, have helped shatter the old bourgeois ego of yesteryear and facilitated new kinds of attunement to an unpredictable emotional landscape. Behaviors that until very recently indicated an outré perversion or the abjection of sex work—dance moves originating in strip clubs, sharing video and images of oneself naked or having sex—are now so culturally de rigueur that American children are participating with their personal cell phones, and this is all precipitating a large-scale handwringing and discomfort about adolescent pornography. At every level of society, older sexual norms and expectations are being liquidated. As Andrew Sullivan put it: "There can, in fact, be no queer without the hegemony of the normal."[18] This sharp formulation cuts both ways.

While Sullivan thought that the alignment of queer politics with a struggle for recognition and acceptance implied the self-abolition of queer politics through its subsumption into the normal, he failed to imagine a world in which the reverse process also occurred in tandem. Intellectuals and activists initially reappropriated the "queer" epithet, in true ethnographic fashion, to designate the forms of sex radicalism and emotional attachments they thought were threatened with extinction. The word and standpoint have now been adopted by many people with any claim whatsoever to outsider status (a status not limited to sexuality). Popular culture's new avatars of queerness have universalized the classically homosexual narrative of coming out of the closet, as well as its demand for recognition and the acceptance of the legitimacy of a spectrum of variegated differences.[19] The projection of the normal into an ever more nebulous and free-floating vision of "normativity" and the expanded currency of the concepts of the "queer" and the "closet" are themselves antinomies produced by a collapsing hegemony of the normal. Although this ongoing crisis of modern sexual categories may initially have produced a utopian sense that societies were moving beyond rigid binary systems, such celebrations of intransitivity have missed the ways in which gender and sexual flexibility have also been forced upon subjects as a consequence of precarity. The intellectual valorization of fluidity has also, crucially, missed the historical ways in which "fixed" sexual binaries provided the gay and lesbian political movement with its terrain of struggle. The structural preconditions for the end of sexual normalcy and the underlying breakthroughs in the politics of homosexuality require further elucidation.

In his essay on Fredric Jameson's theoretical account of postmodernism, Perry Anderson has written about a dedifferentiation of the social order caused by the flattening of moral and cultural differences between classes—the end, in other words, of bourgeois moral hegemony. He writes that "the cultural and psychological markers of position have become steadily more eroded among those who enjoy wealth or power."[20] This dedifferentiation of the social order accounts for the effectiveness of neoliberal political appeals to "threatened middle classes," which appeals found their purchase in the disintegration of lives and life prospects following deindustrialization, successive asset bubbles and collapses, cuts to the public sector, and the spread of new forms of precarity that together mark the era following the economic crisis of the 1970s.[21] Late capitalism has undermined the sociopolitical basis for a sexual hegemony of the normal by replacing the economic foundations of the postwar order with speculative, debt-financed consumption patterns. Easy credit has replaced stable jobs and wages as the foundation of household economy. As Anderson writes, "No stable class structure, comparable to that of an earlier capitalism, has yet crystallized. Those above have the coherence of privilege; those below lack unity and solidarity. A new 'collective laborer' has yet to emerge. These are the conditions, still, of a certain vertical indefinition."[22]

Differences of morality and of sexual norms were once the way that a vertical social order of classes asserted itself, the way classes became conscious of themselves in marriage alliances, property inheritances, and their position in relation to urban police, sanitation, and public health work. A postmodern relativization of sexual morals in high-income countries and the growth of peripheral urban slums in low-income countries signal this vanishing mediator of a vertical class structure. Gross forms of wealth inequality are now distributed horizontally within an urbanized global space, massifying poverty, disease, and existential precarity on scales never witnessed in the modern period, as the last remnants of subsistence agriculture have been eliminated and human populations have piled into irregular forms of urban sprawl.[23] Within this unevenly developed, increasingly urban world space, the liberal sexual ethics of high-income societies—that homosexuals and gender nonconforming individuals be tolerated, that sex be consensual, that youth and children are off-limits, and that sex traffic remains socially invisible—have become the basis for the interventions of a global civil society of NGOs analogous to the charitable organizations of the high Victorian period in Britain. Whereas such phenomena led Victorian reformers to criticize the social relations of capitalism and to view such problems as consequences of a ruthless drive of capital toward extracting ever greater profit, this connection is less apparent to the Ladies Bountiful tending to the new global poor, who have been relegated to the hell of various informal kinds of subsistence and hustle. Lacking any strong social antagonism, neoliberalism has frequently resorted to a combination of shock journalism and law-and-order politics in which police, austerity, and microfinance are the universal solutions to problems of exploitation, sexual or otherwise. The disinhibition of sexual mores indeed reflects this postbourgeois urban dominant, an explosion of popular tabloid forms in which sexual scandal and humiliation have the power to invert an older order of social hierarchy by exalting the low and bringing down the high.[24]

Lauren Berlant describes this present conjuncture as a process of "normative dissolution" in which fantasies of the good life that once bound people to promises of "upward mobility, job security, political and social equality, and lively, durable intimacy" become irreparably damaged.[25] She writes that increasing social, economic, and environmental precarity have transformed "conventions of racial, gendered, sexual, economic, and nation-based subordination" and have "increased the probability that structural contingency will create manifest crisis situations in ordinary existence for more kinds of people."[26] Berlant's *Cruel Optimism* weaves a painful tapestry of fraying norms and expectations that once governed a more prosperous postwar life—expectations of meritocracy, durable intimacy, and health—and the various strategies adopted by those treading water amid these structural contingencies. Berlant's attention to the cultural artifacts of this dissolution of the normal intimates a deep transformation of the sociopolitical structure, a waning of bourgeois hegemony over people's most intimate self-understandings.

As these critical assessments of the present suggest, the ongoing crisis of a bourgeois dominant sustains aspirational fantasies of middle-class life within a morbid cultural-political form, in which the demand for a return to normalcy or the preservation of the present order seem like radical strategies amid widespread structural socioeconomic fallout. This thesis about late capitalist culture was formulated, however, prior to political developments that may have opened up a political horizon beyond the deadlocks identified above. Although they were not exactly antisystemic in the sense that anti-imperialist and socialist movements once claimed to be, the movement of squares from the Arab Spring to the Occupy movement has militantly politicized this downward mobility and normative dissolution. Mike Davis makes the connection between downward mobility and the strange socioeconomic composition of Occupy, which included traditional labor organizers, anarchists, hippies, the homeless, and others.[27] The collapse of trust in traditional political elites and institutions and a counterhegemonic affective habitus—or, as Paul Mason describes it, "the inability to go on living the pre-crisis lifestyle"—have yet to assume any enduring form beyond these massive mobilizations.[28] However, the structural causes and grievances of that conjunctural politicization of a global condition of social and economic disenfranchisement persist, and it is difficult to predict how future mobilizations in one part of the world will, once again, find resonances in others. In any case, the flare-up of new movements of this sort suggests possibilities beyond the morbid forms of slow death or the demands for a return to normal.

Based on such assessments of the present conjuncture, it's possible to pose the following historical question: To what extent are politicizations and neutralizations of homosexuality contingent or structural features of periods of crisis in the historical hegemonies of the capitalist world system? Does a pattern emerge from a comparative consideration of the successive politicizations of homosexuality by the northern Italian city-states, the patricians of the Dutch Republic, the revolutionary-era French and English bourgeoisie, and, finally, the American world system? How might our senses of the way in which sexuality becomes politicized and neutralized be sharpened by such a comparative sociohistorical approach?

To put it schematically: alternate or queer sexualities—primarily homosexuality, intransitive gender identifications, prostitution, and other kinds of sex work—historically emerged along the fault lines of transformed property relations in a process of combined and uneven development. This development involved the displacement from the countryside of populations superfluous to agrarian production, the concentration of those populations in urban centers and in institutions attempting to manage or capture this surplus within either a productive apparatus for valorizing capital or state apparatuses for managing the social fallout of economic development; and these sexualities figured as problematic to a bourgeois moral separation of private acts from public spaces. Irregular work and housing conditions led to irregular patterns of sex and intimacy, casual prostitution, illegitimate births, and casual sex between men.[29] The geographical and historical role of parts of Australia and North and South America as resource frontiers generated anomalous settlement patterns, attracting predominantly male laborers to seasonal, casual, and otherwise precarious forms of employment. The sexuality of settler colonies was often irregular, and honor, rather than a homo/hetero binary, played a regulative role in policing the boundaries of legitimate intimacy between men.[30]

Just as the development of the capitalism was, according to the formulation of world-systems theory, a combined and uneven process, so too were its cultural forms. What too often remains to be accounted for historically is how and why a bourgeois understanding of male homosexuality, as a source of embarrassment, shame, and identity, made forays into these other milieus (especially that of the working class) and, finally, how it gained dominance over a casual, perhaps "non-identitarian" attitude toward sex-sex practices and behaviors. It is my contention that the gay intellectual formation's pendulum has, for various reasons I consider below, swung too far in the direction of downplaying the role of class in the history of sexuality. The principal reason is that historical discourse has played a key role in authorizing gays' and lesbians' bid for respectability—and so downplaying the roles of unsavory working-class, nonwhite, and queer cultures within that history became crucial to a particular kind of struggle for recognition. History and historical discourse provided alibis for the project of envisioning an imagined community compatible with the liberal value of public respect for private lives.

An Imagined Community of Homosexuality

The breakup of bourgeois sexual hegemony implies a foreclosure of certain emancipatory horizons of self-transformation once connected with homosexuality. Although this dissolution initially released immensely creative countercultural energies in the 1960s and 1970s, these radical potentials have been worn out by a neoliberal multicultural politics of recognition, preserving the hegemony of this formation through force and constraint as consent has broken down into a kind of rule without leadership. Homosexuality was once beyond the pale of respectability, for it remained morally incompatible with ideals of family, national belonging, and the legitimacy of the couple form. This criminalized outsider status generated critical distance between those institutions and the forms of self-transformation not possible within them. That once-emancipatory horizon diminishes with the concurrent achievement of formal legal equality and a general crisis of social norms and expectations associated with an earlier period of bourgeois culture and the postwar economic boom.

The emancipatory possibility of a "transgressive reinscription" of homosexuality within these institutions—as if gay marriage could begin to exert some subversive force upon the institution, or as if openly gay soldiering could queer the act of killing enemies abroad—seems implausible.[31] Wider social acceptance of homosexuals, formal legal equality, and the imprimatur of legally recognized relationships almost certainly imply the loss of a shared experience of social exclusion and hostility that once created a sense of belonging and solidarity against church, state, and polite society. It seems likely that as sexual object choice becomes increasingly less determinant of life possibilities in high-income countries, it will continue to weaken as a marker of identity, devolving into a set of consumer preferences and choices exercised in a market, access to which is determined by other factors.[32] This development creates a new political function for flexible sexual norms within an increasingly moribund bourgeois cultural hegemony: as principles of group belonging weaken and sexual identities fracture into ever more queer particularities, there is no longer any counterhegemonic position from which to contest this infinitely more permissive establishment. The political ground of sexual contention and countercultural opposition has crumbled beneath our feet.

In the late 1990s, Michael Warner polemically opposed the homosexual politics of respectability, typified by Andrew Sullivan's argument for normalcy, by identifying himself with "queer counterpublics"—a turn of Nancy Fraser's phrase—which he defined as "scenes of criminal intimacy."[33] Historically, these scenes have been "tearooms, streets, sex clubs, and parks," according to Warner, and together fostered "a common language of self-cultivation, shared knowledge and exchange of inwardness."[34] Warner's book *The Trouble with Normal* attempted to demonstrate how the bid for gay marriage and normalcy threatens a thriving queer counterculture by reinscribing this language community within a "heteronormative" cultural dominant. By opting out of the queer culture and into normative forms of intimacy, homosexuals not only assume a kind of false consciousness with respect to their own desires and interests but also risk withdrawing their solidarity from the imagined community of sexual deviants, leaving its queerer members exposed to more intense stigma and hardship. Sexual stigma, Warner argued, perpetuated the dynamics of shame and denial fueling the HIV/AIDS epidemic among gay men.[35]

Although Warner's definition of "queer" is expressly non-identitarian—emphasizing alternative social architectures for intimacy rather than psychological senses of self—his argument still appeals to some vital queer essence that would be existentially at stake in the politics of respectability. By identifying queer belonging as a language community attached to historical cultural forms, structures of feeling, and architectures of interaction, *The Trouble with Normal* appears, at turns, nostalgic for the weakening forms of bourgeois power that formed the counterpart of a resistant queer culture. While various wellsprings of queer counterculture, admittedly, were mercilessly paved over in the long march toward constituting a palatable, media-friendly image for the achievement of gay rights, the zero-sum logic of representational struggles posited by Warner is forced. It isn't clear that the bid of some gay and lesbian people for normalcy must necessarily come at the expense of more subaltern queer cultures, however much this bid represents an attempt to establish distance from these cultures. Warner's accounts of struggles to overcome the stigmatization of HIV/AIDS and of the gentrification and policing of historically gay neighborhoods make some of these concerns more concrete; however, the phenomena in question are not directly attributable to homophobia. Debt-financed real estate speculation, the preponderance of low-wage service sector labor, and a general politics of slow death have produced socioeconomic phenomena and forms of disempowered political subjectivity not limited to what Warner defines as queer culture. As Lauren Berlant writes, "the temporality of the workday, the debt cycle, and consumer practice and fantasy" are crucial to understanding "scandals of appetite—along with food, there's sex, smoking, shopping, and drinking as sites of moral disapprobation, social policy, and self-medication."[36]

Warner's attack on liberalism from the standpoint of "queer counterpublics" is actually driven by a more philosophical concern (indebted to Arendt) that human capacities are endangered by modern forms of private individualism. The politics of marriage, according to this view, abandons a queer *vita activa* of "world making" for a familial model of coupling and national membership.[37] Warner's argument on behalf of these queer communities in the late twentieth century thus appealed to the republican ideals that formed the basis of Hans Blüher's defense of the erotic culture of Wilhelmine *Männerbund* at the start of the century. Whether or not one accepts Warner's terms or the mutual exclusivity of world making and private coupling—it could be convincingly argued that the very cultural practices he cites are formations of queer kinship, or semipublics, rather than the paragons of the active republican life that Arendt and Blüher had in mind—this romantic conception of human subjectivity cannot grasp how homosexuality had already been captured by alienated private individualism, especially during gay liberation.[38] It cannot seriously grapple with the dedifferentiation of public and private that informed both Habermas's and Arendt's assessments of contemporary culture. The capture of homosexuality by alienated private individualism and the blurring of public and private spheres implied by it formed necessary preconditions for a movement politicizing sexuality.[39] The historical establishment and decomposition of the bourgeois public sphere were both crucial developments for the social development of the category of homosexuality.

At its Enlightenment inception, the notion of the individual or private person was advanced by juridical reformers as a limit on state power in the revolutionary struggle of the bourgeoisie against the ancien régime. Liberal thinking thus made private individuals the site, however fictional, of a generic humanity and the seat of natural rights that represented, at least theoretically, universal claims that could be made on the state. An increasing division of labor enabled individuals of certain classes to elaborate a private life that in turn became the basis for the performance of a personality for a wider public sphere.[40] This historical expansion of selfhood in the late eighteenth and early nineteenth centuries, and its displacement of an older form of representative publicness, formed necessary preconditions for the kind of intimacies and institutions associated with normative bourgeois family life *and* those of a homosexual identity.

The enjoyment of time away from work and the free development of the human personality was a privilege resulting from one's position in the division of labor. Bourgeois women were, for this reason, the largest reading publics of the French novel.[41] This subjective freedom for some individuals rested on the exploitation of others in brutal working conditions that kept workers just above abject poverty and prevented the free development of their human potential. Bourgeois male homosexual self-understanding was inseparable from the fear of losing this privileged status in the division of labor. These men subjectivized the incompatibility of their desires with prevailing standards and institutions of respectability. This sometimes led to scandals and unseemly forms of solidarity with criminal classes, or to more socially acceptable concerns for the public welfare of working-class boys (or girls, in the case of female-identified bourgeois women in the settlement house movement).[42]

The defeat of sodomy laws throughout the advanced capitalist world comes as a late liberal development of the idea of the private person as a limitation on state power, one positing sexual activities once considered revolting to bourgeois society as potentially universal and requiring protection against state incursions, one perhaps worthy of the officially sanctioned status of marriage. It is supremely appropriate that utilitarian philosopher Jeremy Bentham gave this liberal demand its birth certificate. "Offenses against One's Self," composed by Bentham around 1785 but never published, poses the paradox of the formal legal recognition of homosexuality nearly two centuries before the debate between Sullivan and Warner:

> The persecution [pederasts] meet with from all quarters, whether deservedly or not, has the effect in this instance which persecution has and must have more or less in all instances, the effect of rendering those persons who are the objects of it more attached than they would otherwise be to the practise it proscribes. It renders them the more attached to one another, sympathy of itself having a powerful tendency, independent of all other motives, to attach a man to his own companions in misfortune. This sympathy has at the same time a powerful tendency to beget a proportional antipathy even towards all such persons as appear to be involuntary, much more to such as appear to be the voluntary, authors of such misfortune. When a man is made to suffer it is enough on all other occasions to beget in him a prejudice against those by whose means or even for whose sake he is made to suffer. When the hand of every man is against a person, his hand, or his heart at least, will naturally be against every man.[43]

The structures of feeling that once attached men with same-sex desires to one another and propelled them toward certain kinds of antipathy for the state and for trappings of bourgeois life were to a large extent products of shared suffering and outlaw status. Homosexual enclaves were established in capital and port cities central to mobilizations for the First World War, and repressive measures increased over the course of the Second World War to rein in this socially visible sexual deviancy. Senses of belonging thus intensified into a sexual identity and political consciousness seeking redress against such harms. The achievement of formal legal equality and general social acceptance may weaken these structures of belonging and cross-class solidarity, as these may undermine the historical basis for a shared homosexual grievance.

A profound structural transformation has accompanied the increasing social acceptance of homosexuality, forming an essential condition of its possibility. Warner's own reading of Habermas acknowledges this transformation but demurs as to what possibilities, if any, it may offer to queer cultures, reducing the matter to a question of whether decentralized technologies can counter the force of an increasing capitalization of media.[44] Habermas identified the present dedifferentiation of the public and private spheres as a "refeudalization" in which institutions of public welfare increasingly serve the apparent needs once met by private family units and publics assume strange new dimensions of private closeness by abandoning disinterested rational-critical debate in favor of a public culture of feeling, opinion polls, focus groups, and the now ubiquitous personality pageant of social media.[45] Weakened family units and the advent of a semipublic, semiprivate gray zone together constituted, as Warner writes, "the context of modern social movements, including identity politics," precisely because "movements around gender and sexuality do not always conform to the model of 'rational-critical debate.'"[46] In addition to the ability of identity politics to navigate new cultures of public feeling, the dedifferentiation of public and private eliminated the very basis for bourgeois moral hegemony.

Warner's catastrophism concerning the threatened institutions of queer culture relies on a hypertrophied vision of "heteronormativity" at a moment when all signs point toward an epochal decline in the power of the family to shape human subjectivity as it did at the height of bourgeois culture or during the generalization of the Fordist nuclear family. The relation of this tendency to queer culture and life stories is obscured by the fact that, as the family evanesces into a more diffuse structure, media technologies interpellate children as sexual subjects at increasingly younger ages. The family's social importance thus exists in inverse proportion to its narrative function as a backdrop for stories of sexual awakening. Here, too, the situation is a muddle. The lack of economic opportunities has prolonged various kinds of family dependency, signaling both a failure of capitalist social relations to reproduce normative family structures from one generation to the next and a continued, spectral existence of families formed in better economic times.

CHAPTER SIX

This "refeudalization" of postmodern societies accounts for the resonance of the early modern period with queer theory, including Warner's
flirtation with a republican basis for opposing neoliberalism. Early modern
forms of sexual subjectivity were both protocapitalist and nonbourgeois,
producing self-conceptions that were not yet saturated by bourgeois con-
ceits but nonetheless dependent on markets and new forms of waged labor. Grasping such historical phenomena requires questioning historical
thinking based on models of progressive development or of discontinuous
breaks—models that were themselves products of bourgeois societies—and
exploring temporal relations more closely synced with the historic cycles of
economic boom and bust in the Mediterranean littoral.[47] Developmentalist
and discontinuous models of history were connected to particular bourgeois
experiences of an interior self and life process, experiences bearing directly
upon how one can conceive of sexuality and its history.

Warner's identification of "queer counterpublics" with "scenes of criminality" that produce "a common language of self-cultivation, shared knowledge and exchange of inwardness" could be enriched by making a connection between counterhegemonic queer activities or senses of belonging and
a historically proletarian public sphere. Warner follows Habermas's conceptualization and "leaves aside the plebeian public sphere as a variant that
in a sense was suppressed in the historical process."[48] However, the suppression of a queer plebian counterpublic is precisely the problem Warner
identifies in his polemic against Sullivan's politics of homosexuality. The
historical connection of queer counterpublics to the proletarian or plebeian
public sphere could be articulated in neither the polemical context of *The
Trouble with Normal* nor the abstract theoretical frame of the essays assembled in *Publics and Counterpublics*. An exploration of this theme would
have required bringing these theoretical reflections back to bear on the history of queer counterhegemonic participation in a plebeian public sphere or
incursions on the bourgeois public sphere.[49] Consideration of the "plebeian"
character of the scene of male homosexuality—a sexual public made up of
workers and heterogeneous urban lower classes, including elements of the
bourgeoisie—would also account for the longer history of how this plebeian
public was suppressed and eclipsed by a middle-class homosexual formation
that became hegemonic.

Oskar Negt and Alexander Kluge's critical reply to Habermas sought
to rework his conceptualization to incorporate considerations of how the
classical bourgeois public sphere was in fact a contingent "product" that
actively concealed its own conditions of production. They discuss the ways

in which proletarian experience was blocked temporally and spatially by conditions of work. In the concrete production process, workers interacted with partial objects of machines without any view of the whole, just as the life cycle of proletarian experience attenuated any coherent identity by compartmentalizing it into cycles of childhood, adolescence, and an adulthood hemmed in by the two forces of work and "the terrifying structure of the modern nuclear family."[50] By contrast, the amenities of bourgeois subject formation—stable forms of sexual subjectivity generated by the interiority of rooms, an epistolary subjectivity produced by letter writing, predictable patterns of domestic intimacy and separate beds and bedrooms for children and intimate partners—were completely foreign to the proletarian experiences of crowded boardinghouses; shared beds; institutions of confinement such as workhouses, prisons, brothels, labor camps, ships, and barracks; and irregular patterns of work and intimacy. Furthermore, what proletarian sexual subjectivity had to gain by publicizing itself—a meal or some other material exchange, life options however precarious, a modicum of pleasure in an otherwise brutalized existence—bourgeois sexual subjectivity had to lose: property, status, and marriageability.

Homosexuality has historically been an imagined community whose principles of belonging were based upon differing, perhaps fundamentally incompatible, self-understandings. Here it is necessary to part ways with Warner's concept, for the Foucauldian assumption that "a common language" implies either "shared knowledge" or "exchanges of inwardness" is based upon a story that attributed sweeping powers of subjective transformation to an intellectual formation of sexual science that never had the means of exerting such an influence over proletarian self-understandings. Instead of making the bourgeois model of shared senses of interiority into the principle of group belonging, it is crucial to ask how criminal intimacies and cross-class encounters shaped multiple sexual subjectivities and principles of group cohesion and recognition by appropriating urban space in a struggle with forces seeking to impose a hegemonic moral order over such spaces. Rather than viewing the private individual as the container of an inward-looking subjectivity, a critical approach seeks to understand how social space generated same-sex desires and sexual subjectivities that externalized themselves in the world.

Proletarian queers' association with gender-variant self-presentation—and the state repression of such activities in the public sphere—have been historically documented in taverns, bars, and public thoroughfares since the early eighteenth century in France and England.[51] As Chauncey writes of the early twentieth-century same-sex sexual culture in New York, "the prominence" of the predominantly working-class "fairies" of the flamboyant, effeminate homosexual type "offered many men a means of constructing public personas they considered more congruent with their 'inner natures' than conventional masculine ones." Paradoxically, what many contemporaries may have considered transgressive gender behavior was, Chauncey argues, "consistent with the terms of the dominant gender culture in which they had been socialized," enabling men who did not identify as homosexuals to play the active sexual role without any threat to their masculinity or sexual subjectivity.[52] Flamboyant self-presentations made homosexuality socially visible both to potential sexual partners and to state authorities; as such, they represent a strategy primarily adopted by people unconcerned with losing their status. As long as homosexuality had a limited basis in the bourgeois public sphere, its flourishing in the plebeian public sphere subjected men of status to a local proletarian sexual hegemony. This power gradient flipped in the opposite direction as homosexual institutions were increasingly commercialized and the plebeian basis of queer counterpublics was liquidated.

The broad cultural shift away from identification with the gender-variant type in the 1970s and 1980s represented an attempt to construct a more masculine self-image during gay liberation struggles and distanced gay men from a historically working-class queer subjectivity that had been comparatively unconcerned with the loss of bourgeois status. This shift and the oblivion into which a swishy working-class dominant has fallen is particularly dramatic in the disappearance of English homosexual cant, or Polari, from British gay culture. Although many of the words have been preserved—"trade," "cruising," and so on—little remains of this earlier language community. Polari, which linguists believe emerged from a lingua franca spoken by Mediterranean sailors—later circulating in the milieus of the traveling circus, the theater, and prison—percolated into working-class queer culture by the start of the twentieth century as a counterlanguage grouping in which men could speak freely without fear of being understood by potentially hostile outsiders. As it had become associated with an improper, flamboyant self-expression, and as homosexuality achieved greater social acceptance in the 1970s, Polari fell into disuse.

The evolving dialect by which an imagined community of homosexuals historically publicized itself—asking for a light, red ties and cosmetics, women's names and green suits, "excessively bright feathers" in a hat, brown and gray suede shoes—interpellated an ever wider group of gender-conforming men into a sexual community dominated by proletarian counterhegemony.[53]

So long as homosexuality was a street culture, men of status risked black-mail, theft, and other forms of predation for participating in a lawless sexual counterculture. Working-class codes of recognition declined in importance as the syntax of the language community was formalized in commercial establishments openly catering to gay clientele. These new spaces of acceptance formalized previously criminal cultures of public sex, creating a buffer zone against legal forces of repression and strengthening group identity around the project of politically defending these institutions against police encroachment. The basis of the imagined community in a plebeian counterpublic was replaced by a new foundation in small businesses allowed to operate unperturbed by the state. As state violence receded, markets stepped in to meet and shape a consumer profile of gay identity.

Interregnum

As the social infrastructures of normality, reliable employment, state welfare assistance, and stable families were eroded by successive political and economic crises after the 1970s, the hegemony of a restrictive sexual morality exerted a significantly weakened influence over the lives of ever fewer people. This ongoing crisis of the normal within late capitalism produced an intellectual crisis of modern sexual categories in which these categories were projected back into time—providing a unified field of historical inquiry, as with the terms "queer" and "homosexuality"—and expanded to encompass the entirety of the social field, as with the concept of "normativity." This intellectual confusion may indicate a paradoxical universalization of social conditions once understood under the category of "homosexuality," less through an extension of subjective sexual freedoms than through a generalization of precarious intimacy. Forms of love and life not limited to same-sex object choice but nonetheless "queer" correspond structurally to the historical position occupied by homosexuals, one outside the institutions of family, state, and couple form. As a social category, "queer" would then describe the morbid cultural forms by which the normative logics of gender and sexuality become irreparably damaged, desperately reasserted, and perversely renaturalized within a generalized social crisis—rather than marking some utopian release from these logics in the pursuit of self-transformative play. Against the background of widespread infrastructural fallout, the normal persists within decrepit forms, remaining in force but with significantly weakened powers.

An antagonistic homosexual subject and a stable family form are both undermined in this dissolution of the normal, and yet no new sexual order can be born—signaling a type of conjuncture that Gramsci called an "interregnum," full of "morbid phenomena of the most varied kind":

> If the ruling class has lost consensus, that is, if it no longer "leads" but only "rules"—it possesses sheer coercive power—this actually means that the great masses have become detached from traditional ideologies. . . . The crisis consists precisely in the fact that the old is dying and the new cannot be born: in this interregnum, morbid phenomena of the most varied kind come to pass.[54]

Gramsci's optimism that a worsening material situation and the end of old ideologies would provide favorable terrain for the expansion of Marxist theory, as well as his case for the necessity of maintaining a cynical realism toward this conjuncture, remain compelling. Only a consciousness cleared of old ideologies could be attentive to those fragile points in which the crisis reveals strategic overlaps between structure and superstructure, offering the possibility and even necessity of "creating a new culture" that would break with these morbid phenomena.

Perhaps due to some of the antinomies indicated above, the articulation of "queer" as a social category has provided a diagnostic for the forms of physical and psychological breakdown, the exhaustion of the libidinal body by late capitalism. An earlier biopolitical concern for the welfare of populations in high-income countries has now given way to varieties of managed slow death, a situation resulting from an economy relying on an affect-heavy service sector employment and on public welfare requirements in which disability is increasingly the only path to social safety nets. Taking David Harvey's observation that capitalism defines sickness as an "inability to work," Lauren Berlant writes that

> the bodies of the U.S. waged workers will be more fatigued, in more pain, less capable of ordinary breathing and working, and die earlier than the average for higher-income workers, who are also getting fatter, but at a slower rate and with relatively more opportunity for exercise. . . . They will live the decay of their organs and bodies more explicitly, painfully, and overwhelmingly than ever before; and it has become statistically clear that between stress and comorbidity they will die at ages younger than their grandparents and parents.[55]

By articulating these sick, worn-out laboring bodies as morbid phenomena resulting from the managed fallout of the social welfare state and late capitalism, Berlant calls attention to the ways in which normative dissolution ideologically blocks apprehensions of the structural causes of human misery by creating morally culpable subjects. The experience of the AIDS epidemic prepared the intellectual formation of queer theory for understanding public health discourses as "inevitably part of an argument about classification, causality, responsibility, degeneracy, and the imaginable and pragmatic logics of cure."[56] Whereas these experiences of the physical deterioration of the body might be expected to create a new kind of class consciousness, a liberal moralization of health in terms of individual decisions and risk calculus blocks such apprehensions.

Whatever the possibilities of "creating a new culture" in the present conjuncture, consideration of the possibilities thrown up by past conjunctures may help sharpen a sense of what's possible. The dissolutions of previous formations of sexual hegemony and previous crises in sexual categories have marked all previous crises of the world system. Following the French Revolutionary wars, the political crises and revolutions of 1848, the Great Depression of 1873–96, the First World War, and the Great Depression of the 1930s, new intellectual formations crystallized around radical transformations of sexual morality and behavior. Crises have been as generative for new formations of sexual hegemony as they have been disruptive of older formations.

The historical terrain of conjunctures of crisis is a privileged site for examining how sexual categories and behaviors are undone and reformed and for observing which social forces are brought to bear upon this process. Assessing the relative significance of these forces requires careful consideration of the relationship between forces of opposition and a cultural dominant. Raymond Williams makes the point that the major theoretical problem for understanding the hegemonic is categorically distinguishing counterhegemonic forces from forms of opposition that may ultimately be absorbed by a specific hegemony—bound by certain specific limits, neutralized, changed, or wholly incorporated. In other words, nearly all forms of opposition may in practice be "tied to the hegemonic"; in other words, "the dominant culture . . . at once produces and limits its own forms of counter-culture."[57] Arguing for the importance of this understanding of cultural domination for the analysis of homosexuality, Jonathan Dollimore writes that "the most effective Marxist cultural critique of this century has attended to the reasons for the failure of potential to be realized in circumstances which should have enabled it." Western Marxism's experience of defeat after the First World War, when conditions thought to be ripe for socialism favored the rise of fascism, have made the tradition "acutely aware of the fact that human potentialities have not only been savagely repressed, but also abandoned and repudiated by their former adherents and those with the most to gain from them."[58]

The experience of defeat allows for a retrospective differentiation of what was counterhegemonic in homosexuality from what was oppositional but ultimately subsumable by a more flexible postbourgeois sexual hegemony. To be sure, the homosexual appropriation of companionate marriage is capable of supporting semipublic cultures of stranger intimacy, which theorists have argued is essential to the queer counterculture.[59] Such seemingly incongruent practices have become nonsubversive life options in high-income societies. What was counterhegemonic about homosexuality—its appropriation of urban spaces for public sex, its identification with other antisystemic movements—may no longer be so for a postbourgeois cultural dominant. Although the freedom to participate in queer cultures of stranger intimacy presently depends upon a sexual health infrastructure to which there is still uneven access, and although wealth inequalities continue to deepen, it is hard to imagine that homosexuality will provide the basis for any future politicization of sex. It seems far more likely that any future politicization of sexual health will be part of a wider social movement responding to worsening conditions of life, further cuts to public-sector spending, and hostility toward the ruling elite. How the precarity of some bodies will link up with that of others in future struggles is difficult to predict.

The dedifferentiation of public and private spheres has produced a mixed cultural dominant. Mass culture generalized a bourgeois epistemology of homosexuality by popularizing psychological models of self. The decomposition of bourgeois sexual morality enabled a movement politicizing homosexuality to meet with some success. Whereas the conditions of possibility for an earlier socialist movement politicizing sexual identity in fin-de-siècle Germany exploited a crisis of the liberal ego that ultimately galvanized the conservative forces of reaction that would become the movement's undoing, the present crisis has enabled a partial overcoming of antihomosexual prejudice by affirming the threatened values of family and intimate coupling. Whether this forward position provides the imagined community with a strategic beachhead within the establishment for launching further offensives against the fortifications of "normativity" (or deeper retreats into various conservative defensive maneuvers) seems like a moot point. Without the strong antagonism of a bourgeois dominant against which a homosexual counterculture once asserted itself, this language and these categories may no longer be relevant to a depoliticized sexual field. Sexual role play, then, for a postbourgeois cultural theater: the options of tea-room trade or trophy husband, masculine or feminine, phone app or bathhouse, now appear to be matters of personal taste, culturally recombinable to varying degrees even within a single individual's highly compartmentalized social milieus and self-presentations. Such, anyway, are the conditions of a partially emancipated order of gender and sexuality.

Hence the cowardly spectacle of the San Francisco Pride board of directors, repudiating the decision of its electoral committee to extend an invitation to Chelsea Manning to be a Pride Grand Marshal in 2013. In a public statement stigmatizing Manning as a criminal "facing the military justice of this country" and signaling SF Pride's "responsibility to serve a broader community," the president of the board, Lisa Williams, affirmed the group's commitment to defend the American establishment against political dissent.[60] Ironically, Manning might have been considered by the board if she had been discharged for her gender, which was compatible with the agenda of SF Pride; her exposure of state corruption, war crimes, and gross abuses of power was not. Thus, the very same political discourse that had once excluded homosexuals from American society by appealing to the interests of a silent majority is now used by homosexuals to keep members of its community in check. These new fault lines of fragmentation and division within American identity offer little room for the countercultural and subjective freedoms of an earlier period of hegemonic dissolution and gay liberation. Rather, as cultural hegemony has become more diffuse and postwar sexual communities have fragmented, authorities, including gay and lesbian elites, have tended to preserve their power by resorting to repression and force. The gay establishment found itself on the opposite side of police barricades, as a small handful of queers protesting San Francisco Pride and the Chelsea Manning decision were asked by organizers, without any hint of irony or camp, not to rain on their parade.

notes

Introduction

1 Beverly J. Silver and Giovanni Arrighi, "End of the Long Twentieth Century," in *Business as Usual: The Roots of the Global Financial Meltdown*, ed. Craig Calhoun and Georgi Derluguian (New York: New York University Press, 2011), 53–68.

2 Silver and Arrighi, "End of the Long Twentieth Century," 65.

3 Michel Foucault, *The History of Sexuality, Vol. 1: An Introduction*, trans. Robert Hurley (New York: Vintage, 1990), 123.

4 Foucault, *The History of Sexuality, Vol. 1*, 120.

5 Foucault, *The History of Sexuality, Vol. 1*, 166–68.

6 D'Emilio, "Capitalism and Gay Identity," in *The Lesbian and Gay Studies Reader*, ed. Henry Abelove, Michèle Aina Barale, and David Halperin (New York: Routledge, 1993), 474.

7 D'Emilio, "Capitalism and Gay Identity," 474–75.

8 D'Emilio, "Capitalism and Gay Identity," 473.

Chapter 1. Homosexuality and Capitalism

Epigraph: Larry Mitchell, *The Faggots and Their Friends between Revolutions* (New York: Calamus Books, 1977), 34.

1 Françoise Barret-Ducrocq, *Love in the Time of Victoria: Sexuality, Class, and Gender in Nineteenth-Century London*, trans. John Howe (New York: Verso, 1991), 2.

2 Jeffrey Weeks, *Sex, Politics, and Society: The Regulation of Sexuality since 1800* (New York: Longman, 1981), 19.

3 Lytton Strachey, *Eminent Victorians: Cardinal Manning, Florence Nightingale, Dr. Arnold, General Gordon* (Garden City, NY: Garden City Publishing, 1918), 246.

4 Andrew Sullivan, *Virtually Normal: An Argument about Homosexuality* (New York: Vintage Books, 1996), 76.

5 Michel Foucault, *The History of Sexuality, Vol. 1: An Introduction*, trans. Robert Hurley (New York: Vintage Books, 1990), 32.

6 "We, Victorians" is a better translation of Foucault's colloquial chapter heading "Nous autres victoriens."

7 Göran Therborn, *Between Sex and Power: Family in the World, 1900–2000* (New York: Routledge, 2004), 193.

8 Therborn writes: "In Eastern Europe there is no clear pattern of marital decline until the 1990s, except in East Germany and Slovenia. . . . By 1975 the first marriage rate was going down all over Western Europe north of the Alps and the Pyrenées, although the decline was not yet historical in Belgium, France, and the British Isles. Outside Europe it was declining strongly in Australia and New Zealand, more cautiously in Canada and the USA. . . . By 1980 a significant, epochal change had occurred all over Western Europe, although from and to quite different levels of marriage" (*Between Sex and Power*, 194).

9 George Chauncey, *Why Marriage? The History Shaping Today's Debate over Gay Equality* (New York: Basic Books, 2004), 22.

10 Margot Canaday, *The Straight State: Sexuality and Citizenship in Twentieth-Century America* (Princeton, NJ: Princeton University Press, 2009).

11 There is a strong analogy between this response to state oppression and the way in which Benedict Anderson has shown "anti-nationalist" colonial states imagined their domination; see Benedict Anderson, *Imagined Communities: Reflections on the Origin and Spread of Nationalism* (New York: Verso, 1991), 163–85; Marc Stein, "'Birthplace of the Nation': Imagining the Lesbian and Gay Communities in Philadelphia, 1969–1970," in *Creating a Place for Ourselves: Lesbian, Gay, and Bisexual Community Histories*, ed. Brett Beemyn, 253–88 (New York: Routledge, 1997); and George Chauncey and Elizabeth A. Povinelli, "Thinking Sexuality Transnationally: An Introduction," *GLQ: A Journal of Lesbian and Gay Studies* 5, no. 4 (1999): 444.

12 John D'Emilio, *Sexual Politics, Sexual Communities: The Making of a Homosexual Minority in the United States, 1940–1970* (Chicago: University of Chicago Press, 1998), 31–33, 49–53, 146–50, 182–95.

13 "For long, sociologists had debated the term *embourgeoisement* of the working-class in the West—never a very happy term for the processes at issue. By the nineties, however, the more striking phenomenon was a general *encanaillement* of the possessing classes—as it were: starlet princesses and sleazeball presidents, beds for rent in the official residence and bribes for killer ads, disneyfication of protocols and tarantinization of practices, the avid corteges of the nocturnal

underpass or the gubernatorial troop": Perry Anderson, *The Origins of Post-modernity* (New York: Verso, 2002), 85–86.

14 Therborn, *Between Sex and Power*, 268.

15 Estelle B. Freedman and John D'Emilio, "Problems Encountered in Writing the History of Sexuality: Sources, Theory, and Interpretation," *Journal of Sex Research* 27, no. 4 (November 1990): 481–95.

16 Queer realism is not subscribed to the tenets of the realist school of international relations theory, although it shares many of the same inspirations, considerations, and foundational texts as this formation. See, for example, Jonathan Joseph, *Hegemony: A Realist Analysis* (New York: Routledge, 2002); Joseph S. Nye, Jr., "The Future of American Power," in *War, Peace, and Hegemony in a Globalized World: The Changing Balance of Power in the Twenty-First Century*, ed. Chandra Chari, 36–49 (New York: Routledge, 2008); Andrew C. Sobel, *Birth of Hegemony: Crisis, Financial Revolution, and Emerging Global Networks* (Chicago: University of Chicago Press, 2012).

17 This conceptualization avoids the paternalism of arguing that the desire for normalcy is a kind of false class consciousness for queers, on the one hand, and the smug elitism of the assumption that such aspirations are passé.

18 Comparing sexual status to educational qualifications, Pierre Bourdieu writes that in "each case, what is at stake is as much a status-linked right to politics as a simple political culture, the prerequisite to the exercise of this right which those who feel entitled to exercise it provide for themselves. . . . The marking produced by the imposition of properties such as educational status or sexual identity impresses itself both on the marked individual, who is called upon to 'live up' to his or her social definition, and on others, who expect him or her to actualize his or her essence. (The psychological translation of this relationship is particularly visible in the relations within couples.) That is why competence in the sense of specific culture is to competence in the sense of status property as existence is to essence: only those who ought to have it can really acquire it and only those who are authorized to have it feel called upon to acquire it": *Distinction: A Social Critique of the Judgement of Taste*, trans. Richard Nice (London: Routledge, 2013), 411.

19 I align this more limited use of the term with Cathy Cohen's still-relevant critique of the political uses and potential alliances of the term "queer": Cathy J. Cohen, "Punks, Bulldaggers, Welfare Queens: The Radical Potential of Queer Politics?" *GLQ: A Journal of Lesbian and Gay Studies* 3 (1997): 437–65.

20 Stuart Hall, "Gramsci's Relevance for the Study of Race and Ethnicity," *Journal of Communication Inquiry* 10, no. 5 (1986): 5–27.

21 Nathan Stewart Rosenstein, *Rome at War: Farms, Families, and Death in the Middle Republic* (Chapel Hill: University of North Carolina Press, 2004), 185–87.

22 Michael Perelman, *The Invention of Capitalism: Classical Political Economy and the Secret of Primitive Accumulation* (Durham, NC: Duke University Press, 2000), 13–16.

23 Fredric Jameson, *Brecht and Method* (New York: Verso, 1998), 43–45.

23 Fredric Jameson, *Brecht and Method* (New York: Verso, 1998), 43–45.

24 James Clifford, *Returns: Becoming Indigenous in the Twenty-First Century* (Cambridge, MA: Harvard University Press, 2013), 41.

25 Douglas Crimp, *Melancholia and Moralism: Essays on AIDS and Queer Politics* (Cambridge, MA: MIT Press, 2004), 1–26.

26 Aristotle, *Politics*, trans. Ernest Barker (New York: Oxford University Press, 2009), 2. The claim is made by Benveniste; see citation in note 27.

27 Émile Benveniste, *Le Vocabulaire des institutions indo-européennes: 1. Économie, parenté, société* (Paris: Gallimard, 1966), 205–8, 239.

28 Louis Crompton, *Homosexuality and Civilization* (Cambridge, MA: Harvard University Press, 2003); Rudi C. Bleys, *The Geography of Perversion: Male-to-Male Sexual Behaviour outside the West and the Ethnographic Imagination, 1750–1918* (New York: New York University Press, 1995), 160–85.

29 David F. Greenberg, *The Construction of Homosexuality* (Chicago: University of Chicago Press, 1988), 25–89, 94–100, 110–14.

30 George Dumézil, *Mitra-Varuna: An Essay on Two Indo-European Representations of Sovereignty* (New York: Zone Books, 1988); William Percy has recently argued that, despite fulfilling these functions and despite surface-level similarities, pederastic institutions among Indo-European cultures were too scattered to have any common origin; see William Armstrong Percy, *Pederasty and Pedagogy in Archaic Greece* (Urbana: University of Illinois Press, 1996), 15–26.

31 Eve Kosofsky Sedgwick, *Epistemology of the Closet* (Berkeley: University of California Press, 1990), 44–48.

32 Eve Kosofsky Sedgwick, *Touching Feeling: Affect, Pedagogy, Performativity* (Durham, NC: Duke University Press, 2004), 147.

33 Walter Benjamin, "Paralipomena to 'On the Concept of History,'" in *Walter Benjamin: Selected Writings, Vol. 4, 1938–1940*, trans. Edmund Jephcott et al., ed. Howard Eiland and Michael W. Jennings (Cambridge, MA: Harvard University Press, 2006), 406.

34 Benjamin, "Paralipomena," 407.

35 Sedgwick, *Touching Feeling*, 148.

36 Benjamin, "On the Concept of History," in *Selected Writings, Vol. 4*, 396.

37 Benjamin, "On the Concept of History," 394.

38 Dagmar Herzog, "Syncopated Sex: Transforming European Sexual Cultures," *American Historical Review* 114 (December 2009): 1295.

39 Herzog, "Syncopated Sex," 1297.

40 Gilbert Herdt, "Introduction: Moral Panics, Sexual Rights, and Cultural Anger," in *Moral Panics, Sex Panics: Fear and the Fight over Sexual Rights*, 1–32 (New York: New York University Press, 2009); Stanley Cohen, *Folk Devils and Moral Panics* (1972; New York: St. Martin's Press, 2002); Mary Douglas, *Purity and Danger: An Analysis of Concepts of Pollution and Taboo* (1966; New York: Routledge, 2003).

41 George Chauncey, *Gay New York: Gender and the Making of the Gay Male World, 1890–1994* (New York: Basic Books, 1994), 355–66; Robert Aldrich, "Ho-

mosexuality and the City: An Historical Overview," *Urban Studies* 41, no. 9 (August 2004): 1719–37; Nayan Shah, *Stranger Intimacy: Contesting Race, Sexuality, and the Law in the North American West* (Berkeley: University of California Press, 2011), 54–61.

42 Chauncey, *Gay New York*, 111–15.

43 The fairy, Chauncey writes, "embodied the very things middle-class men feared most about their gender status. His effeminacy represented in extreme form the loss of manhood middle-class men most feared in themselves, and his style seemed to undermine their efforts to shore up their manly status" (*Gay New York*, 115).

44 Clarence Hooker, "Ford's Sociology Department and the Americanization Campaign and the Manufacture of Popular Culture among Assembly Line Workers, c. 1910–1917," *Journal of American Culture* 20, no. 1 (spring 1997): 47–53.

45 Canaday, *The Straight State*; Allan Bérubé, *Coming Out under Fire* (New York: Simon and Schuster, 1990); Marilyn E. Hegarty, *Victory Girls and Khaki-Wackies and Patriotutes: The Regulation of Female Sexuality during World War II* (New York: New York University Press, 2008); Sabine Frühstück, *Colonizing Sex: Sexology and Social Control in Modern Japan* (Berkeley: University of California Press, 2003); George L. Mosse, *Nationalism and Sexuality: Respectability and Abnormal Sexuality in Modern Europe* (New York: Howard Fertiv, 1985); Dagmar Herzog, *Sexuality in Europe: A Twentieth-Century History* (New York: Cambridge University Press, 2011).

46 Samuel Delany, *Times Square Red, Times Square Blue* (New York: New York University Press, 1999), 111–27.

47 Chauncey and Povinelli, "Thinking Sexuality Transnationally," 444.

48 Giovanni Arrighi, *The Long Twentieth Century: Money, Power, and the Origins of Our Times* (New York: Verso, 2010); Immanuel Wallerstein, *World-Systems Analysis: An Introduction* (Durham, NC: Duke University Press, 2004), 1–22; Fernand Braudel, *Civilization and Capitalism: 15th to 18th Century, Vol. 2—The Wheels of Commerce*, trans. Siân Reynolds (Berkeley: University of California Press, 1992); Samir Amin, *Unequal Development: An Essay on the Social Formations of Peripheral Capitalism* (Delhi: Oxford University Press, 1979).

49 Raymond Williams, *Writing in Society* (New York: Verso, 1991), 152–53.

50 Robert Brenner, "Bourgeois Revolution and the Transition to Capitalism," in *The First Modern Society: Essays in English History in Honor of Lawrence Stone*, ed. A. L. Beier, David Cannadine, and James M. Rosenheim (Cambridge: Cambridge University Press, 1989), 286.

51 John D'Emilio, "Capitalism and Gay Identity," in *Powers of Desire: The Politics of Sexuality*, ed. Ann Barr Snitow, Christine Stansell, and Sharon Thompson (New York: Monthly Review Press, 1983), 104.

52 David Harvey, *The Urban Experience* (Baltimore, MD: Johns Hopkins University Press, 1989), 33.

53 Harvey, *The Urban Experience*, 32.

54 Chauncey, *Gay New York*, 355–66; Aldrich, "Homosexuality and the City"; Shah, *Stranger Intimacy*, 54–61.

55 Fredric Jameson, *Valences of the Dialectic* (New York: Verso, 2009), 515–32, 552–64; Carla Freccero, *Queer/Early/Modern* (Durham, NC: Duke University Press, 2006), 31–41.

56 See Perry Anderson, "The Notion of Bourgeois Revolution," in *English Questions*, 105–18 (New York: Verso, 1992).

Chapter 2. Sodomy and the Government of Cities

1 Quoted in Michael Jesse Rocke, *Male Homosexuality and Its Regulation in Late Medieval Florence, Volumes 1 and 2* (Ann Arbor: University of Michigan Press, 1989), 179–80.

2 Lauro Martines, *Fire in the City: Savonarola and the Struggle for the Soul of Renaissance Florence* (New York: Oxford University Press, 2006), 1.

3 Ten florins was the most common penalty for poor men convicted of sodomy during this period. Twenty years after Pacchierotto's death, Francesco Guicciardini ironically remarked to Machiavelli that "the wool guild's charge to Machiavelli to procure a preacher was as preposterous as commissioning Pacchierotto, while he was still alive, to find a wife for a friend" (Rocke, *Male Homosexuality*, 180).

4 Although the greater part of these revenues was collected from those individuals paying a higher fine of fifty florins, likely upper guildsmen and master tradesmen, the fines collected from fourteen wealthy individuals were nearly equivalent to those 274 individuals each fined a mere ten. Even this much-diminished fine was considered an exorbitant price to pay by many of the city's sodomites, as the example of Pacchierotto demonstrates (Rocke, *Male Homosexuality*, 176).

5 Or 1.3 percent of the much expanded revenues of Florentine wool cloth production the year previous; Arrighi, *The Long Twentieth Century*, 102.

6 Rocke, *Male Homosexuality*, 100–101.

7 Guido Ruggiero, *The Boundaries of Eros: Sex, Crime, and Sexuality in Renaissance Venice* (New York: Oxford University Press, 1985), 128, table 6. This figure probably refers to both convictions and absolutions, as another study of the Venetian record by another scholar claims only 268 convictions for sodomy between 1406 and 1500; see Elisabeth Pavan, "Police des mœurs, société et politique à Venise à la fin du Moyen Âge," *Revue Historique* 264, no. 2 (1980): 276.

8 Pavan, "Police des mœurs," 276–77.

9 Henry Kamen, *The Spanish Inquisition: A Historical Revision* (New Haven, CT: Yale University Press, 1998), 267–69.

10 Christian Berco, *Sexual Hierarchies, Public Status: Men, Sodomy, and Society in Spain's Golden Age* (Toronto: University of Toronto Press, 2007), 67.

11 Richard C. Trexler, *Public Life in Renaissance Florence* (Ithaca, NY: Cornell University Press, 1991), 10–11.

12 Giovanni Cavalcanti, "Tratto Politico-Morale," quoted in Trexler, *Public Life*, 16.

13 Richard A. Goldthwaite, *The Economy of Renaissance Florence* (Baltimore, MD: Johns Hopkins University Press, 2009), 373.

14 Robert C. Davis, "The Geography of Gender in the Renaissance," in *Gender and Society in Renaissance Italy* (London: Longman, 1988), 24–26.

15 Fynes Moryson, *The Itinerary of Fynes Moryson, Vol. 4* (Glasgow: James MacLehose and Sons, Publishers to the University, 1617), 96.

16 Rocke, *Male Homosexuality*, 9; Ruggiero, *The Boundaries of Eros*, 109–45.

17 Quoted in Davis, "The Geography of Gender in the Renaissance," 27.

18 Michael Jesse Rocke, "Gender and Sexual Culture in Renaissance Italy," in *Gender and Society in Renaissance Italy* (London: Longman, 1988), 165.

19 Samuel K. Cohen Jr., *Women in the Streets: Essays on Sex and Power in Renaissance Italy* (Baltimore, MD: Johns Hopkins University Press, 1996), 29.

20 Rocke, "Gender and Sexual Culture," 165.

21 John A. Najemy, *A History of Florence 1200–1575* (Malden, MA: Blackwell, 2006), 37.

22 Nassau William Senior, *Poor Law Commissioners' Report of 1834* (London: Darling and Son, 1905), 6.

23 Rocke, *Male Homosexuality*, 300–301.

24 Giorgio Agamben writes: "He who has been banned is not, in fact, simply set outside the law and made indifferent to it but rather abandoned by it, that is, exposed and threatened on the threshold in which life and law, outside and inside, become indistinguishable. It is literally not possible to say whether the one who has been banned is outside or inside the juridical order. (This is why in Romance languages, to be 'banned' originally means both to be 'at the mercy of' and 'at one's own will, freely,' to be 'excluded' and also 'open to all, free.') It is in this sense that the paradox of sovereignty can take the form 'There is nothing outside the law.' The originary relation of law to life is not application but Abandonment. The matchless potentiality of the *nomos*, its originary 'force of law,' is that it holds life in its ban by abandoning it"; see Giorgio Agamben, *Homo Sacer: Sovereign Power and Bare Life*, trans. Daniel Heller-Roazen (Stanford, CA: Stanford University Press, 1998), 28–29.

25 Wally Seccombe, *A Millennium of Family Change: Feudalism to Capitalism in Northwestern Europe* (New York: Verso, 1995), 136–42.

26 Oliver Cox, *The Foundations of Capitalism* (London: Peter Owen Ltd, 1959), 153.

27 Arrighi, *The Long Twentieth Century*, 105.

28 Rocke, *Male Homosexuality*, 323.

29 Rocke, *Male Homosexuality*, 330–39.

30 Rocke, *Male Homosexuality*, 341.

31 Quoted in Rocke, *Male Homosexuality*, 344.

32 Rocke, *Male Homosexuality*, 462.

33 Trexler, *Public Life*, 438–41.

34 Niccolò Machiavelli, *The Florentine Histories, Vol. 2* (1843; New York: Paine & Burgess, 1845), 151–52.

35 Rocke, *Male Homosexuality*, 464.

36 Niccolò Machiavelli, *Discourses on Livy*, trans. Harvey C. Mansfield and Nathan Tarcov (Chicago: University of Chicago Press, 1996), III.6, emphasis added.

37 Machiavelli, *Discourses*, III.26.2; Aristotle, *Politics*, 1303b15–1304a18.

38 Aristotle, *Politics*, 1314b20–40.

39 Machiavelli, *Discourses*, III.26.2.

40 Machiavelli, *Discourses*, II.28.2.

41 James N. Davidson, *The Greeks and Greek Love: A Bold New Exploration of the Ancient World* (New York: Random House, 2009), 3–36.

42 Thomas F. Scanlon, "The Dispersion of Pederasty and the Athletic Revolution in Sixth-Century B.C. Greece," in *Same-Sex Desire and Love in Greco-Roman Antiquity and the Classical Tradition of the West*, ed. Beert C. Verstraete and Vernon Provencal (Binghamton, NY: Harrington Park Press, 2005), 62–84.

43 William Armstrong Percy, "Reconsiderations about Greek Homosexualities," in Verstraete and Provencal, *Same-Sex Desire and Love*, 13–61.

44 E. Will, "La Grèce archaïque," in *Deuxième conférence internationale d'histoire économique/Second International Conference on Economic History*, Aix-en-Provence, 1962, vol. 1 (Paris: Mouton, 1965), 62.

45 Michel Foucault, *Lectures on the Will to Know: Lectures at the Collège de France 1970–1971 and Oedipal Knowledge*, trans. Graham Burchell (London: Palgrave Macmillan, 2013), 123.

46 Foucault, *Lectures on the Will to Know*, 127–28; A. French, "The Economic Background to Solon's Reforms," *Classical Quarterly*, n.s., 6 (1956): 11–25.

47 Foucault, *Lectures on the Will to Know*, 129.

48 See *Discourses* III.6.16, where Machiavelli cites the offense against much-celebrated Athenian lovers Aristogeiton and Harmodius, celebrated in Athens as the Tyrannicides with a statue group in the Agora. The offence involved both the shaming of a woman, Harmodius's noble-born sister, and Aristogeiton's jealous rage at the advances of one of the tyrants toward his boy, Harmodius. The full account is given by Thucydides in *History of the Peloponnesian War*, trans. Thomas Hobbes (London: Bohn, 1843), 6.54.

49 Machiavelli writes that "as men hate things either from fear or from envy, two very powerful causes of hatred come to be eliminated in past things since they cannot offend you and do not give you cause to envy them. But the contrary happens with those things that are managed and seen. Since the entire knowledge of them is not in any part concealed from you, and, together with the good, you know many other things in them that displease you, you are forced to judge them much inferior to ancient things, even though the present may in truth deserve much more glory and fame than they" (*Discourses*, II.Preface.I).

50 Leo Strauss, *Persecution and the Art of Writing* (Chicago: University of Chicago Press, 1988), 25.

51 "And there is nothing that consumes itself as much as liberality: while you use it, you lose the capacity to use it; and you become either poor and contemptible or, to escape poverty, rapacious and hateful. Among all the things that a prince should guard against is being contemptible and hated, and liberality leads you to

both. So there is more wisdom in maintaining a name for meanness, which begets infamy without hatred, than in being under a necessity, because one wants
to have a name for liberality, to incur a name for rapacity, which begets infamy
with hatred"; see Niccolò Machiavelli, *The Prince*, trans. Harvey Claflin Mansfield (Chicago: University of Chicago Press, 1985), 65.

52 Machiavelli, *Discourses*, 1.5.2, emphasis mine.

53 Machiavelli, *Discourses*, 1.5.4.

54 Najemy, *Between Friends: Discourses of Power and Desire in the Machiavelli-
Vettori Letters of 1513–1515* (Berkeley: University of California Press, 1993).

55 Niccolò Machiavelli, *The Chief Works and Others, Vol. 2*, trans. Allan Gilbert
(Durham, NC: Duke University Press, 1989), 939.

56 Machiavelli, *Chief Works*, 940.

57 Machiavelli, *Chief Works*, 941.

58 Machiavelli, *Discourses*, 1.7.

59 Machiavelli, *Discourses*, 1.7.4.

60 Michael Jesse Rocke, *Forbidden Friendships: Homosexuality and Male Culture in
Renaissance Florence* (New York: Oxford University Press, 1998), 222.

61 Rocke, *Forbidden Friendships*, 229.

62 Antonio Gramsci, *Prison Notebooks, Vol. 1*, ed. and trans. Joseph Buttigieg (New
York: Columbia University Press, 1992), 219.

63 Michel Foucault, *Histoire de la sexualité I: La volonté de savoir* (Paris: Gallimard,
1976), 59.

64 Rocke, *Forbidden Friendships*, 4.

65 Rocke, *Male Homosexuality*, 8; northern Italian city-states were notorious long
before the Renaissance for harboring heretics of all stripes. Frederick II said that
Milan was a city "omnium haereticorum, Paterinorum, Luciferanorum, Pub-
licanorum, Albigensium, usurariorum refugium et receptaculum"; quoted in
John C. L. Gieseler, *A Text Book of Church History, Vol. 2: A.D. 720–1305*, trans.
Samuel Davidson and John Winstanley Hull (New York: Harper and Brothers,
1871), 577.

66 Gen. 19:28 (King James Version).

67 Gen. 19:17 (KJV).

68 Benjamin, "On the Concept of History," 396.

69 Rocke, *Male Homosexuality*, 524.

70 Benjamin, "On the Concept of History," 396.

Chapter 3. Sexual Hegemony and the Capitalist World System

1 Arrighi, *The Long Twentieth Century*, 31–41.

2 Fernand Braudel, *The Mediterranean and the Mediterranean World in the Age of
Phillip II, Vol. 1*, trans. Siân Reynolds (Oakland: University of California Press,
1996), 246–67.

3 "1. There exists what I shall call a 'Sotadic Zone,' bounded westwards by the
northern shores of the Mediterranean (N. Lat. 43°) and by the southern (N. Lat.

30°). Thus the depth would be 780 to 800 miles including meridional France, the Iberian Peninsula, Italy and Greece, with the coast-regions of Africa from Marocco [*sic*] to Egypt. . . . Within the Sotadic Zone the Vice is popular and endemic, held at the worst to be a mere peccadillo, whilst the races to the North and South of the limits here defined practice it only sporadically amid the opprobrium of their fellows who, as a rule, are physically incapable of performing the operation and look upon it with the liveliest disgust"; Richard Burton, *Thousand and One Nights, Vol. 10* (The Burton Club, 1886), 206–7.

4   For a recent take on the controversy surrounding Richard Burton's essay, see Joseph A. Massad, *Desiring Arabs* (Chicago: University of Chicago Press, 2007), 10–11.

5   Richard C. Trexler, *Sex and Conquest: Gendered Violence, Political Order, and the European Conquest of the Americas* (Ithaca, NY: Cornell University Press, 1997), 39–47.

6   Arrighi, *The Long Twentieth Century*, 55.

7   Braudel, *The Mediterranean, Vol. 1*, 60–80.

8   Karl Polanyi, "Ports of Trade in Early Societies," *Journal of Economic History* 23, no. 1 (1963): 31.

9   Polanyi, "Ports of Trade," 30–31.

10   Polanyi, "Ports of Trade," 31.

11   Adam Smith admits as much: "The inhabitants of a city, it is true, must always ultimately derive their subsistence, and the whole materials and means of their industry from the country. But those of a city, situated near either the sea-coast or the banks of a navigable river, are not necessarily confined to derive them from the country in their neighbourhood. They have a much wider range, and may draw them from the most remote corners of the world, either in exchange for the manufactured produce of their own industry, or by performing the office of carriers between distant countries, and exchanging the produce of one for that of another. A city might in this manner grow up to great wealth and splendor, while not only the country in its neighbourhood, but all those to which it traded, were in poverty and wretchedness"; Adam Smith, *The Wealth of Nations*, (Chicago: University of Chicago Press, 1976), 427.

12   Braudel, *The Mediterranean, Vol. 1*, 278.

13   Braudel, *The Mediterranean, Vol. 1*, 40.

14   Braudel, *The Mediterranean, Vol. 1*, 45–48.

15   Braudel, *The Mediterranean, Vol. 1*, 146.

16   Braudel provides colloquial names for the Ufficiali di notte in *The Mediterranean, Vol. 1*, 146.

17   Albert Habib Hourani, *A History of the Arab Peoples* (Cambridge, MA: Belknap Press of Harvard University Press, 2002), 111–31.

18   Hourani, *A History*, 119–20.

19   Hourani, *A History*, 259–60.

20   Everett K. Rowson, "Homoerotic Liaisons among the Mamluk Elite in Late Medieval Egypt and Syria," in *Islamicate Sexualities: Translations across Temporal*

Geographies of Desire, ed. Kathryn Babayan and Afsaneh Najmabadi (Cambridge, MA: Harvard University Press, 2008), 204–30.

21 Khaled El-Rouayheb, *Before Homosexuality in the Arab-Islamic World, 1500–1800* (Chicago: University of Chicago Press, 2005); Stephen O. Murray, "Homosexuality among Slave Elites in Ottoman Turkey," in *Islamic Homosexualities: Culture, History, and Literature*, ed. Will Roscoe and Stephen O. Murray (New York: New York University Press, 1997), 174–86.

22 Dror Ze'evi, "Changes in Legal-Sexual Discourses: Sex Crimes in the Ottoman Empire," *Continuity and Change* 16, no. 2 (2001): 226.

23 Ze'evi, "Changes in Legal-Sexual Discourses," 228, table 3.

24 Ze'evi, "Changes in Legal-Sexual Discourses," 233–34; there is to my knowledge no detailed study of records of actual homosexuality persecutions under the Ottoman Empire.

25 Scanlon, "The Dispersion of Pederasty and the Athletic Revolution in Sixth-Century B.C. Greece," 62–84.

26 Percy, "Reconsiderations about Greek Homosexualities," 13–61.

27 Aristotle, *Politics*, 1263b.

28 Aristotle, *Politics*, 1262a1–39, translation adapted.

29 Aristotle, *Politics,* 1264a.

30 Aristotle, *Politics*, 1269a–b.

31 Aristotle, *Politics*, 1269b.

32 Aristotle, *Politics*, 1269b21.

33 This discussion was addressed in my reading of Machiavelli above.

34 Aristotle, *Politics*, 1303b20–25.

35 Aristotle, *Politics*, 1272a1–2.

36 Aristotle, *Politics*, 1272a.

37 The other use of the word in *Politics* is in reference to sexual relations between men and women, with the valence of a "mode of conduct" as in "sexual relations" or "mode of slaying each other sexually" (1260b10).

38 J. T. Killen, "Thebes Sealings, Knossos Tablets, and Mycenaean State Banquets," *Bulletin of the Institute of Classical Studies* 39, no. 1 (1994): 67–84; William A. Parkinson, Dimitri Nakassis, and Michael Galaty, "Crafts, Specialists, and Markets in Mycenaean Greece: Introduction," *American Journal of Archaeology* 117 (2013): 413–22.

39 Burton, *Thousand and One Nights, Vol. 10*, 88–90.

40 Claude Quétel, *History of Syphilis* (Baltimore, MD: Johns Hopkins University Press, 1990); K. N. Harper, M. K. Zuckerman, M. L. Harper, J. D. Kingston, and G. J. Armelagos, "The Origin and Antiquity of Syphilis Revisited: An Appraisal of Old World Pre-Columbian Evidence for Treponemal Infection," *American Journal of Physical Anthropology* 146, no. 53 (2011): 99–133; B. M. Rothschild, "History of Syphilis," *Clinical Infectious Diseases* 40, no. 10 (2005): 1454–63.

41 In part 1, section 24 of the *Metaphysics of Morals*, Kant delineates a clear distinction between natural and unnatural commercium sexuale, these latter being sex

with "a person of the same sex or an animal of another than human species . . . unnatural vices [crimina carnis contra naturam] that are also unnamable." Immanuel Kant, *Grounding for the Metaphysics of Morals*, trans. James Ellington (Cambridge, MA: Hackett, 1993), 87.

42 As Lukács writes, the commodity "stamps its imprint upon the whole consciousness of man; his qualities and abilities are no longer an organic part of his personality, they are things which he can 'own' or 'dispose of' like the various objects of the external world. And there is no natural form in which human relations can be cast, no way in which man can bring his physical and psychic 'qualities' into play without their being subjected increasingly to this reifying process. We need only think of marriage, and . . . we can remind ourselves of the way in which Kant, for example described the situation with the naïvely cynical frankness peculiar to great thinkers. 'Sexual community,' he says, 'is the reciprocal use made by one person of the sexual organs and faculties of another. . . . Marriage . . . is the union of two people of different sexes with a view to the mutual possession of each other's sexual attributes for the duration of their lives.'" See Lukács, *History and Class Consciousness* (Cambridge, MA: MIT Press, 1972), 100.

43 Rictor Norton, ed., "The Dutch Purge of Homosexuals," Homosexuality in Eighteenth-Century England: A Sourcebook, updated July 28, 2019, http:// rictornorton.co.uk/eighteen.

44 Norton, "The Dutch Purge of Homosexuals," rictornorton.co.uk/eighteen.

45 Norton, "The Dutch Purge of Homosexuals," rictornorton.co.uk/eighteen.

46 *Daily Journal*, July 8, 1730.

47 Gert Hekma, "Amsterdam," in *Queer Sites: Gay Urban Histories since 1600*, ed. David Higgs (New York: Routledge, 1999), 65.

48 Theo van der Meer, "The Persecutions of Sodomites in Eighteenth-Century Amsterdam: Changing Perceptions of Sodomy" *Journal of Homosexuality* 16, no. 1–2 (1989): 263.

49 Dirk Jaap Noordam, "Sodomy in the Dutch Republic, 1600–1725," *Journal of Homosexuality* 16, nos. 1–2 (1989): 207–28.

50 Noordam, "Sodomy in the Dutch Republic," 214–15.

51 Hekma, "Amsterdam," 65.

52 Arrighi, *The Long Twentieth Century*, 145.

53 Van der Meer, "The Persecutions of Sodomites," 269.

54 Van der Meer, "The Persecutions of Sodomites," 270.

55 Or "infernal lewdness," as the local minister of the rural village Faan would have it in his eponymous pamphlet of 1731; L. J. Boon, "Those Damned Sodomites: Public Images of Sodomy in the Eighteenth-Century Netherlands," *Journal of Homosexuality* 16, nos. 1–2 (1989): 244.

56 Simon Schama, *The Embarrassment of Riches* (New York: Vintage, 1997), 25.

57 Schama, *The Embarrassment of Riches*, 25.

58 A. H. Huussen, "Prosecution of Sodomy in Eighteenth Century Frisia, Netherlands," *Journal of Homosexuality* 16, nos. 1–2 (1989): 238.

59　Huussen, "Prosecution of Sodomy," 241.

60　On the ambivalence of exemplary punishments, see Marcus Rediker, *Villains of All Nations: Atlantic Pirates in the Golden Age* (Boston: Beacon Press, 2004), 1–13; see also Michel Foucault, *Discipline and Punish*, trans. Alan Sheridan (New York: Vintage, 1995), 53–69.

61　W. H. McNeill, *The Pursuit of Power: Technology, Armed Force, and Society since A.D. 1000* (Chicago: University of Chicago Press, 1982), 117–33.

62　Julia Adams, *The Familial State: Ruling Families and Merchant Capitalism in Early Modern Europe* (Ithaca, NY: Cornell University Press, 2005), 40–41.

63　Adams, *The Familial State*, 44.

64　Arrighi, *The Long Twentieth Century*, 143.

65　Schama, *The Embarrassment of Riches*, 38.

66　R. E. Kistemaker, "The Public and the Private: Public Space in Sixteenth- and Seventeenth-Century Amsterdam," trans. Wendy Shattes, in *The Public and the Private in the Dutch Culture of the Golden Age*, ed. A. W. Wheelock, A. K. Wheelock Jr., and A. F. Seeff (Newark: University of Delaware Press, 2000), 17.

67　Kistemaker, "The Public and the Private," 19–20.

68　This, at least, is the thesis of Julia Adams in *The Familial State*.

69　Adams, *The Familial State*, 30.

70　Adams, *The Familial State*, 69.

71　A total of 32 percent was invested in stock, 12 percent in houses, and 6 percent in land; other towns reflect similar patterns; see Adams, *The Familial State*, 71.

72　Adams, *The Familial State*, 84.

73　Quoted in Adams, *The Familial State*, 86.

74　Peter Linebaugh and Marcus Rediker, *The Many-Headed Hydra: Slaves, Sailors, Commoners, and the Hidden History of the Revolutionary Atlantic* (Boston: Beacon Press, 2000), 150.

75　Linebaugh and Rediker, *The Many-Headed Hydra*, 151.

76　In early eighteenth-century Vienna, government officials accounted for 60 percent of the working population. Military families made up around a quarter of the Berlin population circa 1789. Royal officials outnumbered the burghers of Stockholm; see Andrew Lees and Lynn Hollenn Lees, *Cities and the Making of Modern Europe, 1750–1914* (Cambridge: Cambridge University Press, 2007), 24.

77　Amsterdam's weapons were, as Braudel writes "the great warehouses—bigger and more expensive than a large ship—which could hold enough grain to feed the United Provinces for ten or twelve years (1670), as well as herrings and spices, English cloth and French wines, salpetre from Poland or the East Indies, Swedish copper, tobacco from Maryland, cocoa from Venezuela, Russian furs and Spanish wool, hemp from the Baltic and silk from the Levant"; quoted in Arrighi, *The Long Twentieth Century*, 141.

78　Quoted in B. R. Burg, *Sodomy and the Pirate Tradition: English Sea Rovers in the Seventeenth-Century Caribbean* (New York: New York University Press, 1995), 63.

79 Jan Oosterhoff, "Sodomy at Sea and the Cape of Good Hope during the Eighteenth Century," *Journal of Homosexuality* 16, nos. 1–2 (1989): 229–35.

80 Quoted in Linebaugh and Rediker, *The Many-Headed Hydra*, 160.

81 Linebaugh and Rediker, *The Many-Headed Hydra*, 162.

82 Linebaugh and Rediker, *The Many-Headed Hydra*, 168.

83 Quoted in Linebaugh and Rediker, *The Many-Headed Hydra*, 169.

84 Burg, *Sodomy and the Pirate Tradition*, 130.

85 Charles Tilly, *Popular Contention in Great Britain, 1758–1834* (Cambridge, MA: Harvard University Press, 1995), 102–3.

86 E. P. Thompson, *The Making of the English Working Class* (New York: Vintage, 1963), 167–68. See also G. E. Manwaring and Bonamy Dobree, *The Floating Republic: An Account of the Mutinies at Spithead and the Nore in 1797* (Barnsley, UK: Pen and Sword Books Limited, 2004), 200, 245, 265–68; and Conrad Gill, *The Naval Mutinies of 1797* (Manchester: Manchester University Press, 1913), 308–9.

87 Arthur N. Gilbert, "The *Africaine* Courts-Martial: A Study of Buggery and the Royal Navy," *Journal of Homosexuality* 1, no. 1 (1974): 111.

88 Gilbert, "The *Africaine* Courts-Martial," 114.

89 Gilbert, "The *Africaine* Courts-Martial," 113.

90 Jody Greene, "Hostis Humani Generis," *Critical Inquiry* 34, no. 4 (2008): 683–705.

Chapter 4. Homosexuality and Bourgeois Hegemony

1 *Le nouveau tableau de Paris, ou La capitale de France dans son vrai point de vue* (Paris: Imprimerie de la Vérité, 1790), 13–15. All translations from French are the author's unless otherwise noted.

2 Louis-Sébastien Mercier, *Panorama of Paris: Selections from "Le Tableau de Paris,"* ed. Jeremy D. Popkin (University Park: Pennsylvania State University Press, 1999), 144. The writer of *Le nouveau tableau* placed his work under the sign of Mercier's: the dedication page reads, "A work destined to become a supplement to *Tableau de Paris*."

3 François Furet, *Interpreting the French Revolution*, trans. Elborg Forster (Cambridge: Cambridge University Press, 1989), 10.

4 *Le nouveau tableau*, 15.

5 Elizabeth Colwill, "Pass as a Woman, Act Like a Man: Marie-Antoinette as Tribade in the Pornography of the French Revolution," in *Homosexuality in Modern France*, ed. Jeffrey Merrick and Bryant T. Ragan Jr., 54–79 (New York: Oxford University Press, 1996).

6 Jeffrey Merrick, "Commissioner Foucault, Inspector Noël, and the 'Pederasts' of Paris, 1780–1783," *Journal of Social History* 32, no. 2 (winter 1998): 287–307.

7 Jürgen Habermas, *The Structural Transformation of the Public Sphere*, trans. Thomas Burger (Cambridge, MA: MIT Press, 1991), 10.

8 Carl E. Schorske, *Fin-de-Siècle Vienna: Politics and Culture* (New York: Alfred A. Knopf, 1980), 24–45.

9   David Harvey, *Paris, Capital of Modernity* (New York: Routledge, 2003), 95–97.

10 "La vérité dirigea mon pinceau; / De mon Pays, voila la triste image. / Paris n'est plus qu'un effrayant tableau, / Une Nation criminelle & sauvage"; *Le nouveau tableau*, title page.

11 Michel Foucault, *"Society Must Be Defended": Lectures at the Collège de France, 1975–76*, trans. David Macey (New York: Picador, 2003), 216.

12 Michel Foucault, *Abnormal: Lectures at the Collège de France, 1974–1975*, trans. Graham Burchell (New York: Picador, 2004), 97–99.

13 Or "Garden of Friendship"; *Les enfans de sodome à l'assemblée nationale* [1790], ed. Patrick Cardon (Lille: Gai Kitsch Camp, 2005), 53. It is difficult to gain purchase on the scale of sexually scandalous accusations in Paris, considering that so many of the pamphlets of this kind have been lost to history.

14 The text specifies "Buggers," "antiphysicals," "tribades," "Berdache," etc. *Les enfans de sodome*, 46.

15 "Requête et Décret en Faveur des Putains, des Fouteuses, des Macquerelles et des Branleuses contre les Bougres, les Bardaches et les Brûleurs de Paillasse," *Les enfans de sodome*.

16 "La Liberté, ou Mademoiselle Raucourt. À toute la sect anandrine, assemblée au foyer de la Comédie-Française," *Les enfans de sodome*, 117.

17 "La Liberté," *Les enfans de sodome*, 117.

18 *Les enfans de sodome*, 54.

19 *Les enfans de sodome*, 53–54.

20 Elizabeth Colwill considers *Les enfans de sodome* and *Le nouveau Dom Bougre à l'assemblée nationale* in relation to the tradition of libertine pornography, of which she considers the Marquis de Sade an apotheosis; however, this reading seems to have been based on an incomplete archive, and there is no evidence that Colwill was aware of several of the texts I will discuss, which explains her focus on the figure of Marie Antoinette rather than on the wider social struggle and the shift in discourse that I will register in the reading that follows; see Colwill, "Pass as a Woman," 54–78.

21 Thierry Pastorello, *Sodome à Paris, fin XVIIIᵉ–milieu XIXᵉ siècle: L'homosexualité masculine en construction* (Paris: Creaphis Editions, 2011), 152.

22 "Un vieux paillard, qu'à Rome on accusoit / De pratiquer l'amour antiphysique, / Vit à Paris un Prêtre qu'on cuisoit / Pour même cas dans la place publique. / Hélas, dit-il, le pauvre Catholique, / Que n'est-il né Romain ou Ferrarois? / Pour un écu la Tax Apostolique / L'auroit absous du moins quatre ou cinq fois." *Épigrammes de Jean-Baptiste Rousseau: Publiés sur les recueils manuscrits et les éditions du XVIIᵉ siècle e précédées d'un avant-propos par un bibliophile parisien* (Paris: E. Sansot and Cie, 1911), 55–56.

23 Denis Diderot, *Œuvres complètes*, vol. 6, ed. Jules Assézat and Maurice Tourneux (Paris: Garnier Frères, 1875), 252–53.

24 Trexler, *Sex and Conquest*, 82.

25 Quoted in Pastorello, *Sodome à Paris*, 34.

26 Voltaire, *Dictionnaire philosophique, portatif* (London, 1764), 18.

27 Voltaire, *Dictionnaire philosophique portatif*, 18–19.

28 Montesquieu, *The Spirit of the Laws*, ed. and trans. Anne M. Cohler, Basia Carolyn Miller, and Harold Samuel Stone (New York: Cambridge University Press, 1989), 193–94.

29 Montesquieu, *The Spirit of the Laws*, 193–94.

30 Cesare Beccaria, *On Crimes and Punishments*, trans. David Young (1764; New York: Hackett, 1986), 60.

31 Beccaria, *On Crimes and Punishments*, 58.

32 This sentence was discovered by the lawyer Mathieu Marais in 1723 in a review of criminal records in the Paris Provost; Chausson Mathieu Marais, *Journal et mémoires de Mathieu Marais, avocat au parlement de Paris: Sur la régence et le règne de Louis XV, 1715–1737* (Paris: Dido Frères, Fils, and Co., 1864), 65.

33 Foucault, *Discipline and Punish*, 48; Foucault, *Abnormal*, 93–94.

34 Crompton, *Homosexuality and Civilization*, 448–49.

35 Edmond Jean-François Barbier, *Chronique de la régence et du règne de Louis XV, 1718–1765: ou Journal de Barbier, avocat au parlement de Paris*, vol. 4 (Paris: Charpentier, 1857), 447.

36 Barbier, *Chronique de la régence*, 447–48.

37 Foucault, *Discipline and Punish*, 285.

38 For this mise-en-scène, see the beautiful novella *No Tomorrow*. Vivant Denon, *No Tomorrow*, trans. Lydia Davis (New York: New York Review Books Classics, 2009).

39 Julien-Joseph Virey, *De la femme: Sous ses rapports physiologique, moral et littéraire* (Paris: Chez Crochard, 1825), 369.

40 Jeffrey Merrick, "The Marquis de Villette and Mademoiselle de Raucourt: Representations of Male and Female Sexual Deviance in Late Eighteenth-Century France," in Merrick and Ragan, *Homosexuality in Modern France*, 30–53.

41 Habermas, *The Structural Transformation of the Public Sphere*, 10–11.

42 Habermas, *The Structural Transformation of the Public Sphere*, 50.

43 Ernst Kantorowicz, *The King's Two Bodies: A Study in Mediaeval Political Theology* (Princeton, NJ: Princeton University Press, 1997), 436.

44 Foucault writes that in the eighteenth century "there was a transposition into different forms of the methods employed by the nobility for marking and maintaining its caste distinction; for the aristocracy had also asserted the special character of its body, but this was in the form of blood, that is, in the form of the antiquity of its ancestry and of the value of its alliances; the bourgeoisie on the contrary looked to its progeny and the health of its organism when it laid claim to a specific body. The bourgeoisie's 'blood' was its sex. And this is more than a play on words; many of the themes characteristic of the caste manners of the nobility reappeared in the nineteenth-century bourgeoisie, but in the guise of biological, medical, or eugenic precepts" (Foucault, *History of Sexuality, Vol. 1*, 124).

45 Brian Joseph Martin, *Napoleonic Friendship: Military Fraternity, Intimacy, and Sexuality in Nineteenth-Century France* (Durham: University of New Hampshire Press, 2011), 19.

46 Quoted in Martin, *Napoleonic Friendship*, 25.

47 Michel Vovelle, *La chute de la monarchie, 1787–1792: Nouvelle histoire de la France contemporaine* (Paris: Éditions du Seuil, 1972), 1:144–45.

48 Martin, *Napoleonic Friendship*, 34–35.

49 *Les confédérés vérolés et les plaints de leurs femmes aux putains de Paris* (Neuchatel: Les Presses de la Société, 1873), 3–4.

50 *Les confédérés vérolés*, 4.

51 *Les confédérés vérolés*, 6.

52 Quoted in Claude Maillard, *Les vespasiennes de Paris ou les précieux édicules* (Paris: La Jeune Parque, 1967), 31.

53 James Wright, *Plumbing Practice* (London: Engineering and Building Record, 1891), 246.

54 Johanna Drucker, *Graphesis: Visual Knowledge Production and Representation* (Cambridge, MA: Harvard University Press, 2014), 2.

55 Robert Brenner, "Bourgeois Revolution and Transition to Capitalism," in *The First Modern Society: Essays in English History in Honour of Lawrence Stone*, ed. A. L. Beier, David Cannadine, and James M. Rosenheim (Cambridge: Cambridge University Press, 1989), 286.

56 Brenner, "Bourgeois Revolution," 286.

57 Seccombe, *A Millennium of Family Change*, 43–46.

58 Seccombe, *A Millennium of Family Change*, 55–56.

59 Tacitus, *Germania* (London: Penguin), 107–8.

60 Seccombe, *A Millennium of Family Change*, 83–89.

Chapter 5. Historicizing the History of Sexuality

Epigraph: Jeremy Bentham, "Offenses against One's Self: Paederasty, Part I," ed. Louis Crompton, *Journal of Homosexuality* 3, no. 4 (1978): 393.

1 Jean Genet, *Querelle de Brest* (Paris: Gallimard, 1953), 72, 77. Translations author's own, unless otherwise cited.

2 Didier Eribon, *Insult and the Making of the Gay Self*, trans. Michael Lucy (Durham, NC: Duke University Press, 2004), 108.

3 Adrienne Rich, "Compulsory Heterosexuality and Lesbian Experience," *Signs* 5, no. 4 (summer 1980): 648–49.

4 Rich, "Compulsory Heterosexuality," 650.

5 Jonathan Katz, *Gay American History* (New York: Avon, 1976), 11.

6 Florence Tamagne, *History of Homosexuality in Europe: Berlin, London, Paris 1919–1939*, vol. 1 (New York: Algora, 2007), 152–54.

7 Tamagne, *History of Homosexuality*, 59.

8 Bleys, *The Geography of Perversion*; Matthew C. Gutmann, "Trafficking in Men: The Anthropology of Masculinity," *Annual Review of Anthropology* 26 (1997): 385–409.

9 Marx writes that "each new class which puts itself in the place of one ruling before it, is compelled, merely in order to carry through its aim, to represent its

interest as the common interest of all the members of society, that is, expressed in an ideal form: it has to give its ideas the form of universality, and represent them as the only rational, universally valid ones." Karl Marx, *The German Ideology* (New York: International Publishers, 1970), 66. On the wider crisis of liberal historiography and the challenge posed to that tradition by Nietzsche and Marx, see Hayden White, *Metahistory: The Historical Imagination in 19th-Century Europe* (Baltimore, MD: Johns Hopkins University Press, 1973), 267–80.

10 Mike Hawkins, *Social Darwinism in European and American Thought, 1860–1945: Nature as Model and Nature as Threat* (Cambridge: Cambridge University Press, 1997), 75–76, 219–20.

11 Freedman and D'Emilio, "Problems Encountered."

12 Herdt, "Introduction"; Cohen, *Folk Devils*; Douglas, *Purity and Danger*.

13 Michel Foucault, "The Mesh of Power," trans. Christopher Chitty, *Viewpoint Magazine* 2, September 12, 2012, http://viewpointmag.com/2012/09/12/the-mesh -of-power/.

14 "I do not maintain that the prohibition of sex is a ruse; but it is a ruse to make prohibition into the basic and constitutive element from which one would be able to write the history of what has been said concerning sex starting from the modern epoch"; Foucault, *The History of Sexuality, Vol. 1*, 12.

15 "This is the essential thing: that Western man has been drawn for three centuries to the task of telling everything concerning his sex; that since the classical age there has been a constant optimization and an increasing valorization of the discourse on sex, and that this carefully analytical discourse was meant to yield multiple effects of displacement, intensification, reorientation, and modification of desire itself"; Foucault, *The History of Sexuality, Vol. 1*, 23.

16 Foucault, *The History of Sexuality, Vol. 1*, 137.

17 "But through a circular process, the economic—and primarily agricultural— development of the eighteenth century, and an increase in productivity and resources even more rapid than the demographic growth it encouraged, allowed a measure of relief from these profound threats: despite some renewed outbreaks, the period of grave ravages from starvation and plague had come to a close before the French Revolution; death was ceasing to torment life so directly. But at the same time . . . Western man was gradually learning what it meant to be a living species in a living world, to have a body, conditions of existence, probabilities of life, an individual and collective welfare, forces that could be modified and a space in which they could be distributed in an optimal manner." Foucault, *The History of Sexuality, Vol. 1*, 142.

18 Compare the foregoing citation to Marx's argument from *Capital*: "The greater the social wealth, the functioning of capital, the extent and energy of its growth, and therefore also the greater the absolute mass of the proletariat and the productivity of its labor, the greater the reserve army. The same causes which develop the expansive power of capital, also develop the labor power at its disposal." Karl Marx, *Capital, Vol. 1*, trans. Ben Fowkes (New York: Penguin), 798.

19 Michel Foucault, *Security Territory Population: Lectures at the Collège de France,*

1977–1978, ed. Michel Senellart, trans. Graham Burchell (New York: Palgrave Macmillan, 2007), 23–79; Michel Foucault, *The Birth of Biopolitics: Lectures at the Collège de France, 1978–1979*, ed. Michel Senellart, trans. Graham Burchell (New York: Palgrave Macmillan, 2008), 160–65, 203–7.

20 Foucault, *The History of Sexuality, Vol. 1*, 139.

21 Foucault, *The History of Sexuality, Vol. 1*, 143.

22 Hence James Clifford's wry comment that Foucault was "scrupulously ethnocentric"; see James Clifford, *The Predicament of Culture* (Cambridge, MA: Harvard University Press, 1988), 265.

23 Foucault, *The History of Sexuality, Vol. 1*, 49.

24 See Foucault, *The History of Sexuality, Vol. 1*, 126–27; translation here is author's own from Michel Foucault, *Histoire de la sexualité 1* (Paris: Gallimard, 1976), 166–68.

25 David M. Halperin, *One Hundred Years of Homosexuality: And Other Essays on Greek Love* (New York: Routledge, 1990), 29.

26 Halperin, *One Hundred Years of Homosexuality*, 8–9.

27 Sedgwick, *Epistemology of the Closet*, 47.

28 David Halperin, *How to Do the History of Homosexuality* (Chicago: University of Chicago Press, 2004), 109.

29 Williams, *Writing in Society*, 152–53.

30 Jameson, *Valences of the Dialectic*, 546–65.

31 John D'Emilio, "Making and Unmaking Minorities: The Tensions between Gay Politics and History," *Review of Law and Social Change* 14 (1986): 915–22.

32 David F. Greenberg and Marcia H. Bystryn, "Capitalism, Bureaucracy, and Male Homosexuality," *Crime, Law, and Social Change* 8, no. 1 (1984): 35.

33 D'Emilio, "Capitalism and Gay Identity," in *The Lesbian and Gay Studies Reader*, ed. Henry Abelove, Michèle Aina Barale, and David M. Halperin (New York: Routledge, 1993), 470.

34 Kathleen Canning, *Languages of Labor and Gender: Female Factory Work in Germany, 1850–1914* (Ann Arbor: University of Michigan Press, 2002), 103–7.

35 August Bebel, *Woman under Socialism*, trans. Daniel De Leon (New York: New York Labor News Company, 1923).

36 Wally Seccombe, *Weathering the Storm: Working-Class Families from the Industrial Revolution to the Fertility Decline* (New York: Verso, 1995), 71–80.

37 Shah, *Stranger Intimacy*; B. R. Burg, *An American Seafarer in the Age of the Sail: The Erotic Diaries of Philip C. Van Buskirk, 1851–1870* (New Haven, CT: Yale University Press, 1994); William Benemann, *Men in Eden: William Drummond Stewart and Same-Sex Desire in the Rocky Mountain Fur Trade* (Lincoln: University of Nebraska Press, 2012).

38 See chapter 15, "Machinery and Large-Scale Industry," and chapter 25, "The General Law of Capitalist Accumulation," in Marx, *Capital, Vol. 1*, and specifically pages 592–610, 808–28.

39 Steven Epstein, "Gay Politics, Ethnic Identity: The Limits of Social Constructivism," *Socialist Review* 93–94 (May–August 1987): 23–25.

40 Epstein, "Gay Politics," 25.

41 Carla Freccero discusses the way in which this "acts versus identities" debate has also produced a paradigm neglecting literary sources whose subjective accounts are at variance with official institutional discourses and texts. Her reading of Halperin demonstrates that the emphasis is based on a misreading, however productive, of a single passage of Foucault's *The History of Sexuality, Vol. 1*; see Freccero, *Queer/Early/Modern*, 32–38.

42 Jonathan Katz, "Jonathan Ned Katz Papers, 1947–2004" (Series V. Research Notes and Papers, c. 1978, Box 41.6, Jonathan Ned Katz Papers, New York Public Library), 15.

43 Michel Foucault, quoted in Didier Eribon, *Michel Foucault et ses contemporains* (Paris: Fayard, 1994), 280.

44 Guy Hocquenghem, *Homosexual Desire*, trans. Daniella Dangoor (Durham, NC: Duke University Press, 1993).

45 Chauncey, *Gay New York*, 355–56; Aldrich, "Homosexuality and the City," 1719–37.

46 Justin Spring, *Secret Historian: The Life and Times of Samuel Steward, Professor, Tattoo Artist, and Sexual Renegade* (New York: Macmillan, 2010).

47 Paula A. Treichler, "AIDS, Homophobia, and Biomedical Discourse: An Epidemic of Signification," in Treichler, *How to Have Theory in an Epidemic: Cultural Chronicles of* AIDS, 1–41 (Durham, NC: Duke University Press, 2004); Lee Edelman, "The Plague of Discourse: Politics, Literary Theory, and 'AIDS,'" in Edelman, *Homographesis*, 79–92 (New York: Routledge, 1994).

Chapter 6. Homosexuality as a Category of Bourgeois Society

Epigraph: Gramsci, *Prison Notebooks, Vol. 1*, 235.

1 Chauncey, *Gay New York*, 155–63; George Chauncey, "Christian Brotherhood or Sexual Perversion? Homosexual Identities and the Construction of Sexual Boundaries in the World-War-One Era," *Journal of Social History* 19, no. 2 (winter 1985): 189–211.

2 S. N. Eisenstadt, "Archetypal Patterns of Youth," *Daedalus* 91, no. 1 (winter 1962): 28–46; Kenny Cupers, "Governing through Nature: Camps and Youth Movements in Interwar Germany and the United States," *Cultural Geographies* 15, no. 2 (April 2008): 173–205; Klaus H. Pringsheim, "The Functions of the Communist Youth Leagues (1920–1949)," *China Quarterly* 12 (December 1962): 75–91; Matthias Neumann, "Revolutionizing Mind and Soul? Soviet Youth and Cultural Campaigns during the New Economic Policy (1921–1928)," *Social History* 33, no. 3 (2008): 243–67.

3 Walter Laqueur, *Young Germany: A History of the German Youth Movement* (New Brunswick, NJ: Transaction Books, 1984), 50–52.

4 Isabel V. Hull, *The Entourage of Kaiser Wilhelm II, 1888–1918* (New York: Cambridge University Press, 1982), 133–45; James D. Steakley, "Iconography of a Scandal: Political Cartoons and the Eulenburg Affair," *Studies in Visual Communication* 9, no. 2 (spring 1983): 20–51.

5 Tamagne, *History of Homosexuality in Europe*, 106–25; Ronald Hyam, *Empire and Sexuality: The British Experience* (New York: Manchester University Press, 1990), 34–37, 66–74.

6 Antonio Gramsci, *Prison Notebooks, Vol. 2*, ed. Joseph Buttigieg (New York: Columbia University Press, 2011), 215.

7 Janet Zollinger Giele, *Two Paths to Women's Equality: Temperance, Suffrage, and the Origins of Modern Feminism* (New York: Twayne, 1995); Joseph Gusfield, "Social Structure and Moral Reform: A Study of the Woman's Christian Temperance Union," *American Journal of Sociology* 61, no. 3 (November 1955): 221–32.

8 Magnus Hirschfeld, *The Sexual History of the World War*, ed. Victor Robinson (New York: Cadillac, 1941), 109.

9 Chauncey, "Christian Brotherhood"; Canaday, *The Straight State*, 71–77.

10 Josh Sides, *Erotic City: Sexual Revolutions and the Making of Modern San Francisco* (New York: Oxford University Press, 2009), 22–24.

11 Hirschfeld, *Sexual History of the World War*, 92–108. For comparison, the British troops stationed in India also had enormous losses of man hours due to VD; see D. Arnold, "Sexually Transmitted Diseases in Nineteenth- and Twentieth-Century India," *Genitourinary Medicine* 69, no. 1 (February 1993): 3–4.

12 Gramsci, *Prison Notebooks, Vol. 2*, 216.

13 Gramsci, *Prison Notebooks, Vol. 2*, 217.

14 Hooker, "Ford's Sociology Department."

15 Dennis Altman, *Homosexual: Oppression and Liberation* (St. Lucia, Australia: University of Queensland Press, 2012), 165–66.

16 Altman, *Homosexual*, 166.

17 Chauncey, *Why Marriage?*, 5; see also Kathleen Battles and Wendy Hilton-Morrow, "Gay Characters in Conventional Spaces: *Will and Grace* and the Situation Comedy Genre," *Critical Studies in Media Communication* 19, no. 1 (2002): 87–105; and Karin Quimby, "*Will and Grace*: Negotiating (Gay) Marriage on Prime-Time Television," *Journal of Popular Culture* 38, no. 4 (2005): 713–31.

18 Sullivan, *Virtually Normal*, 89.

19 J. Jack Halberstam, *Gaga Feminism: Sex, Gender, and the End of Normal* (Boston: Beacon Press, 2012).

20 Anderson, *The Origins of Postmodernity*, 85–86.

21 David Harvey, *A Brief History of Neoliberalism* (New York: Oxford University Press, 2005), 75–78.

22 Anderson, *The Origins of Postmodernity*, 62.

23 Edward W. Soja, *Postmodern Geographies: The Reassertion of Space in Critical Social Theory* (New York: Verso, 1998), 190–220; Mike Davis, *Planet of Slums* (New York: Verso, 2006).

24 In this sense, the founders of Sex Panic! were wrong to diagnose AIDS hysteria as evidence of some general cultural fever of homophobia or panic concerning homosexuality. They were using modern sociological categories to understand a postmodern cultural form in which the older sensorium of "shock" or "panic"

was no longer operative. Deaths from AIDS and revelations of HIV infections played precisely this tabloid role of bringing down the high (consider the Andrew Sullivan scandal, Rock Hudson, Magic Johnson, etc.) and elevating the low (consider the Harlem Ball scene as captured in *Paris Is Burning*, political funerals, David Wojnarowicz, Keith Haring, Félix González-Torres, etc.).

25 Lauren Berlant, *Cruel Optimism* (Durham, NC: Duke University Press, 2011), 3.

26 Berlant, *Cruel Optimism*, 11.

27 "Since 1987, African Americans have lost more than half their net worth; Latinos, an incredible two-thirds. Five-and-a-half million manufacturing jobs have been lost in the United States since 2000, more than 42,000 factories closed, and an entire generation of college graduates now face the highest rate of downward mobility in American history." Mike Davis, "No More Bubblegum," *Los Angeles Review of Books*, October 21, 2011.

28 Paul Mason, *Why It's Still Kicking Off Everywhere: The New Global Revolutions* (New York: Verso, 2013), 261.

29 Seccombe, *Weathering the Storm*, 40–43, 50–53; George Chauncey, "Privacy Could Only Be Had in Public: Gay Uses of the Streets," in *Stud: Architectures of Masculinity*, ed. Joel Sanders, 223–67 (New York: Princeton Architectural Press).

30 Shah, *Stranger Intimacy*, 54–61; Kristen McKenzie, *Scandal in the Colonies: Sydney and Cape Town, 1820–1850* (Carlton, Australia: Melbourne University Press, 2004).

31 Jonathan Dollimore, *Sexual Dissidence: Augustine to Wilde, Freud to Foucault* (New York: Oxford University Press, 1991), 318–25.

32 Although Nancy Fraser's judgment that sexuality isn't determined by political economy is bizarre and completely ahistorical, remaining blind to the material benefits of legally recognized relationships, her observations concerning the sense of exclusion driving the postwar movement for gay and lesbian rights are sharp: "Sexuality in this conception is a mode of social differentiation whose roots do not lie in the political economy, as homosexuals are distributed throughout the entire class structure of capitalist society, occupy no distinctive position in the division of labour, and do not constitute an exploited class. Rather, their mode of collectivity is that of a despised sexuality, rooted in the cultural valuational structure of society. From this perspective, the injustice they suffer is quintessentially a matter of recognition"; Nancy Fraser, "From Redistribution to Recognition? Dilemmas of Justice in a 'Post-Socialist' Age," *New Left Review* (series 1) 212 (July–August 1995): 77. Iris Marion Young has critiqued this position by complicating the stark division Fraser draws between culture and political economy; see Iris Marion Young, "Unruly Categories: A Critique of Nancy Fraser's Dual Systems Theory," *New Left Review* (series 1) 222 (March–April 1997): 147–60.

33 Nancy Fraser, "Rethinking the Public Sphere: A Contribution to the Critique of Actually Existing Democracy," in *Habermas and the Public Sphere*, ed. Craig Calhoun, 109–42 (Cambridge, MA: MIT Press, 1992).

34 Michael Warner, *Publics and Counterpublics* (New York: Zone Books, 2005), 42, 201–2.

35 Michael Warner, *The Trouble with Normal: Sex, Politics, and the Ethics of Queer Life* (Cambridge, MA: Harvard University Press, 2000).

36 Berlant, *Cruel Optimism*, 105.

37 Warner, *Publics and Counterpublics*, 60.

38 Here it's difficult not to think of the queer idiom of "houses" of drag, "drag mothers," "daddies," "house music," queer "sisterhood," "gay family," etc. The transitory and embodied performativity of this kinship suggests some middle ground between stranger intimacy and kinship of a more traditional sort; Brian Currid, "'We Are Family': House Music and Queer Performativity," in *Cruising the Performative: Interventions into the Representation of Ethnicity, Nationality, and Sexuality*, ed. Sue-Ellen Case, Philip Brett, and Susan Leigh Foster (Indianapolis: Indiana University Press, 1995), 165–96.

39 During the postwar period, gay and lesbian struggles against the censorship of lifestyle magazines, pornography, films, and pulp novels and struggles against police crackdowns on bars and other public spaces of socialization galvanized a political consciousness known to no other period of the existence of such institutions; D'Emilio, *Sexual Politics, Sexual Communities*, 31–33, 49–53, 146–50, 182–95.

40 The public sphere, as Jürgen Habermas writes, "arose in the broader strata of the bourgeoisie as an expansion and at the same time completion of the intimate sphere of the conjugal family. Living room and salon were under the same roof; and just as the privacy of the one was oriented toward the public nature of the other, and as the subjectivity of the privatized individual was related from the very start to the publicity, so both were conjoined in literature that had become 'fiction'"(Habermas, *The Structural Transformation of the Public Sphere*, 50).

41 Here, the limitations of Habermas's masculinist conception of the public sphere as one of rational-critical discourse are clear; see Rachel Bowlby, *Just Looking: Consumer Culture in Dreiser, Gissing, and Zola* (New York: Routledge, 2009).

42 Seth Koven, *Slumming: Sexual and Social Politics in Victorian London* (Princeton, NJ: Princeton University Press, 2004).

43 Bentham, "Offenses against One's Self," 403.

44 Warner, *Publics and Counterpublics*, 49–53.

45 Habermas, *The Structural Transformation of the Public Sphere*, 156–58.

46 Warner, *Publics and Counterpublics*, 50–51.

47 Freccero, *Queer/Early/Modern*; Carolyn Dinshaw, *Getting Medieval: Sexualities and Communities, Pre- and Postmodern* (Durham, NC: Duke University Press, 1999); Jonathan Dollimore, *Sexual Dissidence*, 279–328.

48 Habermas, *The Structural Transformation of the Public Sphere*, xvii.

49 The project would then be analogous to what Joan B. Landes does for the history of women's participation in the French public sphere in *Women and the Public Sphere in the Age of the French Revolution* (Ithaca, NY: Cornell University Press, 1988). Robert Darnton's remarkable study of the underground Enlightenment

reflected in the plebeian public sphere of cafes, musées, and lycées explicitly connects this counterpublic to sexual sensationalism and political opposition; see Robert Darnton, *The Literary Underground of the Old Regime* (Cambridge, MA: Harvard University Press, 1982), 23–24.

50 Alexander Kluge and Oskar Negt, *Public Sphere and Experience: Toward an Analysis of the Bourgeois and Proletarian Public Sphere*, trans. Peter Labanyi, Jamie Owen Daniel, and Assenka Oksiloff (Minneapolis: University of Minnesota Press, 1993), 29–31.

51 Rictor Norton, *Mother Clap's Molly House: The Gay Subculture in England, 1700–1830* (Stroud, UK: Chalford Press, 2006); Louis Canler, *Mémoires de Canler, ancien chef du service de Sûreté* (Paris: F. Roy, 1882), 117–27.

52 Chauncey, *Gay New York*, 49–50.

53 Chauncey, *Gay New York*, 52.

54 Gramsci, *Prison Notebooks, Vol. 2*, 33.

55 Berlant, *Cruel Optimism*, 114.

56 Berlant, *Cruel Optimism*, 103.

57 Raymond Williams, *Marxism and Literature* (New York: Oxford University Press, 1977), 113–14.

58 Dollimore, *Sexual Dissidence*, 83.

59 Warner, *Publics and Counterpublics*, 201–3; Douglas Crimp, "How to Have Promiscuity in an Epidemic," *October* 43 (winter 1987): 237–71.

60 Lisa L. Williams, "SF Pride Statement about Bradley [*sic*] Manning," *San Diego LGBT Weekly*, April 26, 2013.

index

Filipepi, Simone, 42, 43, 65
financialization, 4, 15, 35
Florence: and early modern capitalism, 58–72, 77–78, 81, 83, 94, 108, 110; and Machiavelli's *Florentine Histories*, 55, 58–68, and the Officers of the Night, 42–56, 60–62, 64–67, 70–72, 94; and the regulation of sodomy, 2, 5, 39, 42–56, 72, 110; and use of "Florenzer" as antigay derogation, 68
Federici, Silvia, 14
Ford Motor Company, 33–34, 135, 172, 184
Foucault, Michel: and the Collège de France lectures, 110, 153; and critique of the "repressive hypothesis," 6, 21, 22, 31, 41, 137, 142, 144, 150–59; and postwar French intellectual history, 29, 67, 164; and sexual science, 6, 16, 137–38, 142, 144, 146, 152, 154–55, 186; and theorization of power, 7, 8, 117, 144, 154
free love, 168
French Revolution, 39–40, 104, 107–11, 113, 119–23, 136, 178, 190
Freud, Sigmund, 150, 151, 169
Furet, François, 107

gardens, as public space for sex between men, 106–7, 108–9, 112. *See also* Tuileries
gay liberation, ix, xi, 28, 173, 182, 187, 192
Germany, 68, 77, 126, 130–31, 148–49, 169, 170, 191
gonorrhea, 89, 110, 123, 170
Greece, 30, 58–59, 64, 81–87, 111–12, 115, 159, 196n30
Genet, Jean, 141–43
Gide, André, 142
Gramsci, Antonio, 2–5, 27, 156, 167, 170–72, 189; on Fordism, 170–72; and the notion of "interregnum," 189; and *Prison Notebooks*, 3, 27, 167. *See also* hegemony
Greenberg, David, 159–62
guilds, 39, 45, 49–54, 60, 66, 77, 83, 134

Habermas, Jürgen, 109, 120, 182, 184, 185, 215n40
Hague, 91, 94, 98, 100, 78
Halperin, David, 31, 156–59, 212n41

handicraft production, 11, 30, 59, 72, 87, 88, 134
Harden, Maximilian, 169
Harvey, David, 36, 189
Haussmann, Georges-Eugène, 109, 124
hegemony: and American culture, 12, 168, 173–74, 179, 192; and Ancient Greece, 58, 59; and bourgeois sexual hegemony, 32–34, 37–40, 106, 110, 138, 165, 173, 178–80, 184; and British capitalism, 75, 170; and "compulsory heterosexuality," 13, 146; crises of, 35, 39, 40, 43, 59; and the Dutch Republic, 90, 97, 133; and Florence, 67–70, 87; and the French Revolution, 123; Gramsci's conceptualization of, 2–5; "hegemony of the normal," 175–76; and proletarian counterhegemony, 142, 156, 187–88; sexual hegemony, ix, 13, 22, 25–26, 37, 155, 172, 176, 179, 187, 190, 191
Herzog, Dagmar, 32
heterosexuality, 9, 11, 13, 14, 146, 147, 157–61
Hirschfeld, Magnus, 149
Hocquenghem, Guy, 164
Holland, 78, 91
homophobia, viii, 3, 11, 23, 26, 32, 33, 39, 41, 159, 163, 164, 181, 213n24
homoeroticism, 58, 59, 96, 116, 126–27, 150, 168
Hülsen-Haeseler, Dietrich von, 169

identity politics, 5, 10–13, 16, 146, 160, 163, 168, 184, 188, 191
Italy, 35, 43, 45, 50–51, 58–59, 68, 70, 72, 73, 88, 94, 105, 138, 201n65
imagined community, 23, 39, 41, 142, 165, 179–81, 186–88, 191

Jacobins, 104, 110, 111, 113, 122
Jennings, George, 40, 126
Johnson, Samuel, 101

Kamen, Henry, 47
Kant, Immanuel, 90, 121, 151, 154, 203n41, 42n204
Kantorowicz, Ernst, 121
Kanun-i Osmani, 81
Katz, Jonathan Ned, 147

Kluge, Alexander, 185–86
Krafft-Ebing, Richard von, 150

labor, and class formation, 1, 3, 6, 12, 16; and craft production, 82; division of, 30, 115, 129, 132, 144, 159–62, 170, 182, 183; itinerant, 80, 161; and Florence's class structure, 45, 49–50, 51, 53, 54; and Fordism, 171–73; and Foucault, 7–8, 153, 155; and gender, 9, 13, 38, 45, 50, 80, 83, 87, 115, 130 133, 134, 160; and "labor power," 15, 23, 210n18; and the law, 36, 51; low-wage, 121, 181, 185, 190; maritime, 74, 77–78, 83, 100; organized, 33, 178; precarious, 27, 87; rural, 92, 130–31, 134; and settler colonialism, 179; unfree, 85, 95, 130, 134, 186
Lacan, Jacques, 9
Lawrence v. Texas, 161
lesbians: and feminism, 13, 14; and the French Revolution, 107, 112, 123; and the postwar gay and lesbian rights movement, 11, 12, 23, 147, 160, 163, 173, 176; and respectability politics, 9, 179, 181, 192; and Adrienne Rich, 13, 14, 146
libertinism: bourgeoisie's fight against, 39, 111; and pornography, 113, 121, 207n20; policing of same-sex relations, 113, 119
Livy, Titus, 56–57, 60–64
Lombroso, Cesare, 150
London: and birth of modern homosexuality, 157, 162; and domestic service, 133; as hub in capitalist world system, 24, 68, 77, 199; and the Napoleonic Wars, 104; and nineteenth-century capitalism, 123; press coverage of Dutch sodomy prosecutions in 1730, 90, 91; and public urinals, 124
Lot (biblical figure), 46, 68–69, 81, 93

Macchietti, Girolamo, 56, 69
Machiavelli, Niccolò, 3, 27, 39, 55–66, 71, 89, 198n3, 200n48, 200n49
Manning, Chelsea, 192
Marcus, Sharon, 4, 14
maritime labor, 1, 74, 78, 100
Marx, Karl: and *Capital*, 15, 85; and Foucault,

7, 153, 155; and primitive accumulation, 24; and "queer realism," 3, 16, 27, 28; theory of ideology, 189, 210n9; and Western Marxism, 159, 190
Mason, Paul, 178
master-servant relations, 77, 82, 83, 116
Medici family: decline of, 68; Medici, Giuliano de', 66, 67; Medici, Lorenzo de', 42–44, 55–57; and Machiavelli, 39, 59, 60, 62; rise to power of, 51, 54
Mediterranean Ocean, 100, 101, 185, 187
Mediterranean world in the early modern era, 5, 38; male homosexuality in, 45, 47, 49, 50, 60, 68, 70–83, 87, 88, 116; and transition to capitalism, 131–34
menservants, 133
Mercier, Louis-Sébastien, 107, 108
modernity, 37, 40, 67, 81, 123 154; and "sexual modernity," 5, 16, 35, 135
"molly-houses," 157
"monkey closet," 126–27
Montaigne, Michel de, 114
moral panic, 32–33, 150–51, 168, 188
Morel, Bénédict, 150
mutiny, 99, 104, 105
Mycenae, 83, 86, 87

Najemy, John, 51, 62
Napoleonic Code of 1811, 91, 149
Negt, Oskar, 185
new social history, 150, 166
Nordau, Max, 150
normativity, 26, 49, 176, 188, 191
Nouveau tableau de Paris, Le (Anonymous). *See* Paris
novel, the, 174, 182

Occupy movement, 16, 65, 178
Officers of the Night, 39, 42–44, 47–48, 50, 56, 63–64, 72, 94; decline of, 66, 67, 70; establishment of, 45, 53; and history of class struggle in Florence, 49, 53, 54; and Machiavelli, 60–62, 65, 71
Orwell, George, 28
Otto di guardia (the "Eight Judges"), 65, 71
Ottoman Empire, 80–81

CPSIA information can be obtained
at www.ICGtesting.com
Printed in the USA
BVHW081935251120
594000BV00006B/479